D0911034

EVERYMAN, I will go with thee,
and be thy guide
In thy most need to go by thy side

JOHN HOLLINGSHEAD

Born in Hoxton, London, on 9 September 1827. Journalist and theatre manager and reformer. Wrote for Dickens's *Household Words* and *All the Year Round*, Thackeray's *Cornhill Magazine*, and *Punch*. Author of twenty-six books. Drama critic of the *Daily News* from 1863 to 1868. Stage director of the Alhambra theatre from 1865 to 1868. Manager of the Gaiety theatre from 1868 to 1886. Died on 10 October 1904.

JOHN HOLLINGSHEAD

Ragged London in 1861

Introduction and notes by
Anthony S. Wohl
Professor of History, Vassar College

Dent: London and Melbourne
EVERYMAN'S LIBRARY

© Introduction and notes, J.M. Dent & Sons Ltd, 1986
All rights reserved

Phototypeset in 10/11½pt Linotron 202 Sabon by
Book Economy Services, Sussex
Made in Great Britain by
Guernsey Press Co. Ltd, Guernsey, C.1. for
J. M. Dent & Sons Ltd
Aldine House, 33 Welbeck Street, London W1M 8LX

First published as an Everyman Classic, 1986

This book if bound as a paperback is
subject to the condition that it may
not be issued on loan or otherwise
except in its original binding

No 1583 Paperback ISBN 0 460 11583 4

Contents

Introduction

When John Hollingshead was tramping through the streets of London, collecting material for his *Ragged London in 1861*, the city was in the grip of one of the worst winters on record. As early as 2 November 1860, the temperature dipped into the thirties (Fahrenheit) and although early December brought some relief, the temperature dropped to 30° on the 17th and, except for just two days, remained below freezing for an entire month. For several days on end the thermometer did not rise above the teens.[1] With the ice on the Serpentine some thirteen inches deep, Hyde Park took on the appearance of a winter carnival: it was reported that crowds of up to 50,000 people were cavorting on the ice, and ice-skating competitions, impromptu ice-dancing, band concerts, the carriages of the fashionable, refreshment tents serving beer and ale, some 300 chestnut stalls, charcoal braziers, fireworks, accidents and heroic rescues all added to an air of excitement and frivolity. *Punch* grasped the opportunity to regale its readers with humorous accounts of frozen toothbrushes, shaving water, and punch bowls.[2] The harsh winter undoubtedly brought excitement and an engaging diversion to some, but to far more it meant deprivation and even death.

It was to discover the exact extent and depth of the distress and the impact of the weather on the labouring poor that the *Morning Post* in January 1861 commissioned the journalist John Hollingshead (1827-1904). The results of his inquiry, a series of articles entitled 'Horrible London', formed the basis for his *Ragged London in 1861* which was published later that year. Transcending the immediate confines of his assignment, Hollingshead undertook an ambitious survey, incorporating interviews, house-to-house visitations, and considerable research into statistical and other evidence, to produce a remarkable picture of the social, domestic, and working lives of the working classes and of their mores and survival techniques. His book is a brilliant example of Victorian social reportage and investigative journalism, yet it remains a neglected classic, strangely overlooked by historians.[3]

Hollingshead's training as a journalist equipped him splen-
didly for the task. He was born in Hoxton in 1827 into what he
called 'a lower middle-class family'. His father, a failed
merchant, spent a term, like Charles Dickens's father, in debtor's
prison. As a youngster, Hollingshead was a 'respectable street
arab' who developed the love of roaming the streets and the
fascination for street life, and especially street entertainments
and 'penny gaffs', which lasted throughout his life.[4] After a brief
spell at a soft-goods warehouse and as a 'bagman' (commercial
traveller), Hollingshead successfully turned his hand to writing.
Among the journals he contributed to in that golden age of
journalism were *The Press*, Dickens's journals *Household
Words* and *All the Year Round*, Thackeray's *Cornhill Magazine*,
Lloyd's Journal, *London Review*, *Leader*, *Good Works*, *Sphinx*,
Man of the World, *National Observer*, *Sketch*, *Table Talk*,
Whitehall Review, and *Saturday Review*.[5] From 1863 to 1868 he
was the drama critic for the *Daily News* and he later wrote
occasional pieces for *Punch*, including a celebrated attack on the
'Duke of Mudford' (Bedford).[6]

Hollingshead described himself as Dickens's 'champion out-
door young man' at *Household Words* and it was under
Dickens's editorship of that journal that he developed his skills
as an investigative journalist and special correspondent on
London life.[7] He later claimed that his essay, 'All Night on the
Monument', which appeared as a lead article in the issue for 30
January 1858, was perhaps the earliest example of 'graphic
reporting' and 'special correspondence', and in its obituary, *The
Times*, taking him at his word, wrote that 'he may be regarded as
practically the inventor of "graphic reporting"'.[8] But by mid-
century investigative reporting by 'special correspondents' was
well established, and Hollingshead's claim to be the originator is
certainly questionable. What is indisputable, however, is that he
was, together with Henry Mayhew and George Sala (another of
Dickens's bright young men), a leading exponent of it in the
1850s and 1860s.[9] Hollingshead could turn his hand at short
notice to any subject and his range was astonishing – cabs, tap
rooms, advertising, ideal houses, neighbours, bohemian London,
art investment, panaceas and patent medicines, pawn brokers,

dandyism, dog homes, the British Museum, chimney sweeps, the police, boxing matches, umbrellas and their hazards, auctions, traffic jams, spiritualism, street sharps, food stalls, the stock market, debtors and creditors, mad dogs, evangelical literature, postal services, working-class drinking habits, and a host of other topics which, taken together, add up to a marvellously idiosyncratic, kaleidoscopic evocation of life in the metropolis. Inevitably much of his work was rushed and somewhat superficial, but it was always entertaining and enlivened by deft and witty touches. Above all he had the knack of conveying the variety and character of the town he loved. 'No man', he once wrote, 'loves the metropolis more than I do', and among his hobbies he included 'trampling into every hole and corner of London, or any other city'.[10] Like Dickens, he was fascinated by both the variety of life in London and its unpredictability. Scattered throughout his essays and short stories are examples of turns of fortune, debts, foreclosing, evictions, and bankruptcies both genuine and contrived. 'The whole human race', he wrote, 'must range themselves under two classes, viz. debtors and creditors. . . .'[11] But for the most part his contributions were designed to make a 'good read'. 'Shrewd, terse, picturesque, humorous', as the *Daily News* put it, they were colourful, and full of the sounds, sights, and smells of street life and city living.[12]

Hollingshead would certainly have had an assured career as a journalist and writer, and, indeed, he never completely forsook that career (his total output included some twenty-six books); but his greatest passion was reserved for the theatre. At the age of thirty-eight he realized a great ambition when he became a theatre manager (of the Alhambra), and three years later, in 1868, he took over the management of the Gaiety in the Strand. Although he certainly had some anxious moments – a fire destroyed all the scenery just before opening night – Hollingshead continued to manage the Gaiety with great flair and commercial success for eighteen years. From an initial outlay of only £200 he made £120,000 from the Gaiety – money which he unfortunately lost in later theatre speculation.[13] At one stage or another he managed the Empire, the Globe, the Canterbury, the Paragon, the Royal, the Ampitheatre, and the Opéra Comique theatres.

Hollingshead was engagingly, and it would seem genuinely, self-deprecating about his role in the life of the Victorian stage. He was, he said, primarily 'a licensed dealer in legs, short-skirts, French adaptations, Shakespeare', and his function was not to elevate the public's taste but to give them what they wanted. Theatre managers, he stressed

> must never forget the fact that in a comfortable gallery the lower orders of society can obtain a degree of physical warmth for a penny an hour which it is impossible for them to obtain at home with coals at thirty shillings a ton, and gas at three-shillings-and-sixpence the thousand cubic feet.

Nor should they lose sight of the fact that both men and women attended the theatre partly to admire the opposite sex in the audience and the beauty displayed on stage. Above all managers

> must never commit the folly and impertinence of suggesting to a customer who asks for a baked potato the propriety of selling a rose or a volume of poems. He is not a director of public taste. . . . He is only a follower.[14]

In fact Hollingshead was something of a leader and innovator and did far more than just keep 'the sacred lamp of burlesque', as he put it, burning at the Gaiety. He introduced matinées (up to six a week), and in 1878 brought the new wonder of the electric light to the Gaiety.[15] He agitated vigorously for what he termed 'Free Trade in Theatres', fighting the patent theatre monopoly of the Drury Lane and Covent Garden theatres, and the dramatization of novels without the authors' consent. He helped to form the Authors' Protection Society and campaigned against the closure of theatres on Ash Wednesday (a restriction finally removed in 1885).[16] He also had the courage, while manager of the Alhambra, to bring the scandalous can-can to London. It was perhaps that, as much as the display of 'pink silk tights' by his Gaiety girls, which, despite the support of John Bright, prevented his election to membership of the Reform Club.[17] While his greatest contribution was to the robust world of burlesque, he also staged serious drama. He brought Ibsen to the English public and produced Shakespeare, Vanbrugh,

Charles Reade, Dion Boucicault, W.S. Gilbert, and also opera and operetta. He was an enterprising impressario, who introduced Sarah Bernhardt and the Comédie Française to London audiences. Among those who performed in his theatres were some of the leading actors of the day – Charles Mathews, Samuel Phelps, J.L. Toole, Mrs Kendall, Henry Irving, and Edward Terry.[18] The Victorian theatre in general, and especially the vigorous world of music hall, comic opera, and melodrama were considerably richer for Hollingshead's spirited management.

If Hollingshead casually brushed aside his contribution to the theatre, he was equally modest when it came to his other life as a journalist. He was, he wrote, a mere 'dabbler in this eccentric profession'.[19] His type of writing was, he acknowledged, a minor tributary in the great stream of Victorian literature – 'it hangs on the skirts of literature without being literature'.[20] But he clearly saw that he was part of an important new development in journalism. In 1859 he wrote that 'within the last twenty years there has risen a new profession [of investigative journalism]'. It 'requires a strong chest, a power of doing without sleep, of sleeping upon shelves, stones, clay, or hurdles, an observant eye, an even temper, and a good memory'. Significantly, in view of the assignment Hollingshead accepted in 1861, he compared investigative reporting to the exploration of foreign lands. Special correspondents were men of dynamic energy and curiosity, bringing back to their comfortable middle-class readers wondrous tales of unknown regions, 'men who live only in action, who feed only upon excitement. They belong', he continued, 'to the same race who have wandered over parched deserts, who have sailed out into unknown seas, who have thrown themselves amongst howling savages, who have sat upon powder mines to gather information, and to spread it, when gathered, before an ever ravenous public.'[21] Hollingshead's concept of the journalist as intrepid explorer was certainly not original to him and he was undoubtedly influenced by both Dickens and, as we shall shortly see, Henry Mayhew, but he brought to that concept his own standards of honesty and integrity. Certainly, as the range of his subjects indicate, no explorer could be more enterprising in unearthing quirks of conduct and hidden sub-cultures. No sooner had he returned from his travels through the dense terrain of the London slums than he was off again, this time through subterranean London, exploring the sewers of the city. Typically, his *Underground London* (1862), which first appeared as a five-part series in *All the Year Round* in July and August 1861, was both fascinating and informative, analytical, statistical, yet eminently readable; and it touched only lightly upon the obvious horrors to concentrate on the terrain and its inhabitants – the old river courses which had 'degraded into dark underground sewers' and the lives and character of the sewer cleaners (whom he led in a chorus of the National Anthem as they conducted him through a sewer beneath Buckingham Palace!). From his journey through underground London the reader gained a clear picture of the state of the old sewers, the scale and significance of Bazalgette's new sewerage system (1858-68), the sad state of the lost rivers of London, and the progress of the new underground railway lines. In short, Hollingshead's approach was not to be sensational or colourful so much as factual, informative and soberly evocative.

It was these characteristics of his craft and an earnest yet never dull determination to inform accurately – which makes his *Ragged London in 1861* superior to the many other exposés of working-class London which appeared in the mid-Victorian years.[22]

The idea of a series of articles on the condition of the poor was suggested to Hollingshead by the editor and later owner of the *Morning Post*, Algernon Borthwick.[23] The *Morning Post* has been described as a reactionary paper, 'the inveterate foe of reform movements and the intrepid champion of lost causes, most of which deserved to be lost, it combined political conservatism with social snobbery'.[24] Known as 'Palmerston's paper' for its chauvinistic articles, it became under Borthwick even more of a Court and Society paper.[25] It may seem to be an unlikely vehicle for a series of articles on the poor, but Algernon's father, Peter, who had been the editor of the paper from 1849 to 1852, when his son took over at the age of twenty-two, had been associated with Disraeli's Young England group which had drawn attention to the widening gulf separating classes and had called for sympathy and compassion from the governing classes. In early January 1861 the paper reported that coal barges had become stuck in the frozen rivers and that the price of coal had jumped, which, it stressed, 'will be felt severely by the humbler classes'.[26] A week or so before Hollingshead's first article appeared in the *Morning Post*, it had had a powerful first leader on the precariousness of life at the margin and on the impact of the bitter weather on the lives of the poor:

> The first lesson taught by the present condition of the London poor is the frailty of the tenure by which the working classes hold the means of subsistence. Three weeks ago, although provisions were dear and employment far from plentiful, there was no perceptible increase in the amount of distress. But two or three days' frost made all the difference. Thousands were thrown out of work. Production ceased; only consumption went on. Coals and provisions instantly rose in price; wages were not forthcoming. Savings, where there were any, melted away: the small shops were driven to give credit; but their means of doing so soon came to an end. . . . The more the cold increased without, the greater were the squalor and misery within. Beggary was the last resource.

Benevolent societies, pawnshops, and the poor law unions were 'besieged' and, the paper concluded, 'there lies hidden out of sight every phase of suffering, contrasting in an almost unearthly way with the luxury and refinement of the more fortunate members of the one great brotherhood'. Having drawn attention so accurately to the economic dynamics of poverty, the *Morning Post* looked to 'brother love and Christian charity' for a solution. Perhaps it hoped that Hollingshead would treat the subject in the typical sensationalist manner of the exposé literature of the day and reinforce its message that the only remedy was to draw from the deep 'well-spring of sympathy, pity, and abounding charity' to be found among the middle and upper classes.[27] If that was the case, it must have been disappointed, for Hollingshead was not interested in the well-worn theme of the gulf separating classes or in sensationalist reporting, and his attitude towards philanthropy was in sharp contrast to the *Morning Post*'s and, indeed, to the majority sentiment of the day.

Working with his typical energy, Hollingshead completed his survey in a remarkably short time. His first article appeared on 21 January, his tenth and last on the 31st of the month. They formed the 'germ', as Hollingshead put it, of the book which is reproduced here.[28] Armed with letters of introduction to local clergymen, Hollingshead worked furiously: 'For a whole fortnight I walked about all day, and wrote all night, sleeping from four to seven a.m., between the completion of one report and the preparation for another.'[29] The editor appended the title 'London Horrors' to each article, and though that conveyed rather more sensationalism than Hollingshead probably intended, he felt that he 'could hardly have chosen a better name'.[30]

'The Augustan Age of English journalism', it has been said, 'was the age of anonymity . . . ,' and Hollingshead's name did not appear on any of the articles. He might well have thought that he deserved some credit and a wider readership than the 3,000 or so who bought the *Morning Post* each day.[31] A few months later he published the articles in a rearranged and considerably expanded form under the title *Ragged London in 1861*, a title that may possibly have been suggested to him by Mary Bayly's *Ragged Homes and How to Mend Them* (1859), but more likely one that was influenced by the publicity Dickens and Lord Shaftesbury were giving to the condition of the children in London's ragged schools. 'Ragged' was, in any case, a current term for the very poor, carrying something of the connotation of the 'lumpenproletariat'.[32]

When Hollingshead set out on his investigation as a 'Special Commissioner' for the *Morning Post* he must have realized that, far from being in any sense a pioneer, he was contributing to what had become an accepted genre of Victorian journalism – the voyage of discovery into the 'lower regions' inhabited by the 'submerged', 'outcast' or 'residuum' of society. Carlyle's call for an examination of 'the actual condition of Society' had been answered in works of fiction (most notably by Disraeli in his *Sybil, or The Two Nations* and the novels of Dickens and Elizabeth Gaskell), innumerable articles in the *Journal of the Statistical Society of London* and in the *Transactions of the National Association for the Promotion of Social Science*, countless official inquiries by select committees and royal commissions, and dozens of forays into the slums – all these conveyed a sense of exploration into unknown, 'dark' regions which were, ironically, not in foreign lands but right at home. Indeed, a full decade before the publication of Hollingshead's book, one housing reformer wrote that to describe yet again the lack of sanitation 'and the dilapidated condition of the back streets, courts, and alleys of London is almost superfluous' for 'they have been denounced in every form of letter, leading article and harangue'.[33]

Above all, this body of social literature had been influenced by Henry Mayhew's great *London Labour and the London Poor*, which had first appeared as a series of articles in the *Morning Chronicle* in 1849 and 1850, and was published in two-volume book form in 1851 and 1852 and in an expanded four-volume version in 1861-2, all to enthusiastic reviews. It would have been understandable if Hollingshead had followed the underlying approach and assumptions of Mayhew's work, especially since the classes which Mayhew had concentrated on were precisely those most noticeably affected by the bitter weather which had occasioned the *Morning Post*'s commission. But *Ragged London in 1861* differed significantly from Mayhew's work and from the scores of its imitators, in its tone of dispassionate inquiry, its framework of house-to-house visitation, and its broad coverage of London's heterogeneous lower working classes.[34]

Mayhew's style and vocabulary were geared to shock and thrill the reader. His brilliant interpreter, Gertrude Himmelfarb, has written that he could never resist 'the impulse of the dramatist, satirist, novelist, and activist' that he was.[35] By comparison Hollingshead's style and approach were remarkably muted. In his contributions to *Household Words* he had had to make some accommodation to the house style which another of the contributors, Elizabeth Gaskell, called 'Dickensy'.[36] Percy

Fitzgerald, one of 'Mr Dickens's young men' at *Household Words*, complained that the writers there

> were compelled, owing to the necessity of producing effect, to adopt a tone of exaggeration. Everything, however trivial, had to be made more comic than it really was. This was the law of the paper. . . , this pressure became all but irresistible. A mere natural, unaffected account of any transaction, it was felt, was out of place; it would not harmonise with the brilliant buoyant things surrounding it.[37]

Hollingshead strove to resist the irresistible and to remain true to the 'blunt plain style of my own'.[38] He told Thackeray that his 'very pure style' was derived from the streets and from 'costermongers and skittle-sharps', and he wrote with some pride that Carlyle (admittedly no great stylist!) preferred his 'actuality papers' to 'Dickens's Word-Spinnings'.[39] While he could not be completely true to his own style at *Household Words*, he was able in his *Ragged London in 1861* to 'give up effect for the sake of truthfulness' and 'to become a plain, matter-of-fact guide'. The sights he witnessed were 'horrible' enough and so self-evidently 'disgraceful to humanity' that they did not require the embellishments and exaggeration which Dickens had imposed at *Household Words*.[40]

Hollingshead's lean and detached tone did not go unnoticed. To one reviewer, among the characteristics which made *Ragged London in 1861* so compelling was the absence of the usual hyperbole and striving for heightened effect: 'It is very seldom that the condition of the lower orders', wrote the reviewer in the *Westminster Review*, 'is treated with that sobriety which alone rivets the attention of thinking men. Mr Hollingshead's book is completely free from every trace of sentimentality and factitious feeling'.[41] This is not to say that Hollingshead's book was colourless. Far from it, for he had a keen eye for telling detail and dramatic flair for the phrase which would enliven and drive home the central point he was making. Throughout, for example, he commented without belabouring the point that the homes of the poor were cramped and confined, but at one stage he underscored their size when he wrote that they were so small that they might well serve 'as a penal settlement for dwarfs', a phrase Dickens himself would have been proud of.[42]

Whereas one comes away from Mayhew with a sense that he has lifted the eccentricities of his 'characters' out of context and selected only the most interesting or dramatic examples of London low life, and from Dickens with a sense that all is bustle and excitement, cockney vitality and strutting energy – a kaleidoscopic picture of life which, however disagreeable in detail, is picturesque taken as a whole – what emerges from *Ragged London in 1861* is an overwhelming sense of the dejection, despair and passivity which the graphic artists, Doré and Gavarni, so brilliantly captured in their drawings.[43] Working-class life as depicted by Hollingshead is far from enchanting. There are moments of relaxation and pleasure, but for the most part it is a dull, grinding life of constant fatigue, malnutrition, and the struggle to survive. Too many writers, Hollingshead argued, had painted the lives of the poor 'in colours of imagination, rather than in hard outlines of fact'. But 'if truthfully given', their lives have 'little romance, little beauty, and little variety'.[44] The sullen, empty silence which Mayhew commented on when he described London by night pervades Hollingshead's London by day.[45]

Hollingshead was too good a journalist to miss the dramatic value of the bread riots which occurred at the height of the winter, and indeed he rather exaggerated their significance (see below, p.5). But above all there is a frightening silence in his streets and a dull acceptance of their fate on the part of the 'dull, grey famished masses'. He wrote that 'the saddest sight was the general air of weak, hopeless resignation. A murmur, an act of violence, or a threat, would have been a relief.'[46] Hollingshead himself came away from his investigation feeling that it was 'melancholy work' and 'perhaps the saddest task that ever fell to the lot of a "special" [correspondent].' 'The task of digging out so much social degradation became so monotonous, and the daily stories I had to tell seemed to be so painfully like each other', he wrote in an article in *Good Words*, 'that I closed my note-book in less than a fortnight, worn out and depressed.'[47] It is this sense of melancholy and sadness which permeates his book.

Contributing to the sense of grey apathy was Hollingshead's emphasis upon the 'terrible sameness' and 'little variety' to be found in life at the subsistence level.[48] Others had pointed out that it was not necessary to journey far afield into unknown districts to find slums, but what others had mentioned Hollingshead chose to stress. His newspaper articles in fact ended on that melancholy note:

> Weeks spent in Westminster, near the Abbey, would only multiply these experiences, and weeks spent in and about Whitechapel, St George's-in-the-East, Bethnal-green, and Shoreditch, Clerkenwell, St Pancras, Bermondsey, South-wark, Lambeth, 'over the water' generally, and Marylebone would certainly produce a like result. Wherever you sink a shaft – whether in the centre or the outskirts – and penetrate with a good guide, perserverance, and fair local knowledge, you will find endless veins of social degradation. In all my journeys through the holes and corners of London I have found a terrible sameness – little more than one thing – a dead level of misery, crime, vice, dirt and rags.[49]

If Hollingshead's tone and emphasis are different from Mayhew's, his sense of being a social explorer, conducting his readers on a voyage of discovery was very much the same. Mayhew had written of nomadic 'wandering tribes', and Hollingshead echoed him in the phrase 'the wandering tribes of London'.[50] But while Mayhew invested the poor he described with what amounted to strong racial characteristics, Hollings-head tended to attribute their characters and mores to their social and physical environment.[51] And as an explorer Mayhew painted a picture of tribal life that was shot through with 'gayety and high spirits' – 'his street folk', writes Himmelfarb 'some-times seem to revel in their misery and vice' – while Hollingshead, as we have mentioned, thought that they were beaten down by their hard lives.[52]

Above all they differed significantly in their coverage of that varied and ill-defined social stratum, the working classes. Gertrude Himmelfarb has pointed out that despite the grand sweep of Mayhew's title, *London Labour and the London Poor*, he dealt 'almost entirely with the "street folk" and "those that will not work"', and 'took as his explicit theme the street folk ... street-hawkers and hucksters, dock labourers, and flower girls'. His 'labour' and 'poor' in fact were 'undiluted by the presence of any conventional workers' such as weavers, needlewomen, tailors, shoemakers, dressmakers, or carpenters.[53] Given Mayhew's narrow selectivity, it is not surprising that the sub-culture he claimed to have unearthed appears 'archaic, anarchic, barbaric'.[54] There are passages in *Ragged London in 1861* which would suggest that Hollingshead also concentrated on the same sub-culture and was equally determined to portray the 'working classes' as a race apart. He refers to them as 'human rats' and 'refuse population' and to their dwellings as 'human warrens', 'nests' or 'dust heaps'. They 'skulk'or 'huddle together', 'half-buried' in 'sewer-like' courts and alleys, or 'burrow' in 'holes and corners', rather than merely live in houses like Hollingshead's readers.[55] They are portrayed as 'oozing out on to the pavements and into the gutters' like so much human excrement − literally the 'residuum'.[56] The sense of a savage, animalistic, lower form of life is conveyed by his description of their physical appearance: 'rough, long-haired heads' disappear from view, many of his slum dwellers are 'nearly naked', and the children go barefoot and naked; old women 'howl' at him, and the inhabitants of the slums are 'swarthy', or 'sallow' or have 'yellow faces', or are blackened with soot, or possess 'dark sinister faces' − any colour, it would seem, but white.[57] The Victoria Theatre at the corner of New Cut teems with 'evil, low-browed, lowering faces'.[58] The children are 'ragged, sharp, weasel-like' and 'human child-rats ... digging in the dust-heaps'.[59] The babies are 'dirty brown limp bundles that never look like young children'.[60] Hollingshead reduces the existence of the poor to five main aspects, 'poverty, ignorance, dirt, immorality, and crime', and if one were to read only those passages in which these descriptions of an animalistic and savage existence appear, one would come away from *Ragged London in 1861* questioning the common humanity of the working classes and convinced that Hollingshead had reinforced and confirmed Mayhew's earlier exploration and discovery.[61]

But this would certainly be a misreading of Hollingshead. For although he was unable to free himself from the 'attraction of repulsion' which had so great an influence on the writing of Dickens, he was (surprisingly, in view of his great love of street life and the theatre) less interested in the demi-monde, or bohemian groups, street vendors, and the criminal and semi-criminal classes than in that great pool of casual labour that was so large and representative a section of the working classes of London.[62] He knew that this casual labour force was too large for the unskilled jobs available – in his autobiography he put the distress of 1861 down to 'one of those gluts of labour – the curse of great cities', and despite the passages quoted above, he was generally sympathetic in his treatment.[63] He dealt with far more 'conventional workers' than did Mayhew – road workers and grocers, watch makers and tailors, porters, shoe makers and shoe blacks, cabbies, butchers, vegetable sellers, dockers, silk weavers, toy makers, gaswork employees, French polishers, charwomen, laundresses, railway workers, pig keepers, brick makers, stablemen, and market porters. Unlike Mayhew he was not particularly interested in the 'lowest kind of thieves', 'swell-mobsmen' and prostitutes, although he mentions them.[64]

If Hollingshead's coverage was more comprehensive than Mayhew's, touching upon a broader segment of the 'humbler classes', it was also more balanced and favourable in its interpretation, though not unambiguous. His poor are 'patient, industrious and honest', and, for the most part they 'only ask to be employed'; there are many who will do anything rather than apply for charity, and, Hollingshead generalized, 'I know much of working people of all kinds, and I have seen hundreds of bright, open, honest faces under the battered hats and bonnets of costermongers' – a defence of the costermongers' reputation much needed after Mayhew's emphasis upon their criminal natures.[65] Where he found religiosity and sobriety he gives due praise, and he stated that 'the cases of heroic endurance under the most frightful trials . . . make us respect these poor creatures even in their dirt and rags'.[66]

In short, where others, especially Mayhew, evoke alarm and disgust, fear or horror, Hollingshead's work prompts pity and compassion. But not entirely, for throughout his book there is considerable confusion and ambiguity, typical of the mid-Victorian period. He chose to ignore, or at least pay only brief attention to the criminal and semi-criminal classes and stressed that the most common crime was fraudulent application to soup kitchens and other charities; yet he generalizes, contradicting his own evidence, that 'crime' was one of the five main characteristics of the poor.[67] *Ragged London in 1861* also reveals that Hollingshead, like so many other writers and politicians of his age, vacillated in his analysis of the causes of poverty between the traditional, accepted view that character is fate, and the newer, more daring and as yet unclearly perceived view that poverty resulted from impersonal socio-economic and environmental factors. At times he suggests that bad dwellings cause bad morals, at others that improved morality will result in an improved environment.[68] He never clearly states whether it is the pig that makes the stye or *vice versa*. In his discussion of intense pockets of unemployment and overcrowding, for example, he was one of the first to argue that it was the need 'to be near their bread' that produced the immobility of labour, but at the same time he criticizes the poor for their innate conservatism which led to 'immobility' and 'love of place', while elsewhere he calls them 'wandering tribes'! Although he clearly saw that the casual labour force had to live close to their work (this applied especially to dock and market labourers and all those hired on a daily basis), he calls for greater mobility as one solution to their poverty.[69] He realized that the poverty he witnessed throughout London stemmed from the enormous disparity between the size of the casual labour force and the demand for that labour, yet his vocabulary is full of the moral prescriptions of the middle classes – the poor have basically themselves to blame for their poverty. Much of the evidence he gathered pointed to the hopeless uncertainty of life at the margin yet he was faithful to the doctrines of 'his friend' Sam Smiles (to whom he dedicated one of his books).[70] He emphasized the 'wonders of self-help' and 'the principle of self-help – the only principle that tends to assist the poor without demoralizing them', and laments the 'want of self-reliance on the part of the industrious poor'.[71]

Above all, he concluded, the greatest hope for the amelioration of the condition of the poor lay in the Malthusian form of self-help, namely sexual self-control, and failed to develop his argument, offered elsewhere, that their 'overbreeding' was probably related to their overcrowding. Some thirty years after the publication of *Ragged London in 1861* he emphasized that his main message had been that 'a little less drunken indulgence in marriage and child-breeding will at once better the condition of these miserable people, as the Reverend Mr Malthus told them long ago'.[72] Commenting on the cruel irony of street names such as 'Dove Court' or 'Rose Passage', he wrote that a far more appropriate name might be 'Malthus Yard', and his normally detached tone deserted him when he discussed what he regarded as the working classes' sexual excesses: 'they increase and multiply, and for what? To become paupers; to glut the labour market; to keep their wages down at starvation point, to swell the profits of capital. They look to everyone to relieve them, but make few efforts to relieve themselves.'[73]

Hollingshead's love of sturdy self-help and self-reliance and his impatience with 'political sentimentalists' makes his *Ragged London in 1861* at times less of an objective description of the condition of the working classes than a heated attack upon the evils and dangers of indiscriminate charity.[74] During the winter of 1860-61 the number of paupers in London increased from 96,752 to 135,389 and with typical energy and concern the middle and upper classes threw themselves into organizing special relief committees. 'Happily', declared the *Morning Post* on 11 January 1861, 'there seems no present limit to the liberality of the public.'[75] Hollingshead was far less happy about the readiness of Londoners to put their hands in their pockets, for he insisted that such readily available charity only served to turn the 'deserving poor' into the 'undeserving', or, in his terms, the 'industrious' into the 'idle'.[76] He wrote elsewhere that he had 'carried the principles of philosophical Radicalism into magazines that were edited by Conservatives' and so had been able to spread his message of hard-nosed free-trade liberalism in the pages of journals normally given over to old-fashioned Tory humanitarian sentiment and unthinking, unscientific paternalism.[77]

The free flow of charity on which so many Victorians prided themselves, only served to turn even the most 'honest labourers' into beggars, he argued, and robbed the poor of 'character'.[78] Philanthropy might demonstrate to the poor that the classes above them were not hard-hearted, but, he cautioned, 'the head, after all, is not the worst guide in works of charity'.[79]

Hollingshead's strident attack upon the evils of indiscriminate charity, combined with his scattered references to crime and especially fraudulent requests for charity and with his emphasis upon 'over-breeding', only served to weaken the impact of his carefully gathered evidence of the destructive effects of the slum environment and uncertain employment. In this regard *Ragged London in 1861* may have ultimately had a similar impact to Mayhew's work upon the reader, namely the conclusion that the proletariat as a whole had the same mores, the same low character, as the lumpenproletariat![80] This, at least, is what one reviewer got out of his book: Hollingshead, he wrote, had not shrunk from 'ascribing, as is so justly due, a great portion of their [the lower orders] sufferings to themselves. It requires no little moral courage in the present day to speak out on the truth of the reckless marriages, the hopeless improvidence, and saddest of all, the contented indifference' of the poor, and, it asked rhetorically, 'Who can help them that will not help themselves?'[81] This is doubtless the message which Hollingshead hoped his work would convey – it is a conclusion which is at variance with his evidence which supplied ample proof that there were working-class families who followed all the prescriptions and moral precepts of the middle classes yet, for all their virtuous lives, their careful harbouring of resources, their self-denial, and obedience to the injunctions of Sam Smiles, were dragged down into the ranks of the paupers the moment that their precarious living was hit by the harsh winter. His evidence, so carefully gathered, of families who 'cherish the spirit of independence which a long course of intrusive visiting charity has not been able to crush', and of men and women on the verge of starvation who would try anything rather than become charity cases, was lost in his conclusions, so vehemently presented, that 'this want of self-reliance on the part of the industrious poor is something enormous'.[82]

The strength of *Ragged London in 1861* does not lie in its underlying social arguments, which lacked systematic development and penetrating depth, nor in the remedies for the ills Hollingshead so vividly disclosed. He had little respect for the social reformers of the day, regarding them as intolerable busybodies who wanted to 'teach everybody their business', interfere in the free flow of market forces ('producers and consumers would not be allowed to trade together on their own terms'), regiment life for the masses ('every city would be turned into a huge barracks, and every man in it would be treated as a soldier on duty'), and rob 'honest labourers' of their sturdy independence. The net result, if they had their way, would be expensive 'over-government'.[83] His own reforms were modest – the more cautious and discriminating application of charity, education of the younger generation, major revisions in (or, preferably, abolition of) the 1834 Poor Law which he attacked so vigorously, equalization of the rates, and above all else the inculcation of the virtues of self-help and family planning.[84]

It is as an example of the pioneering social surveys of the mid-Victorian period that *Ragged London in 1861* should be judged, and on that basis it is a most impressive work. Despite his disclaimer that he 'hardly felt inclined to produce a blue-book', Hollingshead's survey in fact had the apparatus, breadth, (and hence value to the historian) of the best of the reports from investigating parliamentary select committees and royal commissions.[85] It was certainly broader in its scope, more penetrating in its coverage, and more carefully researched, than previous journalistic forays into the working-class districts of London. He covered all parts of London, the West End as well as the East, the generally neglected regions south of the Thames as well as the better-known North, and his approach was innovative, incorporating as it did interviews, house-to-house visitations, the reports of that small band of men who worked most closely with the poor and were most knowledgeable about their problems – the slum missionaries, medical officers, and ragged school officials – parliamentary speeches, family budgets, and informative items from the daily press. He covered whole neighbourhoods and had a fine sense of their unity and special character, and yet he could descend to the quite specific enumeration of individual streets and dwellings, and he dealt with both the tenements of the poor and the new model dwelling houses.

The *Saturday Review* in 1859 correctly observed that most writers on the slums 'make a point of conducting us to the very threshold, but they distinctly refuse to go further with us'. Hollingshead crossed the threshold and furnishes us with some of the best descriptions up to that time of working-class interiors and the details of domestic living.[86] Part of his value to the social historian lies in his fine eye for the small details of life – the poor sharing their fires, pawnbroking as the art of survival, the pride of the poor in refusing charity, the support network among the womenfolk, the trials and frustrations of queuing up at the soup kitchens, the lifeless hair and eyes of those suffering from malnutrition, the sanitary condition of the cow-stables where the poor bought their contaminated milk, the penny-saving societies of the poor, the location of schools next to polluting factories, the Sunday shopping for cheaper foodstuffs, roofs depressed 'like crushed hats', window-ledges turned into miniature gardens, complete with gates and railings, the problems of female employment in districts too poor to support either domestic servants or even prostitutes, the social dynamics which caused respectable neighbourhoods to decline into slums, the food offered by philanthropically run cheap eating houses, the terrors of seeking new jobs at mid-life, the intermingling of 'hard-working, would-be-honest strugglers for dear life' with the criminal classes, the various legal and illegal (dog and rat fights) leisure pursuits of the poor – these details accumulate to become a literary photograph or daguerreotype of mid-Victorian London.[87]

Hollingshead was one of the first popular writers to go south of the river, but his treatment of south London was superficial in comparison to his treatment of the other areas: it presents a monolithic, over-generalized picture and concentrates largely on only the haunts of criminals, prostitutes, and drunken sailors. It reads rather like the descriptions of other writers of London as a whole and points up the superiority of Hollingshead to those writers in his cautious and careful analysis of the districts north of the Thames. In his treatment of the East End, for example, he was careful to stress that it was not an area of unrelieved poverty or depravity and that standards of living varied considerably within its borders.[88] He is informative and accurate on rent levels, overcrowding and sanitary conditions (distinguishing carefully between the responsibility of landlords and tenants), and he offered one of the first thoughtful criticisms of the model dwelling-house (five per cent philanthropic) movement, the sweeping slum demolitions, and sanitary legislation which, to other, less well-informed, observers were the panaceas for the problems of the slum.[89] When he contemplated the vast regions of dilapidated and rotten dwellings he wrote in despair that only 'a thorough clearance – a clean sweep for miles and miles' (in Bethnal Green) or only 'an earthquake or new railway' (in Clerkenwell) would improve matters, and that ideally the 'haunts of vice and crime' in south London 'ought to be ploughed up by the roots', but he knew that 'metropolitan improvements' only benefited 'one corner of London at the expense of another' and that 'the inhabitants would only be pushed somewhere else'. His book served as a salutary warning to those contemporaries of his who put their faith in the universal benefits to be gained instantaneously from massive slum demolition schemes.[90] It is his blending of the anthropological approach of earlier writers and the sociological methods of later writers such as Greenwood, Booth, and Rowntree, which makes *Ragged London in 1861* so important a contribution to the Victorian literature of social investigation. Evocative, objective in its descriptions, revealing in its analyses and conclusions, painstaking in its detail, and throughout eminently readable and informative, it deserves to be far better known to students of Victorian London and of working-class life within it.

November 1985   Anthony S. Wohl

Notes to the Introduction

Unless otherwise stated place of publication is London. After the first reference, the abbreviation *RL* is used for Hollingshead, *Ragged London in 1861* (1861).

1 All temperatures are in Fahrenheit at midday in London. I am grateful to my student assistant Thomas Kanaley for gathering weather data from *The Times*. See also A.J. Drummond 'Cold Winters at Kew Observatory, 1783-1942', *Quarterly Journal of the Royal Metereological Society*, Vol.69(1943), quoted in Appendix 2, table 12 of G. Stedman Jones, *Outcast London*(Oxford, 1971), p.384.

2 *The Times*, 9 January 1861, *Morning Post*, 7 January 1861, 9 January 1861, 10 January 1861. There were over 25,000 people on the lake in Regent's Park and 8,000 on the lake in St James's Park, *ibid.*, 7 January 1861. *Punch*, 5 January 1861, p.4.

3 Until recently it has been out of print, but has now been reissued by Garland Publishing, edited by Lynn and Andrew Lees, 1985. Stedman Jones has a few brief references to it in his *Outcast London*, and see my *The Eternal Slum. Housing and Social Policy in Victorian London* (1977) pp.9, 25, 30, 32, 39, 205, 300. Gertrude Himmelfarb has one passing reference to Hollingshead in her superb study of poverty and attitudes towards it, *The Idea of Poverty. England in the Early Industrial Age* (New York, 1984), p.355, and see below, note 61. H.J. Dyos, in his survey of the literature on the London slums, 'The Slums of Victorian London', *Victorian Studies*, Vol.XI, No.1 (September 1967), p.15, says that Hollingshead, 'almost more than anyone, aimed at quantifying his data as far as he could', and that together with G. Godwin was 'probably the most authoritative' of the social writers of the period. The *Dictionary of National Biography* (1901-11) entry on Hollingshead mentions it but his obituary in *The Times* does not, and Hollingshead himself devoted only a little over one page to it in his 475-page two-volume autobiography, *My Lifetime*, Vol.1 (1895), pp.165-166. *Ragged London in 1861* is not mentioned in the flimsy biographical sketch by F. Gibson, 'John Hollingshead. A Notable Victorian', *The Dickensian*, Vol.LXII, No.348 (June 1866).

4 J. Hollingshead, *My Lifetime,* Vol. I, pp.16,7. His father, after failing as a merchant, secured a post as a clerk in the City Corporation, *ibid*, pp.50-1.

5 J. Hollingshead, *According to My Lights*, (1900), p.10. Thackeray described him as 'one of the regular cabs on the stand' at *Cornhill Magazine, ibid.*, p.216 and *My Lifetime*, Vol.1, p.163. Other writers there were Trollope, Sala, Lewes, and Greenwood, *ibid.*

6 He attacked the insanitary state of Convent Garden ('Mud-Salad Market'), calling it 'about the greatest nuisance ever permitted in a great City of Nuisances'. *Punch*, 14 August 1880, p.71. See also *ibid*, 21 August 1880, p.83 for 'The Duke of Mudford in Gloomsbury', where he attacked the Duke of Bedford for not building thoroughfares through his estates.

7 Hollingshead, *According to My Lights*, p.10. Among the contributors to *Household Words* were Wilkie Collins, Mrs Elizabeth Gaskell, Harriet Martineau, George Meredith, George Sala, Leigh Hunt, Savage Landor, Elizabeth Barrett Browning. For a superb analysis of *Household Words* and its writers see A. Lohrli, *Household Words. A Weekly Journal, 1850-1859, Conducted by Charles Dickens* (Toronto, 1973).

8 Hollingshead, *My Lifetime*, Vol.I, p.96. *The Times*, 11 October 1904.

9 Himmelfarb, 'The Culture of Poverty', in H.J. Dyos and M. Wolff, eds., *The Victorian City. Images and Realities* (1973), Vol.II, p.709. P. Collins in his splendid introduction to G.A. Sala, *Twice Around the Clock, or the Hours of the Day and Night in London* (Leicester, 1971), p.11, calls Sala the 'unchallenged Prince' of the special correspondents and says that Dickens created the genre when he sent Sala to St Petersburg for *Household Words*.

10 Hollingshead, *Under Bow Bells. A City Book for All Readers* (1860), p.216. *Who Was Who* (1897-1915), p.347. His other hobbies were music, chess, draughts, cricket, and billiards, *ibid*.

11 Hollingshead, *Under Bow Bells*, p.210.

12 The *Illustrated London News* thought that they were 'powerfully and pathetically written'. For these reviews see the advertisements on the end-paper of Hollingshead, *Rubbing the Gilt Off. A West End Book for All Readers* (1860).

13 P. Hartnoll, ed., *The Oxford Companion to the Theatre* (Oxford, 1951), p.296; Hollingshead, *Gaiety Chronicles* (1898), p.436. For a fine print of the interior of the Gaiety (which was demolished in 1902), see the *Illustrated London News*, Vol.LIV(1869), p.20 reproduced as illustration 59 between pp.214 and 215 of *The Victorian City*, Vol.I.

14 Hollingshead, *Plain English* (1880), preface, p.v, pp.9,11. 'There is no occupation', he wrote, 'more easy and agreeable than theatrical management', *ibid*., p.11.

15 Hollingshead, *My Lifetime*, Vol.II, pp.19,126-9. It was placed outside the theatre.

16 Hartnoll, *The Oxford Companion to the Theatre*, p.370; Hollingshead, *My Lifetime*, Vol.II, p.53, *Dictionary of National Biography* (1901-11), p.285.

17   Hollingshead, *Gaiety Chronicles*, p.454. Hollingshead said he was voted down by the 'nonconformist section' of the Reform, and that their war-cry was 'anti-Gaiety'. He claimed that the leader of the opposition to his membership was the manufacturer of the tights worn by the Gaiety girls.

18   Hollingshead, *My Lifetime*, Vols.I and II, *passim*.

19   Hollingshead, 'Great Eastern Postscript', *All the Year Round*, Vol.I, No.23 (October 1859), p.546, reprinted in his *Odd Journeys In and Out of London* (1860), p.335.

20   *Ibid*.

21   *Ibid*.

22   For the more important of these see note 33, below.

23   Borthwick was knighted in 1880, became an MP in 1886 and was raised to the peerage as Lord Glenesk in 1895. In 1876 he purchased the *Morning Post*. See W. Hindle, *The Morning Post, 1772-1937. Portrait of a Newspaper* (1937), p.204. Hollingshead, *My Lifetime*, Vol.I, p.165.

24   S. Koss, *The Rise and Fall of the Political Press in Britain*. Vol.I *The Nineteenth Century* (Chapel Hill, North Carolina, 1981), p.43.

25   Hindle, *The Morning Post, 1772-1937*, pp.187, 204ff.

26   *Ibid*., p.181. *Morning Post*, 9 January 1861.

27   *Ibid*., 11 January 1861.

28   Hollingshead, *Ragged London in 1861* (1861), preface, p.v. Hereafter, *RL*.

29   Hollingshead, *My Lifetime*, Vol.I, p.165.

30   *Ibid*.

31   Hindle, *The Morning Post, 1772-1937*, pp.216, 186.

32   Himmelfarb, *The Idea of Poverty*, p.372.

33   *A Brief Inquiry into the Evils Attendant upon the Present Means of Erecting, Purchasing and Renting Dwellings for the Industrial Classes, etc*., (Anon) (1851), pp.7-8. For these works see Wohl, *The Eternal Slum*, pp.351-2. To the works listed there might be added G.B. Tremenheere, *Dwellings of the Labouring Classes in the Metropolis* (1856), W. Gilbert, *Dives and Lazarus; or the Adventures of an Obscure Medical Man in a Low Neighbourhood* (1858), see also Dyos, *Victorian Studies*, Vol.XI, No.I (September 1967). Peter Keating in his *Into Unknown England 1866-1913* (Manchester, 1976), p.13, writes 'there is barely an area of nineteenth-century fictional and non-fictional prose, in which the central attitudes and terminology of social exploration do not appear'. Himmelfarb has an excellent analysis of some of this literature in her *The Ideas of Poverty*.

34   It will be readily apparent that I am greatly indebted to Himmelfarb's analysis of Mayhew, *ibid*., in the following section.

35   *Ibid.*, p.318.
36   Quoted in Lorhli, *Household Words*, p.10.
37   P. Fitzgerald, *Memories of Charles Dickens* (1913), pp.170-1, quoted in Collins, ed., *Twice Around the Clock*, introduction, p.19.
38   Hollingshead, *My Lifetime*, Vol.I, p.96.
39   *Ibid.*, pp.162, 158.
40   *RL*, p.39. He admitted that his pieces for *Household Words* 'retained some degree of [the] fancy and imagination' demanded by Dickens. *My Lifetime*, Vol.I, p.158. Hollingshead argued that if some of his *Household Words* articles were superficial 'it was less my fault than Charles Dickens's. He wanted '"readable" papers'. *Ibid.*, p.190.
41   *Westminster Review*, Vol. CXLIX(July 1861), p.132.
42   *RL*, p.86.
43   G. Doré and W.B. Jerrold, *London. A Pilgrimage* (1872). For Gavarni (Sulpice-Guillaume (Paul) Chevalier) see E.D.H. Johnson, 'Victorian Artists and the Urban Milieu', Dyos and Wolff, eds., *The Victorian City*, Vol. II, pp.460-1.
44   *RL*, p.8.
45   Himmelfarb, *The Idea of Poverty*, pp.317-18 for Mayhew's London by night.
46   Hollingshead, *My Lifetime*, Vol.I, p.165.
47   *Ibid.*, pp.165-6; *Good Words*, Vol.II, (1861), p.171.
48   *RL*, pp.232, 8.
49   *Morning Post*, 30 January 1861. Although this appeared in the penultimate article it really concluded his survey, for he wrote that he would not present another district, but would 'endeavour to deal with a few of the social questions arising out of my survey, and shall then hold my peace', *ibid*. Hollingshead used this passage, with minor alterations, to begin the Conclusion of his book, *RL*, p.232.
50   *RL*, p.240.
51   Himmelfarb, *The Victorian City*, Vol.II, p.711.
52   *Ibid.*, p.724.
53   *Ibid.*, p.710; Himmelfarb, *The Idea of Poverty*, p.323, 326, 351.
54   *Ibid.*, p.363.
55   *RL*, pp.130, 140, 165, 166, 167, 136.
56   *Ibid.*, p.40.
57   *Ibid.*, pp.108, 31, 74, 44, 58, 81.
58   *Ibid.*, p.180.
59   *Ibid.*, p.67, 72.
60   *Ibid.*, p.73.
61   He refers to their 'swinish life', *ibid.*, p.136. I disagree with Professor Himmelfarb's observation that *Ragged London in 1861* must be classified alongside the works of Beames, Gavin, Ritchie, and

Godwin, among others, as one of 'those books whose titles were more memorable than their contents and conjured up the most lurid vision of the metropolis', (*The Victorian City*, Vol.II, p.727), despite the passages I have just quoted. But her superb discussion of Mayhew's confusion of the labouring poor as a whole with the lowest of the low, the lumpenproletariat, is certainly applicable to Hollingshead.

62 For the phrase 'attraction of repulsion', see Collins, 'Dickens in London', in *The Victorian City*, Vol.II, p.537. The best analysis of casual labour is Stedman Jones, *Outcast London*. Roughly one family in ten was connected to the casual labour force.

63 Hollingshead, *My Lifetime*, Vol.I, p.165.

64 He did mention that 'the best paid occupation appears to be prostitution', and he commented ironically that their's were the best-kept dwellings, Hollingshead, *RL*, p.49.

65 *Ibid.*, pp.18, 115, 28.

66 *Ibid.*, p.82.

67 *Ibid.*, pp.6, 8.

68 *Ibid.*, p.114.

69 *Ibid.*, pp.18, 8, 240.

70 Hollingshead, *Ways of Life* (1861), dedication.

71 *RL*, p.242.

72 Hollingshead, *My Lifetime*, Vol.I, p.166. He is here quoting or rather slightly misquoting the preface of *RL*, p.vi.

73 *Ibid.*, pp.169, 241.

74 Hollingshead., *Gaiety Chronicles*, pp.453-4, and see below, note 83.

75 Stedman Jones, *Outcast London*, p.45; *Morning Post*, 11 January 1861.

76 *RL*, p.248.

77 Hollingshead, *Gaiety Chronicles*, pp.453-4.

78 *RL*, p.241.

79 *Ibid.*, p.239.

80 See Himmelfarb's discussion, *The Victorian City*, Vol.II, p.537.

81 *Westminster Review*, Vol.CXLIX (July 1861), p.132.

82 *RL*, pp.144, 242.

83 Hollingshead, *Rubbing the Gilt Off. A West End Book for all Readers* (1860), pp.152, 153, and 'Teaching our Grandmothers', in *To-Day. Essays and Miscellanies*. Vol.I *Day Thoughts* (1865), pp.117, 118, 119.

84 *RL*, *passim*. He ends the book on the note that 'the only road out of the slough of pauperism' is the education of the next generation, *ibid.*, p.248.

85 *Ibid.*, preface, p.v.

86 *Saturday Review*, 3 December 1859, p.677, quoted in Collins, ed., *Twice Around the Clock*, pp.17-18.

87 *RL*, pp.24, 47, 56, and *passim*.

88 *Ibid.*, p.40.

89 For the model dwelling-house movement and the impact of demolitions on the housing of the working classes, see my *The Eternal Slum*. Hollingshead was certainly among the first to state that the model dwelling-houses were not housing the class most in need of accommodation and that they were in fact a disguised form of philanthropy. Many of the areas described by Hollingshead were demolished in clearance schemes undertaken by the Metropolitan Board of Works and the London County Council; see notes to the text.

90 *RL*, pp.31, 167-8. The reference to 'a clean sweep' in Bethnal Green is from Hollingshead's third article in the *Morning Post*, 23 January 1861, but he may have had second thoughts for he omitted it from the text. See note to the text, p.72.

Note on the Text

I have used throughout the text square parentheses, [ ], to indicate where Hollingshead made additions to his original articles in the *Morning Post*. A dagger symbol (†) indicates where Hollingshead omitted, or altered, material in his original *Morning Post* series. This material is produced under a † in the Notes at the end of the text. I have not indicated minor changes in the wording or in capitalization and punctuation.

All the footnotes in the text itself which are marked by an asterisk (*) are Hollingshead's.

Hollingshead used an *l.* throughout the text to represent the pound (£) symbol.

RAGGED LONDON

Preface

This book, the germ of which consists of ten letters published in the *Morning Post* during the month of January, 1861, under the title of 'London Horrors', is an attempt to beat the bounds of metropolitan dirt and misery.[1] As a special correspondent of a newspaper is not a parliamentary committee, and I hardly felt inclined to produce a blue-book, this volume contains indications rather than proofs of metropolitan social degradation. The proofs, however, unfortunately are not far off; and for a million of people to live in London as they are now living, and, in the main, are contented to live, is a glaring national disgrace. With all our electro-plated sentiment about home and the domestic virtues, we ought to wince a good deal at the houses of the poor. The evils shadowed forth by this and like books cannot be remedied by Government, nor tinkering philanthropy. Parliament babbles about them occasionally, and a few people, deceived by the babbling, imagine that royal roads to cleanliness and plenty are about to be opened up. Those few of the poor and miserable who wish for improvement (they are not the majority) must shut their ears to such debates, and learn to help themselves. A little less drunken indulgence in matrimony and child-breeding would at once better their condition, as the Rev. Mr Malthus told them long ago.

THE CENTRE

Introduction[1]

The one domestic question at present uppermost in the public mind is the social condition of the humbler classes. It has been forced upon us by a winter of unexampled severity; by an amount of national distress, not at all exceptional in the cold season, which has gone to the very verge of bread riots;* and by agitations in the press and on the platform for an immediate improvement in labourers' cottages.[2] The chief streets of the metropolis have been haunted for weeks by gaunt labourers, who have moaned out a song of want that has penetrated the thickest walls. The workhouses have been daily besieged by noisy and half-famished crowds; the clumsy poor-law system, [with its twenty-three thousand officers, its boards, and its

[*Extract from a report in the *Morning Star*, January 18, 1861.—'Owing to the continuance of the frost, and all outdoor labour being stopped, the distress and suffering that prevail in the metropolis, particularly among the dock labourers, bricklayers, masons, and labouring classes at the East End, are truly horrible. Throughout the day thousands congregate round the approaches of the different workhouses and unions, seeking relief, but it has been impossible for the officers to supply one-third that applied. This led to considerable dissatisfaction, and hundreds have perambulated the different streets seeking alms of the inhabitants and of the passers-by. On Tuesday night much alarm was produced by an attack made on a large number of bakers' shops in the vicinity of the Whitechapel Road and Commercial Road East. They were surrounded by a mob of about thirty or forty in number, who cleared the shops of the bread they contained, and then decamped. On Wednesday night, however, affairs assumed a more threatening character, and acts of violence were committed. By some means it became known, in the course of the afternoon, that the dock labourers intended to visit Whitechapel in a mass, as soon as dusk set in, and that an attack would be made on all the provision shops in that locality. This led to a general shutting up of the shops almost throughout the East End—a precaution highly necessary, for between seven and nine o'clock thousands congregated in the principal streets and proceeded in a body from street to street. An attack was made upon many of the bakers' shops and eating-houses, and every morsel of food was carried away. A great many thieves and dissipated characters mingled with the mob, and many serious acts of violence were committed. The mounted police of the district were present, but it was impossible for them to act against so large a number of people. Yesterday, the streets were thronged with groups of the unemployed, seeking relief of the passers-by. In the outskirts similar scenes were observed, and in some instances acts approaching intimidation were resorted to to obtain alms.']

twelve thousand annual reports,] has notoriously broken down; the working clergy, [and the London magistrates,] worn out and exhausted, have been the willing almoners of stray benevolence; Dorcas societies,[1] soup-kitchens, ragged-schools,[2] asylums, refuges, and all the varied machinery of British charity, have been strained to the utmost; and now† we may sit down and congratulate ourselves that only a few of our fellow-creatures have been starved to death. [The storm to all appearance has passed, but the really poor will feel the effects of those two bitter months—December, 1860, and January, 1861—for years. It is doubtful if there was not more real privation in February than in January of the present year; and the registrar-general's return of deaths from starvation—the most awful of all deaths—for the mild week ending February 16, had certainly increased.] There has been no lack of generosity on the part of those who have been able to give. The full purse has been everywhere found open, and thousands have asked to be shown real suffering, and the best mode of relieving it. A local taxation, cheerfully and regularly paid, of 18,000,000*l.* per annum, beyond the Government burden, is either inadequate for the purposes to which it is applied, or applied in the most wasteful and unskilful manner. The sum, or its administration, is unable to do its work. The metropolis, not to speak of other towns, is not 'managed', not cleansed, not relieved from the spectre of starvation which dances before us at our doors. We are evidently surrounded by a dense population, half buried in black kitchens and sewer-like courts and alleys, who are not raised by any real or fancied advance in wages; whose way of life is steeped in ignorance, dirt, and crime; and who are always ready to sink, even to death, at their usual period of want.†† How many they really number, what they really profess to be, and in what proportion they may be found in different parts of the metropolis, are secrets that no census has ever fully exposed.†††

[We are a little too apt to pride ourselves on our material growth, and to overlook the quality in the quantity of our population. Thirty millions of people in the United Kingdom—one-tenth of whom belong to London proper—make a very pretty figure in returns and official documents, until they come to be carefully sifted and examined. Taken in bulk, with a lofty statistical disregard of minds and souls, they show an undoubted advance in capital and prosperity. Taken in detail, in a kind of house-to-house visitation, they show that the spreading limbs of a great city may be healthy and vigorous, while its heart may gradually become more choked up and decayed.

A vast deal of life that skulks or struggles in London is only familiar to the hard-working clergy, certain medical practitioners, and a few parochial officers. It burrows in holes and corners, at the back of busy thoroughfares, where few know of its existence, or care to follow it. The largest and most painstaking directories pass it by; writers upon London reject it as too mean, too repulsive, or too obscure; and novelists, when they condescend to touch it, for the sake of obtaining contrasts, often paint it in the colours of imagination, rather than in the hard outlines of fact. Its records, if truthfully given, have little romance, little beauty, and little variety. Poverty, ignorance, dirt, immorality, crime, are the five great divisions of its history. Immovability, love of place, a determination to huddle together, are some of its chief characteristics; and the growth of many courts and alleys, disgraceful to humanity, is the sure result.[1] Whatever is demanded in London, whether in defiance of law or public decency, is promptly supplied; and ill-constructed, ill-ventilated lurking nests of dwellings exist in every quarter of the metropolis, in obedience to this rule of trade.

Those who wish to search London for gross examples of overcrowded dwellings may find them in the centre, or in any one of the four outskirts. Soho, St James's, Westminster, and St Martin's-in-the-Fields, can lay no claim to purity in this respect; and that part of Westminster known as Tothill Fields is notoriously one of the greatest offenders.[2] In the west there is Knightsbridge, rendered filthy and immoral by the presence of its large military barracks, with Chelsea, and Brentford; in the south there are Lambeth, Walworth, embracing Lock's Fields, and the Borough, with its notorious Kent Street; in the north there is Agar Town, built on a swamp, and running down to the canal in every stage of dirt and decay, with Somers' Town, Kentish Town, and Camden Town, each contributing its share to the general mass of misery; and in the east there are St George's, Whitechapel, Bethnal Green, and overgrown Shoreditch. A melancholy list like this could be filled up for pages by any one familiar with the back streets of London. I have not touched upon the corners of Clerkenwell, of 'merry Islington', and a dozen other districts; and I have purposely omitted St Giles's and Saffron Hill, because they no longer represent the worst parts of London. I have merely taken a broad glance round the metropolis, to show that overcrowding amongst the poor, with all its attendant evils, is not peculiar to any particular parish or district.

The features of this huddling together vary slightly in different neighbourhoods, being governed, in some degree, by the character of the houses. In neighbourhoods that have 'seen better days'—where family mansions that were once inhabited by city merchants, or the leading clerks and managers in banks or offices, have sunk gradually through all the different grades of lodging-houses, 'classical and commercial' schools, down to workshops for cabinet-makers, turners, or ginger-beer brewers—the overcrowding takes the form of living in what are called 'tenements'. The old mansion, faded and dilapidated, with its garden cut off, it may be, for a skittle-ground or a factory, is let out to a dozen or fifteen families, according to the number of its rooms. Its broad staircase, broken, shattered, and muddy, is always open to the street; and its long, narrow windows are patched with paper. Its broad closets and store-chambers are now filled with ragged children, who share their rough beds with coals, coke, wood, and a few cooking utensils. Its dark wainscotings, scratched and chipped, are hung with damp yellow clothes, that are always 'in the wash'; its passages are often strewn with oyster-shells and broken tobacco-pipes; and its forecourt is filled with ashes, one or two rusty, broken saucepans, like old hats, and sometimes with a dead cat,—the playthings of the crowd of dirty children, who roll about on its hard, black earth. The iron railings that once closed it in from the thoroughfare have been long torn away, stolen, destroyed, sold; and all that remains of the low wall in which they were fixed may be a few rotten, jagged bricks standing on one side. I can find scores of such houses—containing forty, fifty, or even sixty human beings, surrounded by neighbourhoods crowded with gas factories, cooperages, and different workshops, or pierced by the dark arches of metropolitan railways—that stand within two miles of the Bank of England, and that once were looked upon as pleasant country retreats!

Dropping, however, this description of Ragged London, drawn from memory, let us go out into the ragged streets, and ragged houses, and see what the ragged people are doing in January, 1861. We will begin with Ragged London in the centre.]

Clerkenwell and the City Borders

We have been too much accustomed of late years to look upon certain notorious localities as representing the only plague-spots in London. They have been visited by day, inspected by night; have formed the text-books of preachers, the backbones of sanitary reports, and the building materials of popular authors. They have attained an exaggerated importance in the public mind, and have been erroneously regarded as the tumours of our social degradation. The sweepings of society have seldom been carefully traced to their hiding-places, and fancy neighbourhoods have been created upon paper, and peopled with the phantoms of imagination. Where are the emaciated children who have often been dangled before our eyes? Certainly not in the black-holes inhabited by the poor. What is it that gives fulness to the cheeks, agility to the limbs, and even bone and sinew to the form? It cannot be food. A block of coarse bread, taken at uncertain intervals, is far from forming the supposed necessary three meals a day, and yet those children who get nothing but this plain and scanty fare astonish those who know them best with their healthy vigour. These children live in the streets, and draw their nourishment from wind and mud. They are not stunted, far from it, and with few exceptions are stronger than the children of the middle class.[1]

The close, crowded borders of the city of London have been touched upon too frequently in some parts, too little in others. We have heard enough of Saffron Hill, and have been lectured about a certain refuge in Field Lane until we have almost forgotten that there are any more refuges in the world.[1] The homeless wanderer must be housed, the starving castaway must be fed; but the great work to be done is to improve† the habits of the industrious poor. If there were no such thing as 'social science', no meddling legislation, no local Government Act with boards and inspectors, no vestries, no committees, and no guardians (save the mark!), society might settle down in it chosen places, and no one take any heed of any one but himself. While, however, we profess to love our neighbours as ourselves, and establish costly public systems—to say nothing of the efforts of private benevolence—to assist those who are too ignorant or too weak to help themselves, it is high time to inquire what is doing for the people in every corner of the town. There are scores of courts in Bishopsgate Street, scores more in Sun Street, Finsbury, scores more in Chiswell Street, Cripplegate, some in Lower Thames Street, others in parts of Blackfriars, that are not fit for human habitation. There are Golden Lane, Whitecross Street,[*2] and that melancholy avenue of vermin-haunted furniture called Long Alley which runs from the Curtain Road,

[*A correspondent writing January 20, 1861, says:—'The district of which Old Street, Goswell Street, Barbican, and Whitecross Street are the boundaries, is a maze of courts swarming with people in a state of starvation.'

The following report of an earlier date (January 6, 1861) also refers to the same neighbourhood:—On Monday night an inquest was held by the coroner as to the death of Sarah Brasnall, aged seventy-four, who was discovered in a dying condition, at No.4, Graham's Buildings, Bunhill Row, St Luke's, and who died from exposure to the cold. The deceased was a slop-worker, and in the receipt of 1s. 6d. per week and a loaf from the parish. On Thursday night the deceased was not about at her usual time, and on the following morning a lodger went to her room and found her lying upon the bedstead naked. It was very cold and frosty at the time. An alarm was raised, and Mr Cullen, the surgeon, was called, but the deceased soon afterwards expired. The deceased was suffering from strangulated hernia, and her body was much emaciated. Mr Cullen, the surgeon, said that the deceased's death had no doubt been accelerated by exposure to the inclement weather, and the want of sufficient food and clothing. The jury returned a verdict accordingly. The same evening, the coroner held an inquiry concerning the death of Hannah Coward, an infant child, who was found in a wretched condition at a

Shoreditch, across Sun Street, into Moorfields,* which are a disgrace to any country that prides itself upon its civilization. The blind alleys in coal-mines, the slimy passages of district sewers, anything that is dark and filthy, may be compared to these places. It is impossible and unnecessary to visit them all. I have known them for years, and, whatever sanguine clergymen or apologetic inspectors may say to the contrary, they get worse every day, and can never be improved. The tinkering of a drain, the whitewashing of a ceiling, will never remove the evils of their original structure.† They are filled with labourers, artizans, needlewomen, and girls employed in many fancy trades, and the capital and enterprise of the city of London are largely responsible for them all. In the Clerkenwell district, two-thirds of the enormous population of sixty or seventy thousand depend upon the City for their support. It is the old story of workpeople

low and disreputable house, in Sycamore Street, St Luke's. The police deposed that the mother had been taken into custody on a charge of felony, but was discharged by the magistrate, and when the police went to the house they found the children in a most deplorable condition. The constables kindly took them to the workhouse, and every assistance was rendered by the authorities, but the deceased died on Friday. The police said that another child was dying from the same cause, and when the deceased was found, she had a 'teat' made of a small bag of plums, which had been placed in her mouth. Dr Love said the deceased had died from neglect, starvation, and cold; and the other child could not live. The coroner, by the special request of the jury, severely reprimanded the conduct of the mother and father, when they returned a verdict of 'Death from want of the necessaries of life, and exposure to the weather, through the wilful neglect of the parents.'

*The Earl of Derby, speaking in the House of Lords of the parish of St Bartholomew, Moorfields, Cripplegate, February 28, 1861, says:—'The population of this parish amounts to four thousand five hundred odd, but I am informed by the incumbent that it may now be taken as exceeding five thousand. The number of houses in it does not exceed five hundred, which gives a proportion of nine or ten persons to every house in the parish. There is not a single gentleman's house in it, not a single large shopkeeper. The whole population is of the poorest class, the lower order of shopkeepers, costermongers, dock labourers, and others of the poorest order of the population. There are not ten families in it that occupy a single house, though the bulk of these houses contain only three rooms. In fact, to use the expression of the clergyman who called on me yesterday in reference to this subject, the aristocracy in the parish are those who can indulge in the luxury of two rooms; the great number of families have one room only, and in many cases there is more than one family in a room.']¹

who must be 'near their bread', and overcrowding follows as a matter of course.

Clerkenwell is a hard-working, operative district, especially in the interior, and contains few thieves, except those that are bottled up in prison. A penal air is given to the neighbourhood by the Houses of Correction and Detention, but, with this exception, the population is patient, industrious, and honest. Very little prostitution defiles its streets, and this not openly. The watch and watchcase making trades form the chief occupation of the men, and the women and children work at artificial flower-making, mantle-making, &c., for the City warehouses. In its upper portion—towards Pentonville—on the top of the mountain, are numbers of large private residences; and in the lower portion—down in the valley—the parish runs into Smithfield. Many French egg-merchants, importing enormous quantities of these eatables, are scattered about the neighbourhood; and a place called Sharp's Alley was once famous for making common sausages of refuse meat, known in the slang of the district as 'blood-worms'.*

Like most places with pretensions to great antiquity, it is closely built upon. It has its old archways and remains of monastic times, and presents in many places the aspect of a cathedral city. This is a peculiarity which makes it very picturesque, but largely uninhabitable. The back courts of Rouen give materials for charming pictures; but their sanitary condition has yet to be represented. A few rags hanging out of a

[*SANITARY CONDITION OF THE CITY, JANUARY, 1861.—At the meeting of the City Commissioners of Sewers yesterday, February 5, Dr Letheby, the medical officer of health, reported on the state of one hundred and ninety-seven houses that had been inspected during the week, and he submitted a list of thirty-nine places for sanitary improvement. He also reported that the markets and slaughterhouses had been duly inspected in the course of the week, and that the officers had seized 6,090 lbs., or nearly 2¾ tons, of meat, as unfit for human food. Nearly all this was meat in a state of disease. There were the carcases of fifty-six rotten sheep, four pigs, and thirty-four quarters of beef, besides smaller joints. 2,664 lbs. were seized by Mr Fisher in Newgate Market; 1,740 lbs. by Mr Davidson in Leadenhall; and 1,684 lbs. by Mr Newman in Aldgate, and in Tyler's Market, and elsewhere. The mortality returns for the week are still excessively high. Last week the number of deaths in the City was ninety-seven, instead of an average of sixty-two.]

window, a hole without any sash in it, a tattered woman, with a shock-headed baby standing at the side of a winding alley, make a delightful water-coloured sketch when they are touched off by Prout;[1] but not so delightful a sketch in a blue book or a descriptive paper. Clerkenwell, especially near the parish church, was laid out on a plan evidently copied from those old cities that had to be built closely so as to come within the fortified walls which formed their protection from invasion. The old courts, or outlines of courts, in the 'Close', as it is called, still remain, and are, as usual, the worst nests of overcrowding in the district. There is Union Place, a row of houses built within the last few years, and forming an alley of close, ill-ventilated† dwellings. They contain two small rooms, the size of which may be about twelve feet square, with a cupboard of a room about half the size, and they are let for about 5s. 6d. a week. As usual in these places, there is but one public privy for all; and the population, with children, may average ten to a house, giving more than eighty people. The pavement was tolerably clean, and the place may rank as a first-class court; but the rooms smelt musty for want of a through draught of air, which they can never get, as there are no windows at the back. Here we found one woman sick and going to the infirmary, [having been deserted by her husband,] and another trying to support herself, her husband (who was out of work), and eight children, by washing and house cleaning. It is astonishing what miracles a tub, a piece of soap, a brisk pair of arms, and a stout heart will often do.

Opposite this place, in another corner of the Close, is a lower class of court, called Cromwell Place. Here the houses are chiefly let off in rooms at from 1s. 6d. to 3s. a week, and seven persons in one small room—father, mother, grown-up children, and infants—appear to represent the average distribution of tenants. One family of seven—the man a labourer at a greengrocer's—had just been discovered by the working clergy nearly naked, and provided with a few articles of clothing. The next room sheltered another family—equal in numbers, and very little better off in condition. The children were all running about with naked feet; and the rooms were barely furnished, dirty, and musty. [These poor people were once far better off, and they dated their fall from a winter a few years back, when bread was at a very high price. This is not the first time that I have heard a connection traced between present poverty and past scarcity of corn.] The parlour contained another family of six, and the mother had just sold her only bed to a marine-store dealer for two shillings, to stop the many little hungry mouths around her. The father had been out of work for many weeks; one son had enlisted in the army, another had become a sailor, and a girl of fourteen could have got a situation as a domestic servant, but she had nothing but rags to go in. This, I am sorry to say, is a very common case. The best workman in the family was a little stuttering, red-coated shoeblack, who earned his shilling every day, paid his regulation fourpence honestly over to his office, and brought home his eightpence every night to his mother. This small house contained eighteen people.

Near this alley is a lower and complex series of passages, going generally by the name of Pear-tree Court.[1] The open space, where the orchard may have been, if we are to infer anything from the name, is now filled with every description of animal and vegetable refuse. The houses on one side are very old, and chiefly made of wood, which is rotten and black with age; the stunted houses on the other side turn their backs to this space, and show yards that are actually not more than four feet square. The alleys about this place are very numerous, with houses, dark, squeezed up, wavy in their outline, and depressed about the roof, like crushed hats. The population is almost a parish in itself, being so numerous; and in the most open parts hawkers of common china have their store-sheds. Some of the passages are so narrow that it is scarcely possible to creep up them; and tracing one of these to its source we came to an ancient smithy, rusty brown, idle, and crowded with litter. A rotten bellows, full of rat-holes, was lying in a puddle by the side of a dismantled grindstone, and a few splinters of wood. Inside the low door of the smithy, under clusters of old rusty keys, bolts, and rings, which hung from the black, smoky rafters like grapes, were two old yellow-shirted, dusty, grisly men in spectacles, who might have sat to Quentin Matsys for his picture of 'The Misers'.[2] One said he had been in the parish for seventy years, and bemoaned the decay of trade; and the other complained of the competition of 'furriners'. The sunlight shone through a broken window into the hollow forge, showing the black cinders, and a blacker cat.

The landlord of all this unsightly property keeps his own missionary and his own doctor to look after his tenants; but he neither ventilates the rooms nor enlarges the stifling yards. A little more cleanliness might help the missionary, and would certainly lessen the doctor's work.

Near Pear-tree Court is a settlement called Red Lion Gardens—the remains probably of Clerkenwell, when it was a country village. The entrance to this place is between those dingy brokers' shops, which look out upon the bleak hills of dirt accumulated on each side of New Farringdon Street. It is at the upper end, nearly opposite the workhouse, and is not easily found. It contains several rows of low one-roomed cottages, with little square yards in front, and is very much like similar places about Hoxton, Holywell Mount, Shoreditch, and other outskirts. In one room, or cottage, was a labourer with his wife and six children; in another was a poor cabman and family—the man trying to mend a very rotten pair of shoes to go out in, having sold his best pair off his feet. He had just come out of prison, where he had been sent for five days, because he was summoned for hanging about the Great Northern Railway Terminus with his cab, and had no money to pay the fine. He was civil and intelligent, and his room, though poorly furnished, was very clean. At another cottage a young woman was standing, waiting for her mother to return and open the closed door. She had come some little distance to see her father—an old, blind street fiddler—who was ill in bed with a fever. The mother had gone to the public soup-kitchen to try and get some food, and had locked the door; the old man was too ill and helpless to rise and open it. While we were talking to the young woman, who told us that she was a brushmaker, living in Finsbury, and that her husband was a butcher's man, out of work, in consequence of the badness of trade, the mother came back, with her bonnet in her hand, and her apron all in tatters. She had been roughly treated in the crowd at the soup-kitchen, as all the really poor, weak, and helpless always are; and while greasy tramps, low thieves and their girls, and other unworthy objects, got in (as I saw afterwards at Clerkenwell, and also at the Leicester Square soup-kitchen), the decent old fiddler's wife came empty away. She burst into tears as she told her daughter this, and was some time before she could be comforted. They were not beggars, not tramps, and were clean and honest. We went into the cottage—I and the excellent clergymen who accompanied me—where the old fiddler was propped up in bed. The doctor had ordered him some beef-tea—a rather costly luxury for a blind fiddler!

'He's brought up a heavy family,' said the old woman, 'and never asked nobody for anything, until the frost bit him, and now he's dropped from his eating.'

The old man recognized the voice of one of the clergymen, and seemed pleased with the goodness of his memory and ear. The gentleman was the son of some one before whose door the old fiddler had played for many years.

'Very proud I am to hear that voice,' whispered the old man, 'and many's the sixpence I've had from your father, God bless him.'

Street hawkers and street minstrels are not ungrateful vagrants and thieves, and it would be a pity if they were, for the London courts and alleys shelter about one hundred thousand of them. I know much of working people of all kinds, and I have seen hundreds of bright, open, honest faces under the battered hats and bonnets of costermongers.*

[*On Thursday, December 13, 1860, a meeting of street vendors of the metropolis was held at the sale-room of Messrs Keeling and Hunt, Monument Yard; Mr Keeling in the chair. There were a good many costermongers present on the occasion. The chairman said the street vendors were at present the principal means of conveying provisions to the artisan class of the community. But they were interfered with in the pursuit of their useful calling, were subjected to fine and imprisonment, and were told when they were following their occupation that they were violating the law. The great objection made against them was that they obstructed the thoroughfares, but if that was an objection it applied equally to others. Were it not for the street vendors, the goods which they circulated would not be brought to London at all. All they wanted was to be allowed a fair opportunity of following their calling. The hon. secretary then read a very respectful petition to the Court of Aldermen, stating fully the nature of their grievances. Mr H. Isaacs moved the adoption of the petition, and the

The freehold property in Clerkenwell often belongs to charities and corporations. Berry Street, Little Sutton Street, and other places lying off Wilderness Row—very fair specimens of the dull, badly built, badly ventilated, overcrowded streets of the neighbourhood—are laid out on ground belonging to the Charter House. Lamb-and-Flag Court, Fryingpan Alley, and several other branches of the same property—the lowest and most degraded in the parish—were left by one William Sanderson, in 1659, to be divided equally between the poor of Clerkenwell and the poor of Wendover, Buckinghamshire. The property is now divided, doubtless under many leases and sub-leases, amongst tenants who are proud of their dirty habits. Fryingpan Alley is what I should call a rampant court. Its entrance is two feet wide—a long narrow slit in the wall—half paved, with a gutter which constantly trickles with sewage. Its tenants are chiefly gipsies and the lowest class of vegetable vendors. It is worse than anything in Whitechapel or Bethnal Green. The rooms are dustbins—everything but dwelling-places. The women are masculine in appearance; they stand with coarse, folded arms and knotted hair, and are ready to fight for their castle of filth. They dislike the new underground railway that is forming in the neighbourhood; they look upon New Farringdon Street as a Corporation job; and they have got a rude notion that all local improvements put money into the pockets of Government.[1] Children make faces at you; repulsive men smoke down upon you from the holes that serve for windows; old women howl at you from the gloomy cellars; and a spreading heap of wet, muddy vegetable refuse, lying in an open spot that

appointment of a deputation to present it to the City authorities. The resolution was seconded, and unanimously adopted. The next resolution—'That this meeting pledges itself to protect the street vendors from interference when lawfully pursuing their calling, by placing it in their power to employ counsel to defend them when unjustly prosecuted'—was moved by Mr Brooke, seconded by Mr Wallace, and adopted. Solomon Green was afraid there were thieves in other callings besides street vendors. He believed that not much less than 3,000,000*l*. of money was invested in various articles by the costermongers throughout the country, and if they were only true to themselves he had no doubt they would be able to protect their capital.

A vote of thanks to the chairman closed the proceedings.]

an inhabitant called 'the square', was regarded like part of old William Sanderson's freehold. An idle, pipe-sucking giant, who was offered sixpence to clear away this nuisance, walked slowly round it, looked at it reflectively—not to say affectionately—and finally decided that he had better leave it alone. Such a place as this, with its old herring-casks standing at the dark doors, its rags hanging across from house to house, and its swarthy defenders, would make a very telling picture upon canvas, like many of its companions. [Its reform, I am afraid, is beyond the reach of anything, except an earthquake or a new railway, and even then the inhabitants would only be pushed somewhere else.*]

The greater part of this enormous neighbourhood is actively watched over by the Rev. Robert Maguire, the rector of the parish church, and a staff of three hard-working, business-like curates.

[In the fine weather they preach much in the open air, and the rector says:—

'This very successful portion of our summer work was conducted last season with much spirit and energy, not indeed on my part, but through the services of Mr Tindall and Mr Herbert. I felt much disappointed that, from illness and other causes, I could avail myself of so few opportunities of preaching in the streets. My place and duties, however, were well supplied by Mr Tindall, who occupied the station on the Green on Sunday evenings, during my absence, and preached with much profit to the people. The other preaching stations were occupied, more or less, during the summer, with the same gratifying success which has attended all such efforts for the spiritual instruction of the people. One man remarked, a few evenings after hearing an open-air sermon by one of my curates,—"Well, no sermon, in church or anywhere else, ever stuck to me so tight as that did: I can't get rid of it."']

The visiting—to say nothing of the mere church labour—must be enormous. Most rooms in most houses in the greatest part of

[*The Metropolitan Railway projects of 1861 are estimated to destroy one thousand houses in low neighbourhoods, and displace a population of not less than twenty thousand.]¹

the valley district contain one family of many members; some, it may be, contain two families.* Summer has its forms of occasional distress as well as winter; and many a garret, high up in the house-tops, contains poor workmen or sufferers who require help all the year round. There are ragged schools, national schools, evening schools, and Sunday schools, in full operation, and well attended; a district visiting society, which distributed last year (1860) between four and five thousand tickets for bread, grocery, meat, and coals; there is a Dorcas association, which, during the same period, supplied nearly three hundred articles of clothing to the poor at a nominal charge; there is an industrial society for supplying poor women with needlework at their own homes; and there is a ladies' benevolent society which, last year, gave six pensioners, over seventy years of age, 4s. per month, assisted sixty maternity cases with a box of linen and half-a-crown in each case, and relieved 1,200 persons during sickness. There is a Bible society, a working-man's institute, a pure literature society; and, amongst the institutions largely self-supporting, there is a clothing fund, and a provident fund. The latter shows a steady increase, and numbered 2,273 depositors and 1,023l. deposited during 1860. The rector and those who work with him do everything they can to cultivate the friendship of the poorest parishioners, by means of social gatherings at different periods of the year. It is no uncommon thing to see 2,000 of the poor assembled at one of these gatherings, enjoying themselves in a manner they could never hope to do at their own wretched homes. Husbands come with their wives, and children with their parents, and every one is made to feel happy and at ease. Many of them spoke to me

[* The Earl of Shaftesbury, speaking of Cow Cross, an adjoining district, in the House of Lords, February 28, 1861, says:— 'In sixteen courts there I found one hundred and seventy-three houses, having five hundred and eighty-six rooms in all, and in them five hundred and eighty-six families; the number of persons was three thousand seven hundred and fifty-four, being an average of six and a half persons to a room. The rooms were from fifteen feet by twelve to nine by nine. They were low, dark, dismal, and dirty; so low, indeed, that it was with great difficulty I could stand upright in them, and when I extended my arms I could touch the walls on either side with my fingers' ends; in these rooms I found five, six, seven, eight, and even nine persons living.']¹

about these meetings during my morning's walk, and spoke utterly free from cant, or a desire to appear pious. There can be little doubt that such gatherings are not only kindly conceived, but very happily conducted by the curates and the rector. They do their best with the vast district committed to their charge, and will only fail in curing those evils that are beyond the reach of charity or preaching.

THE EAST.

The Back of Whitechapel[1]

If I were writing a partially fancy description of the poverty and wretchedness in a particular district, I should mix the aspects of one street with the aspects of another, and hide my real locality under a very thin veil. I should call Whitechapel by its more appropriate name of Blackchapel, and play with the East of London under the title of St George's-in-the-Dirt. As this book, however, is intended to be a faithful chronicle of what I have seen, what the local clergy and others see every day, and almost every hour, and what every one else may see in a week's walk about the back streets of London, I give up effect for the sake of truthfulness, and strive to become a plain, matter-of-fact guide.

There are many different degrees of social degradation and unavoidable poverty, even in the east. Whitechapel, properly so called, may not be the worst of the many districts in this quarter; but it is undoubtedly bad enough. Taking the broad road from Aldgate Church to old Whitechapel Church, a thoroughfare, in some parts, like the high street of an old-fashioned country town, you may pass on either side about twenty narrow avenues, leading to thousands of closely packed nests, full to overflowing with dirt, and misery, and rags. Many living signs of the inner life behind the busy shops are always oozing out on to the pavements and into the gutters; for all children in low neighbourhoods that are not taken in by the ragged and other charity schools are always living in the streets: they eat in the streets what little they get to eat, they play in the streets in all weathers, and sometimes they have to sleep in the streets. Their fathers and mothers mope in cellars or garrets; their grandfathers or grandmothers huddle and die in the same miserable dustbins (for families, even unto the third and fourth generation, have often to keep together in these places), but the children dart about the roads with naked, muddy feet; slink into corners to play with oyster-shells and pieces of broken china, or are found tossing halfpennies under the arches of a railway. The local clergy, those who really throw themselves heart and soul into the labour of educating these outcasts, are daily pained by seeing one or more drop through into the great pit of crime; and by feeling that ragged schools are often of little good unless they can give food as well as instruction, and offer the children some kind of rude probationary home. At the George Yard Ragged School, Whitechapel, conducted by the Rev. Mr Thornton, and personally superintended by Mr Holland, they have turned part of an old distillery into one of the most useful and active institutions of this kind in the metropolis, and they are already struggling with these and other difficulties. [The secretary, Mr Lewis, writing January 15, 1861, says:—

'We have lately had a number of boys in a most distressing state—homeless, hungry, and almost naked. The teachers and friends have done what they could to help them, and can do no more. Those who teach the 'ragged band' have feeling hearts, and it is painful to lie in one's own bed and feel that there are a number of poor boys wanting even shelter these bitter nights. Should we send them away and they perish in the streets, at our doors certainly would their deaths lie. We have paid for their lodgings, at various lodging-houses, night after night; but now with this severe weather, and the mass of distress it has brought around us, matters have come to such a pass we are compelled to ask the public to lend us a helping hand in our extremity. We have taken a place to shelter them in, and earnestly ask for help to go on. Old boots and shoes, old clothes, old rugs or blankets, rice, potatoes, oatmeal, &c., will be most acceptable. To send these helpless ones adrift is, apart from anything else, to make thieves of them.']

They have gathered some four hundred children, of all ages, and of both sexes; and they give them every encouragement to consider the school as their home. They provide a meal of rice on one day, a meal of bread on another, and a meal of soup, if they can, on the third day; and they have taken eight poor castaways—nobody's children—'into the house', and are endeavouring to train them into honest working boys. The stories of destitution, cruelty, and desertion which these outcasts have to tell are more harrowing than a thousand tragedies. One has lost all traces of his parents, another is a street beggar's orphan, and another owns no parent but a drunken prostitute, who kicked him, swore at him, stabbed him in the cheek, and left a scar which he will carry to his grave. He can now find no traces of such a mother, except in the cruel mark upon his face; and is more happy, perhaps, in calling his schoolmaster father than he ever was before in his life.

The conductors of this school† are anxious to fit up some kind of rough sleeping-loft for the children. They dread to let them go out into the black courts and alleys, knowing what dirt and brutality often await them. It requires very little diving behind the houses on either side of the Whitechapel main road to account for this feeling on the part of the ragged-school managers. Within a few yards of this refuge is New Court, a nest of thieves, filled with thick-lipped, broad-featured, rough-haired, ragged women, and hulking, leering men, who stand in knots, tossing for pennies, or lean against the walls at the entrances of the low courts. The houses present every conceivable aspect of filth and wretchedness; the broken windows are plastered with paper, which rises and falls when the doors of the rooms are opened; the staircases always look upon the court, as there is seldom any street door, and they are steep, winding, and covered with blocks of hard mud. The faces that peer out of the narrow windows are yellow and repulsive; some are the faces of Jews, some of Irishwomen, and some of sickly-looking infants. The ashes lie in front of the houses; the drainage is thrown out of the windows to swell the heap; and the public privy†† is like a sentry-box stuck against the pump in a corner of the court. There may be as many families as there are rooms, cellars, and cupboards in a single house; forty people, perhaps, huddled together in a small dwelling; and if there is not a mixture of different families in one room it is due to the ceaseless vigilance of the sanitary officer, Inspector Price, in carrying out the Lodging-Houses Act.[1] The lowest order of Irish, when they get an opportunity, will take a room and sub-let it to as many families as the floor will hold.[2] Inkhorn Court is a fair sample of an Irish colony; the houses are three stories high, and there is not a corner unoccupied. Tewkesbury Buildings is a colony of Dutch Jews, and, if anything, they are a little cleaner than their Christian neighbours. George Yard[3] is an English colony, numbering about a hundred families; and Wentworth Street, Crown Court, and Castle Alley have the same character. Their inhabitants are chiefly dock labourers, and their families a class who form one-half of the population of this district. [A correspondent, Mr Wilford, of Catherine Street East, writing January 10, 1861, says:—'The dock labourers consist of a mixed class of people—English, Irish, Scotch, Germans, and a few French, and others. There are employed at times as many as 20,000 to 25,000 labourers in the five docks, who are extra men, and about 3,000 or 4,000 permanent men; and at the wharves below London Bridge there are at times as many as 3,000 men employed, making a total of upwards of 30,000 men employed in the docks and wharves below bridge. It is thought at the present time that there are not more than 4,000 or 5,000 who are at work, owing to the adverse winds and the severe frost. The average earnings of thousands of these poor fellows is not more than 7s. 6d. per week all the year round, so that when there is a great stagnation in the shipping trade, many thousands are almost starved to death. It is a lamentable fact that such is the case at the present time.'] The other half of the inhabitants in these streets is made up of thieves, costermongers, and stall-keepers, professional beggars, rag-dealers, brokers and small tradesmen.

[In one court I saw a singular blind labourer, who was out of work in consequence of the frost. He got his living by reading the Bible in the street, feeling the raised letters with his hand, and he complained that he could do nothing now because 'the touch was cold'. He staggered over the mud heaps with a thin stick, and disappeared in the dark, cellar-like lower room of a ragged-school refuge for outcasts. In some of these repulsive courts the inhabitants cling to a rude love of flowers, and many an unsightly window-ledge is fitted up to resemble a garden enclosure, with miniature railings and gates.]

The rents drawn for the wretched apartments in these courts vary from 4s. to 9d. a week, the average being about 2s. a week. This rental often pays for the hire of 'furniture', consisting of a round table, white with age, a couple of bare wooden chairs, a fender and poker, often, unfortunately, not wanted except when the parish coals are being sparingly burnt; a turn-up bedstead, with a rustling bag of straw for a bed, and a very dirty scanty coverlet. The rent for this accommodation is collected painfully, punctually, and incessantly by small instalments; and unpromising as this class of property looks to the superficial observer, thriving tradesmen are found to 'farm' it in the neighbourhood as middlemen, and in some cases it belongs to important local residents. The Jews have bought a little of it up of late years, perhaps because their colony in this quarter is slowly increasing. The Jewish poor are fewer and better provided for than our poor, and the applications for relief are never made except in cases of extreme distress.[1] They are wonderfully independent and self-supporting, and keep up the ceremonies of their nation under the most adverse circumstances. In a very black miserable hut in Castle Alley, a poor Jewess was burning the 'twelve-month's lamp' for her deceased mother, although it was only a glimmering wick in a saucer full of rank oil.

The female population in these courts and alleys, as usual, forms the greatest social difficulty to be dealt with. Their husbands may be dock labourers, earning, when employed, if on the 'permanent list', 3s. a day—if on the 'casual list', only 2s. 6d. a day; their children, after an education in the streets or the ragged schools, may be drafted off into lucifer-match or brush factories, where cheap and juvenile labour is in much demand; but for the woman, and the grown-up daughters, although it may be necessary for them to help in maintaining the poor household, there is nothing but ill-paid needlework, which they may never have learnt. Domestic servitude in this neighbourhood, with a few exceptions, is not to be coveted, as there is little more, for the local-bred servant, than a choice of low gin-shops, or lower coffee-houses. The best paid occupation appears to be prostitution, and it is a melancholy fact that a nest of bad houses in Angel Alley, supported chiefly by the farmers' men who bring the hay and straw to Whitechapel market twice a week, are the cleanest-looking dwellings in the district. The windows have tolerably neat green blinds, the doors have brass plates, and inside the houses there is comparative comfort, if not plenty. While the wretched virtuous population are starving in black holes, or creeping out in the hour of their wildest prosperity to purchase sixpennyworth of refuse meat from the stall opposite the greasy, sawdusty shambles, the inhabitants of this court of vice know little, at least for a few years, of want and suffering. If their ranks are thinned by death or disease, there are always fresh recruits coming forward; and must be while there are as many houseless women as men, and nothing but low threepenny lodging-houses, where [little or] no distinction is made between the sexes. [I heard a child in the street—a boy about eight years of age—telling another boy what a man had given his mother as the price of her shame. The boys and girls here are men and women at ten or twelve years of age.]

The local clergy are painfully aware of these facts, and they have made an effort with some success to check the evils of prostitution. The indefatigable incumbent of St Jude's—the Rev. Mr Thornton before alluded to—with local assistance, has started a temporary refuge for females in Boar's Head Yard, Petticoat Lane, in the very heart of this melancholy district. The work of this refuge commenced in May, 1860. Since that period it appears that sixty-four young women—mostly fallen, some in danger—nearly all from the neighbourhood, have passed through the institution; of these sixteen are in situations doing well, seven have been restored to their friends, one is married, one has died, nineteen have been sent to other institutions; and of the remaining twenty some have left, with approval, to seek an honest living; some have proved failures, having left soon after admission from dislike of the discipline or other causes; and eight are now in the refuge, making the total seventy-two. This excellent institution is in some degree self-supporting, the inmates earning money by washing, mangling, and needlework. By this means the cost of each case has been kept down to about four shillings a week. The receipts from work are small, in consequence of the constant change of inmates, the institution being designed as a temporary refuge, not as a permanent home. The managers, consisting of a committee of ladies, solicit female clothing, assistance in procuring more work for the inmates, and the inspection of visitors, especially ladies.

St George's in the East[1]

Passing from Whitechapel towards the river into the Commercial Road, you find the thoroughfare one of the broadest in London, with stone tramways for waggon traffic laid down on each side as far as Blackwall. This main road, viewed at any hour, shows little evidence of the crowded population who huddle together behind the houses, especially on the river-side. The difference in the superficial appearance of this road, compared with Whitechapel, may be accounted for by the fact that it is pierced by very few courts and alleys, strictly so called, the small dwellings being invariably arranged in streets. There are thousands of these streets spread over Stepney, Limehouse, Shadwell, St George's, and Mile End, having such a family likeness that the description of one in its main features will serve for them all. Their houses look flat and depressed, being only one story high, and they generally contain two small rooms on the ground floor, two more above, with a very close little yard, seldom larger than one of the rooms. When they are new, clean, and in the possession of their original tenants, they shelter a hard-working class, chiefly connected with the shipping trade and the different factories in the east; and when they fall a few degrees in the scale of comfort and respectability, they follow the example of more wealthy neighbourhoods and admit a lower colony of tenants. From being occupied by struggling householders they sink gradually through all the phases of lodging-letting until they are reduced to the condition of being divided into tenements. Each room is then taken by a different family; the doorstep is seldom cleaned; the passage and stairs belong to everybody, and are looked after by nobody; the little yard becomes choked up with dust and filth; the inspector of nuisances is openly defied if he ever goes near the place, and the unfortunate street is doomed; it grows more black and more ragged every day; a yellow mist always seems to hang over it, through which its unsightly inhabitants may be dimly seen from the main thoroughfare into which it runs; ignorant policemen begin to look suspiciously upon it, and overrated 'detectives' put it down as a harbour for thieves. It gets an ill-name, like an unlucky dog, and is hanged by all except the patient district visitors.

It is unnecessary for any writer to go over all the low streets of a particular district to give the public a faint picture of their chief characteristics, and he will do his duty if he carefully selects that representative thoroughfare which seems to him to present most of the features he wishes to depict. Such a representative hole and corner I believe I have found in Star Street, in the Christ Church division of St George's in the East, a locality [of forty-three acres,] with a population of 13,300, untiringly watched over by the Rev. G.H. M'Gill.

Star Street is a narrow avenue, leading out of the Commercial Road towards the river, the entrance to which is half blocked up with fruitstalls, crossing-sweepers, and loiterers. [Unlike most of its neighbours,] it hangs out every sign of overcrowding for the most careless or hurried passer-by to look at, and it contains, perhaps, within an equal area, more hard-working, would-be-honest strugglers for dear life than any similar street in the same district. Its road is black and muddy, half filled with small pools of inky water, in which stand a number of trucks and barrows belonging to the poorest class of costermongers. The end is nearly blocked up with a public-house, which seems to thrive in the very citadel of want. At some of the low dirty doors wet baskets are standing half full of a common fish called 'dabs'; in some of the wretched parlour windows, under sickly yellow curtains, a few rotten oranges are displayed on an old shutter for sale; another miserable front parlour seems to have been scooped out so as to form something like a shop, in which a few coals are thrown down in one corner as a sign of trade; another parlour has been turned into a cat's-meat store, and there is one of those small chandler's-shops where nearly everything is sold, and 'weekly payments' are taken, which invariably flourish in such neighbourhoods.

I went down this thoroughfare with the chief clergyman of the district, and we were immediately surrounded by poor, thin women, in scanty dresses, representing every variety of dirt and poverty. They have nothing to pawn, nothing to take to the marine-store dealers. Their husbands can get no work for the present at the docks,* and they can get little or no needlework from the cheap clothiers in the neighbourhood. Their standard of living is so low that a few days of compulsory idleness brings them to the brink of starvation. One has a story to tell of fever and sickness, another of bread refused by the poor-law authorities on some technicality, another begs to be visited without delay, and a dozen others present letters of recommendation for relief from the funds at the disposal of the clergyman. The same question seems always to bring the same melancholy answer:—

'How many children have you?'

'Eight, sir.'

'What's your husband?'

'A dock labourer.'

'How long has he been out of work?'

'Not done a stroke for thirteen weeks.'

'Come to me, at the parsonage, at three.'

We go into some of the houses to inspect the misery. The ground floor of one is occupied by a sweep. A short broom sticks out over the door. The front parlour contains two women, half covered with soot. A bed, as black as the women, stands in one corner, in which an infant is sleeping, with its little face looking pale, even under the dirt, and its head lying lower than its legs. Two other young children are playing on the black floor in front of the little glow-worm of a fire, eating what is literally bread and soot. Six other children, belonging to the same parents, are playing somewhere about in the inky puddles; and even this family only represents half the population of the small house. The rooms may be ten feet square—certainly not more**—and the rent averages about two shillings a room. The back parlour is also rented by the sweep, and it contains nothing but a mountain of soot—the store resulting from several weeks' work—an empty birdcage, and a fluttering green rag of a window-blind.

---

* January, 1861

** Average height, eight feet five inches; length, nine feet six inches; width, nine feet six inches.

Upstairs, in one room, is a street hawker, with a wife and five children, and in another room is a carpenter, also with a wife and five children. The latter has the same old painful story to tell of no work and no pay. He is a strong, healthy man, nearly fifty years of age, respectable in appearance, and civil in address. He is trying to still his evident hunger with a little weak tea, probably made from boiled tea-leaves, which his wife has begged from some family for whom she works. A few small lumps of precious bread are floating in the tea, and a hungry child is looking over the edge of the table at the remains of a small coarse loaf. Not a crumb is wasted of the scanty store; for the blank days of unproductive idleness may not be near their end, and the hateful workhouse must be kept at arm's length. The other children, if not in the ragged or national schools, are rolling anywhere about the streets, like all other children of the very poor, in every back alley of the town. When they are gathered together at night—if they ever are so gathered—the roof of this stunted dwelling will cover twenty-five inmates. Other houses in the same poor street—not larger, not cleaner—shelter twenty-two and twenty-one inmates respectively; and thirteen lodgers for one house seems to be a very common number. Two of the rooms have eleven inmates, while one particular room has nine, and another room has nine also. The general result seems to be—according to a local census taken by the Rev. Mr M'Gill, on December 19, 1860—that in two hundred and thirty-five small rooms there is, self-crammed, a growing, breeding population of three hundred and forty-four adults and three hundred and fifty-seven children, making a total of seven hundred and one. A few of these unfortunates have been struck off the list since this melancholy account was taken; some by exhaustion, or long-settled disease, brought to an end by want. One labourer gave in, under a low fever, a few hours before we visited the street, and his dead body was stretched upon the only bed in the dark room, covered with a borrowed white sheet. Round the fire was a crowd of weeping women, and amongst them the widow, with two of the dead man's moaning children stricken with the same fever. Wretched as these people were, they would struggle to bury the dead body without assistance from the parish, for there is nothing the poor have such a horror of as a pauper's funeral. No sooner have we left this abode of misery than we are almost dragged over to another, where a mere girl is suddenly left a widow with two helpless infants. Her husband was a dock labourer, twice as old as herself, and he died of asthma. He hung about the docks in the keen weather, day after day, waiting for ships that never came, and the afternoon before he came home wet, miserable, and hungry, took to his scanty bed, and never left it again. Death is bitter enough at all times, and in all places, but it is a hundred-fold more bitter where those who are left are haunted by the dreadful feeling that a few pence would have kept the body and soul together if they could only have been found.

There are other streets in this district, such as Devonshire Street and Hungerford Street in the immediate neighbourhood, which are as full of hunger, dirt, and social degradation as Star Street—my representative thoroughfare. They have all been in the same condition for years, and they show little prospect of material improvement. They contain no thieves, and no threepenny lodging-houses, and are tolerably free from houses of ill-fame. It is a curious social fact that when a particular street reaches a certain depth of poverty it becomes purified from its vice; for though thieves and prostitutes do not become converted in a period of scarcity, they invariably shift their quarters. The lower industrial occupations in the general locality I have been dealing with may be broadly classed as dock-work, needlework, coal-whipping, and streek hawking. The labouring population are independent and honest, and no alms are ever applied for at a period of full labour. The district is industriously 'worked' by the clergy and their assistants. The ragged and national schools, some of them fitted up under railway arches, collect and educate about a thousand children of both sexes—boys, girls, and infants. These schools are supported by government to the extent of 290*l*. (I take the figures of 1860), by the pence of the children to the extent of 300*l*., and by local subscriptions to the amount of 150*l*. more. A movement is on foot to enlarge and improve the old Middlesex Society's National Schools in Cannon Street Road, founded in 1781, which are far behind the pressing wants of the locality. There is a blanket-and-rug society, instituted for the purpose of giving (not lending) these necessaries to the poor, and every year one-fourth of the stock distributed has to be renewed from fair wear and tear. Instances where this property has been pawned, even in periods of great want and suffering, are very rare. There is a small Dorcas society, which dispenses about 25*l*. a year, and which only stops here for want of funds. There is no public soup-kitchen, but the clergy distribute bread, coals, and grocery, as far as their means go; and the Rev. Mr M'Gill receives assistance every year from the Marquis of Westminster, for these and other parochial purposes, to the extent of 100*l*.

The clerical work seems very heavy, as in 1860 there were six hundred and eleven baptisms, one hundred and thirty-five marriages, and five hundred and twenty churchings; and the visiting work, divided amongst twenty-one local visitors, has reached four hundred and fifty-three cases of poverty and sickness in one day during January, 1861. It is proper to mention here that the incumbent is assisted in this part of his labours, by the Metropolitan District Visiting Association, with an annual donation of 100*l*.

Amongst all this charity and benevolent work there is one healthy example of self-help in the Christ Church Penny Bank, the oldest institution of its kind in London. Its total receipts in 1860 were about 944*l*., and its total repayments about 945*l*. It brought over a balance from the former year of about 388*l*., and it begins the present year with a balance of about 387*l*. The detailed accounts for 1860 show that more money was paid in during the winter and autumn than during the spring and summer, and the heaviest withdrawal was made in December.

This is hardly the place to dwell upon certain notorious inequalities in the metropolitan poor-rates; but I cannot close this chapter without referring to the different assessments of the two great docks in the quarter I have been dealing with. The London Dock Company, which usually employs about one thousand five hundred of the men who are now thrown upon the parish or upon chance relief, paid 19,000*l*. as its share of the poor-rate in 1859; and the St Katharine Dock Company, which usually employs about one thousand similar labourers, only paid 720*l.* in the same year. The two properties are only divided by a lane which a man can almost leap over; but the first has the misfortune to stand in part of Shadwell, St George's, [Wapping, and Aldgate,] while the last has covered the whole of an extinct parish, and has pushed the poor upon its neighbour's shoulders.

The latest parochial statistics in St George's in the East (for the week ending January 19, 1861) show that the poor-law guardians relieved 3,720 out of an estimated population of 60,000,† and issued some 600 summonses for the last quarter's rates.

[The whole area of the parish is three quarters of a mile long, by three quarters of a mile broad.]

Behind Shoreditch

That vast district of eastern London familiar to the public under the broad title of Bethnal Green would exhaust a twelvemonth in a house-to-house visitation. It is flat, it is ancient, dirty, and degraded; its courts and alleys are almost countless, and overrunning with men, women, boys, dogs, cats, pigeons, and birds. Its children are ragged, sharp, weasel-like; brought up from the cradle—which is often an old box or an egg-chest—to hard living and habits of bodily activity. Its men are mainly poor dock labourers, poor costermongers, poorer silk-weavers, clinging hopelessly to a withering handicraft, the lowest kind of thieves, the most ill-disguised class of swell-mobsmen, with a sprinkling of box and toy makers, shoe-makers, and cheap cabinet-makers. Its women are mainly hawkers, sempstresses, the coarsest order of prostitutes, and aged stall-keepers, who often sit at the street corners in old sedan-chairs, and sometimes die like sentinels, at their posts.* Its broadest highways are chiefly lined with the most humble shops. There are steaming eating-houses, half filled with puddings as large as sofa squabs, and legs of beef, to boil down into a cheap and popular soup; birdcage vendors; mouldy, musty dens full of second-hand garments, or gay 'emporiums' in the ready-made clothing line; pawnbrokers, with narrow, yellow side entrances, whose walls are well marked with the traces of traffic; faded grocers; small print shops, selling periodicals, sweetstuff, and stale fruit; squeezed-up barbers, long factories and breweries, with the black arches of the Eastern Counties Railway running through the midst. Every street of any pretension is generally guarded at its entrances by public-houses smelling of tobacco, stale beer, and sawdust; and the corners of every leading thoroughfare cutting into the heart of the district are watched over by glittering genii in the shape of gin-palaces.[1] Concerts, which consist chiefly of street 'nigger' singing, held in dingy, long rooms, over the bars of the public-houses in the interior, form the chief amusement of the common inhabitants in their hours of plenty, occasionally varied by dog-fights, rat-

[*Last Monday evening, December 24, 1860, the deputy coroner for East Middlesex held an inquest at the 'Marquis of Cornwallis' public-house, Curtain Road, Shoreditch, relative to the death of Agnes Edgell, aged seventy-three years, who died from exposure to the weather. It appeared from the evidence that the deceased had kept an oyster-stall at the corner of Charles Street, Pitfield Street, and on Saturday night last she was seen sitting on a chair by her stall. When her daughter and a lodger called upon her and asked her if she wanted anything, she replied, 'Yes, I am very cold.' The daughter went for some tea and bread and butter, but about half-past eleven o'clock the deceased suddenly became ill, and died in her chair before medical assistance could be got. The deceased had been in charge of the stall about thirty years, and was a decent woman, much noticed by the neighbours for her cleanly and sober habits. Mr John George Blackall, surgeon, of Pitfield Street, Hoxton, stated that the deceased was dead when he was called. Life had been extinct five minutes, and he found her dead in a chair. He had made a *post-mortem* examination of the body, and found that the various organs were healthy and free from disease. The heart and lungs were congested, and the immediate cause of death was cold and exposure to the severity of the weather. On the night in question the deceased complained of the cold, and had once had some warm rum and water, although she was an abstemious woman. The jury returned a verdict that 'The deceased died from congestion of the heart and lungs, brought on by exposure to the cold and inclemency of the weather while sitting at a public stall.']

matches, and the sport of drawing the badger. On Sundays the whole neighbourhood is like a fair. Dirty men, in their sooty shirt-sleeves, are on the housetops, peeping out of little rough wooden structures built on the roof to keep their pigeons in. They suck their short pipes, fly their fancy birds, whistle shrilly with their forefingers placed in their mouths, beat the sides of the wooden building with a long stick, like a fishing-rod, and use all their ingenuity to snare their neighbours' stray birds. Those they catch are not quite as valuable as the products of the Philo-peristeron Society,[1] but they have a value, varying from tenpence to half-a-crown, and long usage has settled the amount of redemption money which will buy back one of these captives. Down in some of the streets a regular exchange is held for the purpose of buying, selling, and comparing animals; and, as in Whitechapel and all such neighbourhoods, no difficulty is found in obtaining beer or spirits contrary to law, as long as the money to pay for it is forthcoming.

This enormous portion of London is divided into many small district parishes, each one watched over by a very active clergyman. Amongst the principal workers are the Rev. Mr Christie, the Rev. Mr Gibson, and the Rev. James Trevitt. I have taken the lower portion of Bethnal Green (the district parish of St Philip), which has been carefully worked by the latter excellent gentleman for more than nine years, because it enables me to deal with certain social features common also to Shoreditch and Spitalfields.

I have known the neighbourhood I am describing for twenty years, and, if anything, it seems to me to be getting dirtier and more miserable every year. Old houses, in some few places, have been taken away—simply because they fell to pieces; but the new houses erected within the last ten years show little advance in the art of building dwellings for the poor. The whole present plan and arrangement of the district is against improvement, and the new structures sink to the level of the old.†

The first court I go into with my guide is called 'Reform Square'—a bitter satire upon its aspect and condition. It is nearly opposite the Church of St Philip, and is a square yard—not much larger than a full-sized dining-room. It is entered by a mountainous slope of muddy brick pathway, under an archway; and contains half-a-dozen houses, which look out upon two dust-heaps, a pool of rain and sewage, mixed with rotten vegetable refuse, and a battered, lopsided public privy.† The houses are like doll's-houses, except that they are black and yellow. The windows are everywhere stuffed with paper—rags being in too much demand at the marine store-shop, or for the clothing of the human child-rats, who are digging into the dust-heaps, with muddy oyster-shells. Every child must have its toys; and at the back of Shoreditch they play with rusty old saucepans, pieces of broken china, stones torn out of the roadway, or cinders that they search for laboriously. Very often the boys have to mind babies, while their mothers are out at work, and they sit about upon doorsteps with dirty brown limp bundles that never look like young children.

At the entrance to 'Reform Square' is a row of zigzag two-roomed houses, let for about four shillings a week; the street-doors of which open into the lower rooms, almost upon the wretched tenants' beds. The staircases leading to the upper apartments are little more than ladders in one corner, and there is no space for more than the usual furniture—a table, two chairs, and a bedstead. The flooring of the lower rooms in these houses is so high above the pavement in the street, that three stones are placed at each of the street-doors for the inhabitants to climb into their dwellings by. I say climb, for the lower stone is so lofty, and the whole three are so shallow on their flat surfaces, that it is with difficulty a full-sized man can stride up them. When you stand in the narrow doorway, and look down into the street, it is like looking down into a deep pit. The comfort in the inside of these dwellings is about equal to the conveniences outside. The one we went into smelt so close and musty from overcrowding, neglect, and, perhaps, forty years' dirt, that it almost made me sneeze. It was occupied by a sallow-faced woman, who called herself a 'gipsy', and who gets her living amongst servants and others as a fortune teller.

In another house of greater height, with a close, black, uneven staircase, almost perpendicular, we found a mixed population of about fifty people. In one room was a labourer's wife and several children, yellow, eager, and very ragged; in another was a woman with a blighted eye; in another a girl making match-boxes, assisted by a boy, while her father, a hawker of bootlaces, crouched despondingly over the grate, groaning about the badness of trade, and her mother was busy about the room. The dirt in this apartment was the landlord's dirt, not the tenant's—a most important distinction. The walls were chipped and greasy—the one cupboard was like a chimney; but the few plates were clean and neatly arranged—clean, perhaps, for want of being used. The floor had been well scrubbed and sanded, the mantelshelf was set out with a few poor china ornaments, and there were a few pictures stuck up which had been cut out of an illustrated newspaper. [One was a fancy portrait of Lord Brougham.][1] This room was admittedly occupied by this family and another woman—a stranger—from necessity, not from choice. At the top of the house was a weaver's work-room, lighted by two long windows with diamond panes. It contained two idle shuttles, watched over by a sickly woman, almost sinking with anxiety, if not from want. The husband was out seeking work in the silk market, like hundreds of fellow-labourers, with little prospect of obtaining it. A change in fashion, and the inevitable operation of the French Treaty, have affected Spitalfields and Bethnal Green in the same way as Coventry, and a large mass of trained industry finds itself suddenly 'displaced'.[2] It is not easy in middle life, with energies kept down by low living, little recreation, and bad air, to turn the mind and fingers into a fresh trade. The best of us are not always equal to such a task, and a poor weaver's wife may naturally sit on the edge of her scanty bed, and look into the future with little hope.

[The statistics of silk-weaving show a melancholy decline. In 1824 there were 25,000 looms in and about Spitalfields, now there are only 8,000. In 1835 wages were lower by thirty per cent than in 1824, and they did not average more than eight or nine shillings a week. Now they cannot be higher than seven shillings, or seven shillings and sixpence a week, on an average; and there are only from twenty-five to thirty master weavers. Perhaps, 20,000 working weavers are now struggling against this decay of their handicraft, and many of them, in despair, are taking to street hawking. The Rev. Mr Trevitt has set up many of these skilled labourers in this rough calling, with a capital of a few shillings. Mr Corkran, the excellent missionary connected with the London Domestic Mission, who knows more, perhaps, of the misery in Spitalfields proper, than most men, gives a very sad account of the poor in his district. I do not quote his admirable reports, because they deal with a period earlier than what I am dealing with.*]

I entered another street, not far from the one I have been speaking of, to witness more misery and more pain. There is nothing exceptional or transient in the conditions of life I am endeavouring faintly to describe. In Whitechapel, in St George's in the East, and in Bethnal Green, the people have lived for nearly a quarter of a century as they are living now. Strike off a few cases of obvious imposition—of pardonable exaggeration on the part of Scripture readers—and make a little allowance for the late severe weather—and we shall find the social condition of [nearly] one-half of London to be nearly as low and degraded as that of Ireland in its worst days. Here is a representative street of houses—leading off from the road in which stands St Philips's Church—the windows in the lower rooms of which are actually on the ground. These lower rooms are wells, dark and unventilated; and overcrowding, with all its attendant evils, can hardly be avoided in such a place. Just now we saw a row of houses where you had to climb up into the lower rooms; here you have to dive down into them. The first house we enter at random contains a suffering family. A large-headed, gaunt girl, tall and speechless, with arms like thin sticks, sits motionless in a chair. It scarcely requires a second glance at this poor creature to tell that she is an idiot. A man sits shivering by the fire—old-looking though not aged. He is a sawyer by trade. We ask after his health, and his wife, who struggles to speak cheerfully, answers for him:

'He went out, sir, to work, one morning early, without food, and the cold seems to have struck on his chest.'

[* 1850 to 1859 inclusive. 1860 is not yet published.]

The man tries to tell us that he has never been warm since, but the words seem to hiss in his throat. I have spoken to scores of people who have nearly lost their voices from asthma and other diseases of the chest; and I have seen many poor deaf and dumb creatures who could only show their misery by their looks. One youth—a young coal-whipper, with scanty and uncertain work—was maintaining a father and mother who both suffered under this terrible affliction. The most melancholy sight, however, is to watch the blind when they hear that the visiting clergyman is in the street or court. They creep out of dark holes of doorways, feeling their road carefully, and throw out their arms widely as if to embrace the expected loaf.

Christopher Street, with its continuations, is a fair example of an ordinary Bethnal Green street, and though short, it contains many varieties of low and humble life. In one two-roomed house is a notorious dog-trainer, who has lived there for many years, and who keeps a dog-pit for the gratification of his patrons. His yard is often crammed with every kind of terrier and fighting dog, and his upper room, where the pit is built, is reached by a ladder passing through a trap-door. When you enter this room, the ladder can be drawn up and the trap-door shut down, and so far you are secure from interruption. The windows are boarded up behind the blinds, so that no noise within can reach the little street; and when a sufficient number of patrons are gathered together to pay the spirited proprietor of this den, the delights of Hockley-in-the Hole are partially revived. Dogs are set together by the throat, cats are worried and killed by bull-terriers within a certain time, to show the training of the dog, and rats are hunted round the pit for the same purpose.

Within a few doors of this illegal sporting theatre is a family who have just been rescued from the lowest depths of wretchedness. They were found, a few days ago,* without food, without fire, or any other necessary, in a room nearly bare, their furniture having been seized for rent. There were a father, mother, and several children standing shivering within the bare walls, the children having nothing on them but sacks tied round their waists.

[* January, 1861.]

In Old Nichols Street, a turning in this district leading off from Shoreditch, we have a specimen of an east-end thieves' street.[1] Its road is rotten with mud and water; its houses are black and repulsive; and at least fifty dark sinister faces look at you from behind blinds and dirty curtains as you pass up the rugged pavement.

Courts of the filthiest description branch off on either side, filled with the usual dust-heaps, the usual pools of inky water, and the usual groups of children rolling in the dirt. There is a silence about the street and its houses indicative of the character of the place. The few trades that are carried on are in most cases merely masks—industry is the exception, robbery is the rule. A few hawkers, who have eaten up their 'stock money', or capital, and have even pawned their baskets at the baker's for a loaf of bread, are to be found in some of the holes and corners, but the dark public-house with the green blinds is full of thieves, the houses on either side are full of thieves and prostitutes, and a tavern in a side street is full of swell-mobsmen. Even here, as in all these places, there is something to admire. A woman, who works at box-clump-making,[2] with her husband, has picked an orphan boy from the streets, and given him a place amongst her own children. His father was a porter at one of the markets, and died suddenly in the midst of his work. The boy was tossed about for many days, fighting hard for food, until he found a home with people who were nearly as poor as himself. Many cases of such self-sacrifice, such large-hearted generosity, may be easily found amongst the poor. The cases of heroic endurance under the most frightful trials are even more frequent, and they make us respect these poor creatures even in their dirt and rags.

The Rev. Mr Trevitt is unceasing in his labours within his own district, and he has called round him an efficient staff of assistants. He has about forty visitors who watch over the poor, and he draws about 80*l.* per annum from the Metropolitan District Visiting Society. He has two ragged schools, which collect about seven hundred children; two national schools, which collect about two hundred and fifty more; and an infant school, which gathers about one hundred infants. His Sunday schools are attended by about eight hundred children, who have to work during the week, and his evening schools are generally attended by about eighty of the same class.

There is no public soup-kitchen, but the usual miscellaneous distribution at the parsonage, according to means. [Mr Trevitt looks sharply after the many hungry children in his district, and often has a soup-dinner for these alone. A few days ago a thin, sickly man came to the parsonage door, and asked to be admitted amongst the children. He was told that this was against the rules and he went away in tears. He was called back before he had crawled out of the street; he crept in, like a poor dog, and was seated with the little ones. His case was inquired into, and it turned out that he was one of the most wretched of that very wretched class, an hospital 'incurable'. He had been turned out by the doctors a few weeks before, had been tossed about the streets unable to work, and was dying from starvation. His case may be only one out of thousands.*]

There is a maternity society in the St Philip's district, to lend necessaries for child-birth, and an excellent industrial school (built and presented to the district by Mr Edward Thornton, at a cost of 3,000*l.*), where girls and women are taught needlework. The penny bank, in 1860, showed receipts to the amount of

[*The following is another 'incurable' case, from the same neighbourhood, bearing date January 20, 1861:—

'Inspector Armstrong, of the H division of police, mentioned to Mr Leigh, the sitting magistrate at the Worship Street police court, the following pitiable case of distress, to which his attention had been called, and which he had himself visited. The inspector said that on entering the top room of a house situate in Thomas Street, Brick Lane, Spitalfields, he found a man and woman lying in what might with due allowance be termed a bed; covering or blanket there was none. The rooms were nearly bare. The inmates were evidently very ill, and they looked much older than they really were. They were man and wife; Copeland by name. The man was formerly a cabinet-maker. His mother was present, and doing all she could to comfort them. From her the inspector learned that they were both in a consumption, the husband having been turned out of the London Hospital a fortnight since as incurable, after a seven weeks' attendance there. The inspector added that the wretched couple were incessantly obliged to be raised to a sitting position, in consequence of inability to breathe otherwise. The mother of Copeland was called for by Mr Leigh, and vouched for the truth of her miserable relative's condition. A fortnight since a son of Inspector Constable, H division, in pity for the sufferings he witnessed, gave them 10s. Mr Leigh, for present aid, ordered that two blankets and 10s. should be instantly sent them.']

900*l*., and this is the poorest of the Bethnal Green parishes.[1]

[The other side of Shoreditch—the Finsbury side—is quite as full of black courts and alleys as Bethnal Green. Walk along the main thoroughfare from the parish church towards the city, peep on one side of the hay-bundle standing at the corn-chandler's door; look through the group of rough, idle loungers, leaning against the corner of the gin-shop, or dive under the fluttering garments that hang across outside the cheap clothier's window, and you will see a dark, damp opening in the wall, like the channel of a sewer passing under and between the houses, and leading to one of the wretched courts and alleys. You enter the passage, picking your way to the bottom, and find a little square of low, black houses, that look as if they were built as a penal settlement for dwarfs. The roofs are depressed, the doors are narrow, the windows are pinched up, and the whole square can almost be touched on each side by a full-grown man. At the further end you will observe a tap, enclosed in a wooden frame, that supplies the water for the whole court, with a dust-bin and privy, which are openly used by all. In the middle of the little sooty square, standing in the puddles always formed by the sinking stones, you will see three or four barrows belonging to street vendors, and you will gather from this that some of the stallkeepers you have noticed in the thoroughfare outside retire to these dark hiding-places when their labour is done. Glancing over the tattered green curtain at one of the black windows, you will see a room like a gloomy well, and in its depths perhaps a knotted old woman crouching over a small glow-worm of coal, gleaming in a grate full of dust; or the frowning face of some idle male inhabitant of the court, whose expression somehow reminds you of the felon's dock. If you pass to the right or left, you may find other oven-like entrances leading to other similar courts; or you may go out into the main thoroughfare, and, seeing a similar passage a few yards farther on, you may explore it, to find yourself in another twin huddling-place of the poor. The plan and design of this second court will be in all respects the same as those of the first, showing that the same master-mind has created them both. Who the owners of this class of property are may remain a mystery; they draw their rents in short, sharp payments, and they have no reason to complain of the unprofitable character of their investments. These settlements, of which there may be fifty scattered at the backs of the houses on each side of Shoreditch, within the space of half a mile, were all built thirty, forty, sixty, and even eighty years ago, when building regulations were not so strict as they are now; and they were nearly all framed to meet that desire of the English people to have a 'house to themselves'. The value of house property in these holes and corners of Shoreditch must be rising rather than falling. An ordinary room, in one of these courts, will fetch two shillings a week, and an ordinary house, which contains little more than one room covered with a loft, will fetch four shillings a week. In some cases these courts are choked up with every variety of filth; their approaches wind round by the worst kind of slaughter-houses;[1] they lie in the midst of rank stables and offensive trades; they are crowded with pigs, with fowls, and with dogs; they are strewn with oyster-shells and fish refuse; they look upon foul yards and soaking heaps of stale vegetable refuse; their drainage lies in pools wherever it may be thrown; the rooms of their wretched dwellings have not been repaired or whitewashed for years; they are often smothered with smoke, which beats down upon them from some neighbouring factory, whose chimney is beyond the control of the Act of Parliament; rag-warehouses have their close store-rooms looking them full in the face; and cats'-meat preparers boil their cauldrons amongst them without fear. In most cases the inhabitants, as we might fully expect, are not superior to their surroundings, and in places like Bowl Court, Plough Yard, which contains a half-Irish colony, they form the greatest nuisance of all. An Irish landlord or landlady will rent a room at about two shillings a week, and then take in as many families, or individuals, at a small nightly rental, as the floor can possibly hold. This is openly done in defiance of the Lodging-house Act, or any other social reform law.

Red Lion Court, near the Shoreditch corner of the Kingsland Road, is another bad specimen of these alleys, being over-crowded with men and their families engaged in the watercress trade. Pierce's Court, New Inn Yard, Shoreditch, is another of the worst; and the whole line of Holywell Lane, on either side, is full of these holes and corners.

Each one has got its story to tell, like more ambitious thoroughfares, and here is a narrative of a Shoreditch Court, told in the words of the Reporters:—'A middle-aged, poor-looking woman, who stated her name to be Sarah Wilkinson, and who was accompanied by a pale-faced little girl, dressed in black, said to be eleven years old, but who seemed about seven or eight, applied at the beginning of December, 1860, to Mr Leigh, the sitting magistrate at the Worship Street police court, for advice, with the following strange statement:—Mrs Wilkinson said that the object of her application to the magistrate was to learn what she was to do with the little girl she had with her, who had neither home nor food, and was utterly friendless. The child's name was Eliza Clarke, and she was the daughter of an engineer of the same name, who formerly worked for Mr Ramsay, in the same business, near Shoreditch Church, but who abandoned the girl's mother about seven years ago, to go to Australia, and had never since been heard of. About two years ago the mother was taken into custody, and brought to this court, charged with selling spirits without a licence, as she believed, and on her being committed for that offence her child was taken into Shoreditch Workhouse, and remained there as long as the mother's term of imprisonment lasted, for as soon as the mother was liberated she instantly went to the workhouse, and claimed and took away her daughter. The mother and child had since lived in a court called Mark's Place, Leonard Street, Shoreditch, in one of the houses of which she had a small ready-furnished room, which she held up to the morning of the previous Monday week, when she went out, as usual, leaving the little girl at home, and had never again been seen from that time to this. Inquiries had been made about her, but she could not be traced anywhere, and she (the applicant) and all the neighbours felt quite sure that something must have occurred to the woman, as she was such a good and affectionate mother she would be certain to come back to her child if she could. They were all poor people down that court, and, as the mother did not come back, and it was unsafe to leave so young a girl in charge of the room, which was wanted for some one else, the landlady had accordingly resumed possession of her room and goods, and then the child had no place to go to. All the neighbours liked the mother, and pitied the child, and they had all given her something to eat and drink by turns; but they had too many incumbrances of their own for any one to take her in and lodge her; and the little girl had consequently been sleeping about anywhere she could, and on Monday slept all night upon the stairs of one of the houses. She (Mrs Wilkinson) was a widow, and had been so three years, and had three little children to keep. She had only one room herself, and could not possibly take the child in. Besides, she was only a charwoman, and that occupation was so uncertain that she could hardly keep herself and family. She did not live in Mark's Place, but a short distance off; and on going there that morning to see about some work, she met the little girl, sopped through with rain, and in such a pitiable state that, knowing how fond her mother was of her, she could not bear it, and determined to go at once with her to Shoreditch workhouse, and induce them to admit the girl till something was heard of the mother. She accordingly took the child there, and some person seated at a desk told her she must see Mr Cole. Who Mr Cole was she did not know, nor whether she did see Mr Cole, but a thin gentleman inquired her business, and she explained to him the forlorn state of the little girl, and told him everything that she had now told the magistrate. Instead of admitting the child, however, the gentleman did not even take down her name or address, but told the witness she had no business to interfere, and as she had interfered so much, she had better look after her herself, which, as she had already explained, she could not do. On receiving this refusal, she told the gentleman that she must take the little girl before a magistrate, and he replied that she might do so if she liked. She then walked out of the house, leaving the child behind her, thinking that they might perhaps keep her, as she was there, but in a minute or so afterwards the girl was turned out into the street, although a shower of rain was coming down at the time. She had now, therefore, brought the child to the magistrate, to know what was to be done with her, as it was enough to make any heart ache to see a child in such a state as this was. Mr Leigh said it was certainly a strange story the woman had told. The child seemed to him to have been wholly deserted, and if the applicant had really told the workhouse authorities all that she had told him, and she said she had, it did seem surprising that they should see a child like this, with no food, no mother, and no place to go to, and yet refuse to take her in. He thought some explanation would be given of it, and the warrant officer of that district must take the woman and child to the house, state the particulars, and inquire why they did not admit her.—Mr Edwards, of the Shoreditch Board of Guardians, and Mr Cole, relieving officer, waited upon Mr Leigh to explain that part of the above case with which they are connected. Mr Cole stated that the woman did attend with the child, and made the application referred to. She said she was a widow with three children of her own, and that she could not keep the child, and although he told her that she would be compensated by the parish for her trouble, and any expense she might incur by tending it while the inquiry was made, she refused to have anything more to do with it, and took the child away with her without further parley, and expressed her determination to take her before a magistrate. The officer said that if she was resolved upon doing that he could not help it, and the woman went out with the child, and did not leave it behind her at the house, as she stated, nor was it, as she also said, thrust out into the street. Mr Edwards said that every anxiety was felt by the guardians to attend to all cases of this kind, as far as possible, and he could confidently appeal to the warrant officer whether immediate attention was not paid to any recommendation or order of the magistrates, whether verbal or written. The child had been admitted the same night without hesitation, and when he stated that they had an ancillary establishment at Brentwood, now full of children, many of whom had been cruelly deserted by their parents, with the object of getting them there, it was obvious that some previous inquiry was imperative, and Mr Cole had been appointed as an extra overseer for that especial purpose. Some further observations of a similar tenor followed, and ultimately Mr Leigh expressed himself satisfied with the explanation now given, and thanked the gentlemen for their waiting upon him to afford it.'[1]

Some of the alleys, which are sometimes called 'rents', sometimes 'rows', sometimes 'gardens', 'places', 'buildings', 'lanes', 'yards', 'squares', and sometimes 'walks',—situated near Mark's Place, on the other side of the Curtain Road, down Holywell Mount—still maintain a little of a certain rural aspect which they must have had in full bloom when they were first built and occupied. Their houses are not larger, but they have each a piece of ground in front, which, though it grows nothing, to all appearance, but broken, uneven railings, serves to ventilate the place, and keep the opposite dwellings at a proper distance. In other alleys, even in the thickest part of Shoreditch, there is, here and there, a desire shown to be clean; and I may mention one little, ill-constructed court in Holywell Lane, which is quite a flower in the wilderness. Its entrance is low and gloomy, but the rugged stones on its footway are carefully swept, and the uneven steps leading down to its little row of houses are white with hearthstone. The first dwelling—a small room with a staircase like a ladder, leading up into the top loft (the plan upon which nearly all the small houses in these courts appear to be built)—has nothing about it to account for its luxurious look, and yet it seems to be a palace compared with its neighbours. Its owner is an humble working man, with one child, and a cleanly, decent wife, and all the magic that struck me, or that would strike any one who took the trouble to pay it a visit, was produced by nothing more wonderful than a little soap and water.]

THE WEST

Near Westminster Abbey

It seems to be the fate of great cathedrals to be surrounded by 'slums'. I use this slang word for courts and alleys in this chapter, because Cardinal Wiseman has made it classical. When he spoke of the holes and corners of Westminster about the Abbey, he could find no more general and expressive term, and I may be pardoned for following so eminent a leader.[1]

The Church, as an institution, has more authority in poor than in rich neighbourhoods; and, as a building, it shines by the meanness lying at its feet. We are never tired of looking up a narrow avenue of fruit-stalls and old-clothes shops when the prospect closes with spires and a Gothic porch. The lower and more irregular the houses that cluster under the shadow of the temple the more charming is the picture. The blue smoke curls upwards from the red housetops, the sunlight touches the corners of the crumbled cathedral stone, and the solemn gray towers seem to watch over all as they stand amidst the low white clouds. Writers like Longfellow, coming from the raw new cities of America, that were only yesterday reclaimed from the jungle, looking upon such scenes, are lost in admiration of the broken outlines and irregular lines, and the slums become invested with the purple hues of poetry.

Unfortunately, however, there is a period in the history of slums when they become utterly mouldy and putrid. I say unfortunately, for most of us like old houses and old neighbourhoods, and Victoria Street, W., will not please the present generation like old Westminster.[2] The mouldy, putrid period fell upon the old Abbey district some few years ago, and an improved thoroughfare was ploughed through to Pimlico. The diseased heart was divided in half—one part was pushed on one side, and the other part on the other, and the world was asked to look upon a new reformation. A great city, a leprous district, is not to be purified in this manner by a Diet of contractors; and the chief result has been to cause more huddling together.* While the

[* The Bishop of London spoke as follows in the House of Lords, February 28, 1861:—'Their lordships were perhaps in the habit of thinking that the East-end

nightmare street of unlet palaces was waiting for more capital to fill its yawning gulf, and a few more residents to warm its hollow chambers into life, the landlords of the slums were raising their rents; and thieves, prostitutes, labourers, and working women were packed in a smaller compass. The mouldiness and putridity of Westminster—the part popularly so called—have gone on increasing, and of all the criminal districts in London I think it is now the worst.

It matters little on which side of Victoria Street you turn, if you wish to find examples of social degradation.[1] The streets and alleys that may be marked with a black cross, even in the five districts of St John, St Mary, St Stephen, St Mathew, and Holy Trinity, are nearly seventy, and there are others scattered about the neighbourhood. The courts here are the worst kind of courts, both in structure and condition; and the streets present lamentable blocks of overcrowding. In Carpenter Street, which is a working-man's street, nearly every room contains a different family of five or six members, and the rents run about two shillings and three shillings a week for each room. At one of the houses I went into an empty kitchen which had recently contained a mother and three children, the roof of which was not more than five feet ten inches from the floor, and the window of which was not a yard deep. In another street, called Grub Street, the houses were even more faded, dilapidated, and overcrowded; and a place called York Buildings presented some of the worst features of an east-end sweeps' court. The dirt in the latter place, both in and outside the houses, was like a thick cement; and the rents for two dark dustholes of rooms was nominally four shillings a week. A lazy-looking man, who was smoking out of an upper window down the court, remarked

of London was inhabited almost solely by the poor; but he believed that they would find that nearer to their own doors there was more squalid misery than in the East-end. In the very neighbourhood where they then were the clergyman who was entrusted with the spiritual charge of the parish of St John had informed him that evening that when Victoria Street was constructed five thousand poor persons were displaced in his parish, three-fourths of whom went into the already overcrowded parishes on the other side of the river, whilst the other fourth found refuge in his own parish; so that in many instances, where a family had a house before, there were now three or four families in it.'][2]

'that they never paid more than two shillings and sixpence on the average, because they were often out of work'. The energy of some of these men in seeking employment is not very great, and a bricklayer's labourer is never so happy as when he is standing against the archway of his court, with his hands in his pockets, and his eyes looking vacantly into space. On Sunday morning, in places like the Seven Dials, Whitechapel, Somers Town, Marylebone, the New Cut, Lambeth, or the Broadway, Westminster, you may always see a hundred of these men gathered in silent groups, smoking, but seldom talking to each other.[1]

A court, recently rebuilt, called Champion's Alley, may be taken as a model of its class. The rooms are small, and the dimensions of the passage in front are not greater than those of many other similar passages, but each house is ventilated at the back, and is complete in itself. A dwelling of two rooms in a court like this seems to satisfy the most ambitious workman. The landlords in this neighbourhood, with a few exceptions, apologize for the wretched condition in which they let and maintain their property, by saying that they dare not fit up a cistern or an outbuilding with anything that would sell for sixpence at the marine store-shop. There may be some truth in this assertion, though it is an obvious excuse for neglecting the tenants.

Tripp's Buildings is an example of a court whose inhabitants struggle to be clean and decent, even in the face of bad building arrangements. The houses have no outlet, no air-hole at the back, and are, therefore, unhealthy and illegal. They have each two rooms, one over the other, the size of which may be about seven feet broad and twelve feet long. Each house lets for about four shillings a week.

The gas-works in this neighbourhood are sure to attract a certain number of labourers, and these labourers are sure to live as near as possible to the factory. Laundry Yard, a long, narrow strip of pavement, covered with every kind of filth, contains a row of dwarfed two-roomed huts, filled with Irish labourers and their families, and closely faced by the high wall of the Chartered Gas Company's premises. It is no uncommon thing to find eighteen people, of both sexes and of all ages, in one of these miserable dwellings. The rooms are dark on the finest day, and the small outlet at the back is nearly full when it contains a dog's house and a pail. The male inhabitants are chiefly Irish, and are mostly engaged at the gas-works.

If some of these places are dirty, repulsive, and overcrowded, they are all brightness and purity compared to other parts of the colony. Enter a narrow street called St Anne's Lane, glance up at a fearful side-court called St Anne's Place, and wonder whether such filth and squalor can ever be exceeded. I went up the last-mentioned court, which had every feature of a sewer, and found a long puddle of sewage soaking in the hollow centre. The passages of the low black huts on either side were like old sooty chimneys, and the inhabitants were buried out of sight in the gloom. As I turned round to leave this place I caught a glimpse of several rough, long-haired heads peeping round the edges of the entrance. They disappeared immediately, like figures in a Punch and Judy show.

I crossed over the road, and entered the openly acknowledged high street of thieves and prostitutes. It is called Pye Street, and has no mock modesty about it—no desire to conceal its real character. Threepenny 'homes for travellers' abound on both sides—yellow, sickly, unwholesome places, many of them far below the level of the road, and entered by a kind of pit. Many of the houses have no flooring on their passages; and there is nothing for the barefooted children to stand upon but the black, damp, uneven earth. A child, dirty and nearly naked, was hanging out of one of the old-fashioned casement windows; and in the summer time it is no unusual thing to see about fifty coarse women exhibiting themselves in the same manner. The yards at the back of the houses contain little mountains of ashes and vegetable refuse; and a dust-contractor's yard, in the centre of the street, seems to have burst its bounds, and to have nearly poured out its oyster-shells, cabbage-stalks, and broken china into the open thoroughfare. Short-haired young men, with showy handkerchiefs round their neck, and tight corduroy trousers, were standing at most of the doors, looking pretty sharply about them from under the peaks of their caps. A fiddler was playing a dancing tune to a mixed assembly of thieves and prostitutes, and a morning ball was being arranged on both sides of the pavement. Many of the side streets and courts about here are shored up with black beams to keep the houses from falling, which adds to their wretched appearance. A few ragged and other schools have been planted in this district in some of those faded shops which were formerly the haunts of receivers of stolen property.

The hilly playgrounds for this hopeful colony lie on both sides of Victoria Street, down by the arches of the roadway. Where the links of new buildings have not yet joined each other you can see fag-ends of courts or interiors of ruined houses lopped, like diseased limbs, but not sewn up and healed. Sometimes the filth of these places runs out in black streams, and winds its way slowly down under the road arches. The interiors, as seen from the highway, are much like what we have been looking at in the last few chapters, and any one who walks leisurely along this broad thoroughfare may observe the kind of life that is boiling within the settlement.

The melancholy row of shops in Orchard Street will remind many of the old days of Field Lane. There is the dismal chandler's shop, with wood, tobacco, and coals mixed up with sooty lard, stale saveloys, a dry knuckle of boiled pork, and a few balls of cotton; a mysterious shop, that may be a lodging-house, or an unlicensed beer-shop; and the low pawnbroker's, with the brown, greasy door, and the many-coloured pocket-handkerchiefs hanging in strings from a hook. In Snow's Rents, in this neighbourhood, you may see a specimen of a very dirty costermonger's colony, with a stream of thick black water and vegetable refuse flowing down the centre of the passage. In King's-head Buildings, in the Broadway, you may see the filthiest court in Westminster. The narrow roadway up it is worse than a sewer, because there is no flow of water; and amongst its swarm of inhabitants are several sweeps. It was near here that I saw the only instance of intoxication that I met with during my journeys, and I mention the fact for what it is worth. A drunken sweep and bricklayer were supporting each other as well as they were able, and exchanging what appeared to be vows of lasting friendship.

The old Almonry, as it was called, near the spot where Caxton's house is said to have stood, and the art of printing to have been first pursued, is now nothing but the dreariest of ruins. A low passage leads out of Tothill Street into the hollow shell of a house, whose rooms seem to have sunk into a few heaps of rotten bricks. Dead dogs, soaking fragments of old placards, and other refuse, lie amongst the bricks and dust, and the space is watched by closed, battered houses, with black, jagged window-panes. In a murky room of one of these houses a few tattered garments were drying; but this was the only sign of life to be seen within the place.†

Near Regent Street

The evils of overcrowding in courts and alleys are, unhappily, not confined to the eastern end of the metropolis. There are almost as many dark holes and corners within a few yards of Regent Street or Charing Cross, which shelter almost as much sickness, crime, and poverty, as any back hiding-places in Whitechapel or Bethnal Green. We may have all hurried for years along the bright open highways, scarcely glancing at the little doorways scattered here and there between the busy shops, and yet these doorways—holes—call them by what name we will—are the entrances to many thousands of closely-packed homes. These human dwellings—human in little else but the old familiar house shape—in old central neighbourhoods, like St James's, Westminster, form square openings, reaching up to the little patch of heaven overhead, like the shaft of a mine. The air in them is close and heavy, and they are dark on the clearest day. The infants and mothers suffer because they cannot escape from them; the elder children, as soon as they are able to run, desert them from instinct, and find more comfort in the gutters and streets; and the men leave them to seek for warmth and cheerfulness in the neighbouring tavern. They are penal settlements, not homes, and those who visit them and consider the effect they must have on mind and morals are compelled to wonder that there is not far more vice and drunkenness in the world.

The poverty and low living of London have to be largely dug out. The noisy crowds who clamour at police-courts—who jam against workhouse-doors, like visitors to a theatre—who are foremost at soup-kitchens, and other similar charitable distributions—contain very few of the patient, hard-working poor. These sit in their wretched rooms, looking into each other's faces, drooping over bare shopboards, bare benches, bare tables, and half-empty grates, hoping and praying for work. They only ask to be employed. They tramp through miles of mud—they stand for hours in work-room passages—they bear rain, and cold, and hunger without murmuring, and they clear their little households of every saleable article rather than beg. When they have got their little strip of cloth, or leather, to stitch or cut into shape, they clasp it like some precious treasure, and hurry home to begin their ill-paid task. In times of plenty they are, perhaps, a little wasteful; they look a very short way into the future; but we must think of their education and habits, and their cheerless lives. It is easy to add up their little excursions, their few dissipations, and fewer amusements, and to bring a wholesale charge of improvidence against them when they drop dead from want; but how few would bear the trial of living where they live and come out of it prudent, thoughtful, and pure!

The great central neighbourhood of St James's, Westminster, which is a fair sample of many adjacent districts, such as Soho, part of St Martin's-in-the-Fields, &c., is chiefly occupied in its Berwick Street district by working tailors, porters, and shoe-makers. Nearly every street has got its history in London handbooks, and is famed for having sheltered some celebrity in literature, science, or art. Now, however, the mansions fashionable in the last century are let off in 'tenements'. Every room is crowded with a different family, and four, if not more, landlords are interested in the rent. The leases are invariably sub-let, three deep, and the active inspector of nuisances, Mr J.H. Morgan, has more than enough to do. Dwellings that originally sheltered eight or ten persons are now crowded with thirty, forty, or fifty inmates. The carved wainscotings are torn to pieces, or covered, an inch deep, with black grease. The old banisters are broken down. The stairs are rugged, dark, and uneven, but fortunately broad, according to the original plan of the buildings. Garrets are as much crowded as ground-floors, and even more, because some of these ground-floors have been turned into common shops, and one of the worst features of the district is a tendency to live in kitchens and cellars. Nine of these kitchens, wholly unfit for human habitation, were condemned last year, chiefly in Windmill Street, Haymarket; Pulteney Street, and Francis Street. In some cases they are lighted by a small window, looking out into a shallow area half full of stones, oyster-shells, and dust; and in other cases they are lighted by nothing but a small gridiron grating. In each of these damp, dreary, underground prisons were self-confined a large family, consisting of four, eight, or even ten persons, and the average rental paid for each room was about three shillings a week. Hundreds of these kitchens are still so occupied, although the district has been weeded of the very worst; and some of the condemned apartments are turned into carpenters' workshops, others into dustholes and receptacles for filth. Looking down more than one of these repulsive places, I saw a shelving heap of dust, broken bricks, eggshells, and vegetable refuse. Here it was that the cholera spent its chief fury in 1854; and though every house then felt the weight of that affliction in one or other of its rooms, and the gutters ran with chloride of lime for many weeks, the same crowding and dirty habits still prevail. The dirt arises partly from long-settled carelessness about domestic cleanliness, partly from the impossibility of keeping one room tidy when six or eight people have to eat and sleep in it, and partly from the neglect of landlords to whitewash, paint, and paper the dwellings. The crowding arises from the desire of the working population to be 'near their bread', as they express it; and the high rental of the tenements, averaging four shillings a room per week, arises naturally from this rush upon a particular spot. An empty room is a novelty. The distribution of population is not equal, even in the same parish, because the rents are unequal. About one hundred and thirty-four persons live on an acre in the St James's Square division, about two hundred and sixty-two on an acre in the Golden Square division, and four hundred and thirty-two on an acre in the Berwick Street division, the neighbourhood I am dealing with.

I went into one of the houses in Pulteney Court—within a stone's throw of Regent Street—and was struck by its resemblance to one of the lowest dwellings of Bethnal Green. The small yard seemed rotting with damp and dirt. The narrow window of the lower back room was too caked with mud to be seen through, and the kitchen was one of those black-holes, filled with untold filth and rubbish, which the inspector had condemned a twelvemonth before. The stench throughout the house, although the front and back doors were wide open, was almost sickening; and when a room-door was opened this stench came out in gusts. In one apartment I found a family of six persons, flanked by another apartment containing five. One room was a little better furnished than another, but the gloom of poverty, dirt, and foul air hung over all. A turn-up bedstead, dirty and broken, a small cracked table, a couple of rickety chairs, a piece of soap lying on the table by the side of a greasy knife, a pail full of soaking rags, and a knot of sooty infants in a corner, seemed to be the usual contents of a room. One thin, sharp-faced boy was minding one of these apartments for the tenants, while they (both husband and wife) were out seeking work. I asked him if he lived there: 'No, sir,' he said; 'my house is higher up.' He led the way to one of the garrets, where there were more signs of misery still, and this he told us was his 'house'. The dead cinders had oozed out of the grate into the room; an empty saucepan stood on the table by the side of a piece of soap, a cracked tea-cup was on the floor; an old collapsed bedstead, covered with something like a ragged mat, stood in one corner; and the dismal aspect of the place was heightened by two or three flower-pots full of black earth and dry, sapless sticks. The boy's mother was a poor shirtmaker, deserted by her husband, and left, fortunately, with only this one child. In the next garret were a shoemaker and his family, a wife and three children. The room was tidy, and even comfortable, though the work-bench under the window was idle. The rent of this apartment was three shillings a week, although the low roof had been broken in in half-a-dozen places by the snow. The man, upon being questioned why he lived in such a hole at such a rent, with the ceiling scarcely higher than his head, spoke about his long residence in the parish, his familiarity with its people and its ways, and his dread of going into another neighbourhood, which he said would be like a 'foreign country' to him. This dislike of going amongst strangers[1] is the feeling which often keeps up rents, and often keeps the working population huddled together, and poor. In another room was a consumptive tailor, working on a shop-board under the window, faced by his wife, who was also employed in the same trade. One child was playing between them on the board, another on the floor, and five more were in the street. The man was almost bent double with disease and long stooping; and, bad as he was, he was only like hundreds of his class. Seen dimly through the garret windows opposite were many more similar workers, and many garrets in the neighbourhood contain half-a-dozen yellow, crooked workmen, stitching themselves into their graves as they sit cross-legged on the floor. This man was an out-door patient of the Brompton Hospital, and he held out his letter of recommendation in his long, thin hand. The hand, the voice, the hollow chest were quite sufficient credentials of disease, without any written attestation. His employment, like that of most of the tailors in this district, comes chiefly from the West-End houses, and he has to live in the neighbourhood to be within reach of his masters. He was working painfully on some tough piece of army cloth.

In another small street, called New Street, remarkable for its condemned kitchens, was a little broker's shop, which looked miserably bare of stock. An old bedstead and one or two small articles stood at the door, but the interior was empty. The room at the back of the shop, where the owner and his wife lived, with seven children, was also nearly empty, for the bedstead at the door was almost the last of their own domestic furniture. The man was a French-polisher out of work, and bit by bit his little home had been broken to pieces and sold to passers-by. It was suggested that an application to the parish was a proper thing under the circumstances, but the wife proudly declined to ask for such charity, saying they were well known in the neighbourhood, and after poor-law relief they would never be able to hold up their heads. This is a very common feeling, especially amongst poor ratepayers.

The most singular hole and corner in the district is No. 6, Husband Street. It is a small yard containing a dustbin, a water-tank, a couple of lower rooms or cellars, that look like condemned cells, and a number of rooms with black wooden exteriors, reached by ladders, and supplied with rude balconies. The population of each room on each flat can look over into the yard from these balconies, which help, in some degree, to ventilate the place. Each room is crowded with a distinct family, having many children; and one room contains a mother-in-law in addition to the usual family. In one of the small garrets is an old charwoman, living by herself, who is going into the infirmary in a few days; and in the other garret is a widow with three children, who supports herself as a tailoress. Her few goods were seized for rent at her last lodgings, and she was left without a single article of furniture, except a few rags for a bed. The children were squatting on the bare boards, and she was standing up stitching a piece of scarlet cloth at the window. One advantage of living 'in tenements', as it is called, is that the poor come together and help each other, or their lot would often be harder than it is. The miserable lodger who has no fire can often run up or down and sit with the one who is more comfortably situated; and many a hungry mouth is filled, or naked form partly clothed, by those who have little more than a few crumbs to share.

The sanitary work of this neighbourhood is perhaps heavier than that of most districts, except the Strand district; certainly far heavier, taking equal areas. The inspector of nuisances is that rare workman, a man whose heart is in his work, and the poor regard him as a friend and adviser. Besides nuisances arising from overcrowding in ordinary dwellings, or courts and alleys, he has to deal with many troublesome animals. The district contains nearly four hundred stables, in which are kept more than one thousand horses. Over these stables are a number of small close rooms, in which about nine hundred people reside and bring up their families, or one-fortieth part of the whole population of the parish. Another nuisance arises from cows, of which there are at least two hundred kept at eight stations in as many streets. I went into one liquorice-coloured den, where thirty-nine of these animals were standing with their faces against the wall, being milked. There was no light except a glimmer from one or two murky windows in the roof, and the whole place was ankle-deep in slush. Whether the milk supplied to the neighbourhood from this dark stable is an invigorating fluid or not, I leave the able officer of health, Dr Lankester, to determine; and, I believe, in his reports, he has spoken against the system and its product more than once.[1] Slaughter-houses, belonging to small, struggling butchers, in the closest part of the neighbourhood, form another sanitary difficulty, which is only got over by incessant inspection. Something like one thousand two hundred distinct nuisances found, and one thousand six hundred abated during the year, represent a very low social condition for a small West-End district.

THE NORTH

Near King's Cross

Some of our most densely populated, faded parishes—like some of our most degraded streets—are known by names that mock their present condition. Paradise Row, Mount Pleasant, Angel Place, and similar titles are commonly attached to some of the rottenest courts in London; and two of the central parishes—St Martin's, at Charing Cross, and St Giles's, at Upper Holborn—are only legally known as standing 'in the fields'. The latter parish, at one time the most notorious, if not the worst, in London, has been partly purified at the expense of other portions of the town, and we may now ask very fairly where we can find St Giles's-in-the-Fields. Without assuming that the courts off Drury Lane, the dark, close avenues of Endell Street, and the dismal maze of the Seven Dials, are half cleared of their human rats; without shutting our eyes to the troublesome fact that Lambeth, Marylebone, Whitechapel, and St George's in the East have become more crowded with refuse population that certain improvements in Bloomsbury and thereabouts might be carried out, we may conclude that the real St Giles's-in-the-Fields stands exactly where it has stood for nearly twenty years—at Agar Town, in the noisy parish of St Pancras.[1] You may reach it in a walk of half-an-hour from the centre of Clerkenwell, and find it nestling, as snugly as ever, by the side of the Great Northern Railway.

The origin of a very few London eyesores may be traced to a landlord-and-tenant quarrel, and Agar Town apologizes for its present degraded existence by a local tradition. The ground belongs to the Ecclesiastical Commissioners—the whole property belongs to them now—and many years ago it was let to a gentleman on a certain lease, most probably for farming land. Some five-and-twenty years before the expiration of this lease he applied for a long extension, expecting no doubt to profit by the advance of railways on the metropolis. His application was refused by the commissioners, and upon this he resolved to make the most of his remainder, and annoy his landlords. The necessary steps were taken, the proper people were called

together, and Agar Town—the lowest effort of building skill and
arrangement in or near London—arose upon Church property.

It is exactly ten years since I last went over this unsightly
settlement, and I found upon visiting it again that more than one
half of its habitations (it contains about five hundred) are
hopelessly decayed, while its roads and footways are improved.
In 1851—the historical year of civilizing exhibitions—it had
gasworks, but no gas; for what lighting material was made upon
the spot was despatched to more solvent and favoured
neighbourhoods. Its highways were ditches—deep and filled
with mud—and its footways were mere earthbanks on each side
of the channel. Now, thanks to the efforts of the parochial authorities, and [in defiance of] the Ecclesiastical Commissioners,
who could never be brought to any sense of their public
duty, although they have repurchased the property, Agar Town
possesses lamps and pavements.† Still, for all this, it forms a
melancholy social picture—a sample of St Giles's really in the
fields—a collection of the very lowest order of labourers'
cottages. There is no occasion to hunt all over the country for
samples of overcrowding, dirt, discomfort, and even vice in rural
dwellings—here is a Dorsetshire[1] under our very walls, almost
within a mile of Temple Bar.

The inhabitants of [the lower part of] this district are chiefly
poor labourers and the poorest class of costermongers, or men,
as they are called, 'who follow the markets'. The women, if not
laundresses, of which there are a great number, are nothing at
all, and a 'mother's society' strives hard to teach them the
commonest home duties. It is doubtful if they know how to cook
the simplest eatable, or wash a child; and the public soup-
kitchen finds full employment in making up for their domestic
shortcomings. [In the upper portion of the town, near the
railway, the inhabitants are of a higher class—hard-working
mechanics and railway men. Their houses are houses, not hovels,
and not unlike those at Wolverton, Crewe, or any other railway
settlement.] Much soup is given away, under the superintendence of the local clergyman, the [Rev. R.P. Cleminger,] and his
assistants; but the place is largely used as a cheap eating-house,
where men and women come or send to get their dinners. The

soup is generally sold at a price which leaves one-half of the cost to be defrayed by voluntary contributions. When the inhabitants are ill, they can send to this benevolent cook-shop, and get a pint of beef-tea for threepence, a pint of mutton broth for the same money; a basin of gruel for one penny; a basin of arrowroot for threepence: a jug of barley-water for twopence; a jug of lemonade for sixpence; a ration of corn-flower blancmange for sixpence; a sago pudding for the same money; and a tapioca pudding or a ground-rice pudding at the same charge. This institution was started by Miss Margaret Howitt, and though it is excellently managed, and reflects great credit upon its originator, it shows the utter helplessness of the low resident population.

Agar Town, by those who knew it best, has long been regarded as the stepping-stone to or from the workhouse. People use it as a sleeping-place, within the meaning of the act, to entitle them to poor-law relief in St Pancras, or they go from it direct into that stately pauper palace which looks down proudly upon this withered portion of the parish. When they are sent from the union—even other unions besides the local one—they make Agar Town their first residence, while they wait for something to turn up. They must have some hole or corner to go to, as the law will not allow them to huddle together in the gutters, and an open settlement where friends may be found, or where no questions will be asked, is what they naturally look for. One half the houses are cottages or huts, standing in black yards that grow nothing but splintered tubs and palings. There are seldom any apartments but what are upon the ground floor. In some rooms there are no doors, in others no windows; in others the garden walls, moist, soft, like wet gingerbread, have fallen down from very rottenness. The water-pumps in some places have long since been destroyed, and the water is kept in a hole. Dustbins are unknown in that portion of the old town named Cambridge Crescent, and the usual public privies are another rarity. The tiles of the huts are broken off; the interiors represent the lowest condition of poverty and filth; the yards often contain clothes-lines, on which a few wet sole-skins, used by brewers, are drying for sale; the children are barefooted and ragged; the women seem to know no better way of closing a hole in a dirty garment than with a pin or a bit of string; donkeys roam about the place as clean and as well housed as their masters; and under the broken flooring you can often see the rough uncovered earth. The whole population of this district may be six thousand or seven thousand, and the rents vary from one shilling and sixpence to three shillings a week for a room. Of course in this, as in all the neighbourhoods I have been visiting, the apparent high rents must be taken to include rates, taxes, drawbacks, irregularities, losses, and cost of collection.

The huts in Agar Town were built of old rubbish, on a twenty-one years' lease. Some of the builders still live in them, happy and contented, dreading the time—about 1866—when their term will expire. [They are always ready to rally round the place, and to call it a 'pretty little town'.] The landlady of one, who was chief architect, builder, and assistant to her husband in raising some of these hovels, was burrowing in a kind of dog kennel at the side of her tenants—living, in fact, upon her property. Her maxim was, 'Live and let live', and she avoided the crime of being an absentee. In most of these squat places families of five, six, ten, and twelve, were found, leading a swinish life in one room, even when they rented another. In one cottage was a young girl with an illegitimate child still living with her parents. In the road we spoke to a girl who had been turned out of doors by her father and stepmother, and had been found sleeping in privies. To do the miserable inhabitants justice, they are never backward in helping their own class, and here, as in similar places, they share what little they have. They are partial to dogs; probably breeding them for sale; and, at one time, there was scarcely a hut without three or four of these animals. Their answer always is that 'A dog keeps itself'. No known thieves or prostitutes are found in the neighbourhood—its lowest part is too poor and miserable for that; and what vices it has arise largely from dirt, and overcrowding. Intemperance is one of these, and the clergy and others try to check it—as the Rev. Mr Maguire does in Clerkenwell—by a temperance society connected with the church and schools. An old inhabitant, who holds property in the district, and keeps one of those comfortable chandlers' shops—which, as I said in a former chapter, always thrive in such places—thought Agar Town would be a delightful settlement 'if it wasn't for the drink'. The public-houses in this and the surrounding neighbourhood are certainly very numerous, and they endeavour to attract custom by pleasing signs. One calls itself 'The Good Samaritan', standing near the canal, and is largely frequented by coal-heavers from the wharves and dustmen from a neighbouring contractor's. Some of the huts run down to this canal with sloping yards, ornamented with a few laths put together in the shape of an arbour. The better class of houses form part of many short streets, in which three and four roomed dwellings are built, and let to two or three families. Some of the railway men [and decent mechanics] inhabit these, and some are occupied by the wives of sailors. One attempt to build a superior kind of dwelling, on a ninety-nine years' lease, at the extreme end of the town, has been stopped by the purchase of much of the property by the Midland Railway Company. The inhabitants have one advantage not often enjoyed by persons in low districts, their air is remarkably pure. Though some of the roads and most passages between the huts, [are still rivers of mud,] and receive the slops thrown into them from each ill-regulated household; and though the dwellings are low, the spaces between them are very open, and St Giles's evidently gathers health by being a little way out of town.

The efforts of the Rev. R.P. Cleminger, during the last ten years, to improve this wretched district, as far as his means and powers go, have been crowned with considerable success. Starting with a temporary church† he has gathered round him a maternity society; a national school, with a hundred scholars; a mother's society, before alluded to; a Sunday school, with three hundred and seventy scholars; and a penny bank, whose depositors in 1860 numbered six hundred, and the amount deposited 250*l*. There is a girls' school and infant school held for the present in the rooms of two of the small houses, and a day nursery, where children are taken care of while their parents are at work. An institution of this kind in such neighbourhoods saves many infants from being burnt to death, or from many serious accidents. [The schools are liberally supported by Miss

Agar.] There is a district visiting society, a soup-kitchen (before mentioned), a Church missionary society, a Bible society, a working man's institute, and a lending library, but the latter has not been much drawn upon by the adults of the district. There is a clothing fund in connection with the Sunday school, and one of the scholars, a little girl, was asked a few days ago if she would like to have a pair of socks. 'I'm very well off for socks,' she said, 'and should like something else.' 'How many pairs have you got?' inquired the teacher. 'This pair on my feet,' said the child, astonished at the question.

The district employs two ministers,† a Scripture reader, and a Bible woman, and the church and charities draw much of their support from the Agar family, Camden Town, and Highgate Rise.

The whole of Somers Town[1]—the adjacent district at the back of the New Road, near King's Cross—is a worthy neighbour of Agar Town.* It is filled with courts and alleys; it puts forward a gin-palace built in the true Seven Dials' style, even to a clock in the wall near the roof; and is crowded with cheap china-shops, cheap clothiers, and cheap haberdashers. Its side streets have a

[*On Tuesday January 29, 1861, a scene presented itself in the Bloomsbury County Court, Portland Road that has never, since these courts came into operation, been witnessed before. The plaintiff, Mr John Hewitt, son of one of the officers of the above court, who carries on an extensive business as a tallyman and draper, in Pratt Street, Camden Town, had summonsed no less than one hundred and fifty-three defendants, for sums varying in amount from 10s. to 2l. and upwards. This vast number of summonses issued at one plaintiff's suit caused the court to appoint a special day for the hearing. The defendants were summonsed at the respective hours of ten, eleven, and twelve o'clock, and shortly after ten the court was crowded with debtors of various grades. No one who witnessed the scene can fail regret that the system of tally-dealing, which affords such easy access for credit to an improvident wife or gay woman, cannot receive some wholesome check to save a working man's home from desolation. Many of the defendants were residents of Agar Town, St Pancras and its vicinity, a place fertile with filth and rags, and inhabited only by the humblest of labouring men. The court sat till the whole of the cases were disposed of, and gave judgments at 3s., 4s., and 5s. per month, according to the means the parties had for payment.

On Thursday the court again presented a like scene. One tallyman, named Goodwin, of King's Cross, having forty-three on the list, and Clements, of Judge Street, Euston Road, twenty-six, making a total of sixty-nine, averaging more than two thirds of the causes to be tried this day.]

smoky, worn-out appearance; the gas-lamps project jauntily from the walls, the iron posts at the end lean towards each other as if for mutual support; every street door is open; no house is without patched windows; and every passage is full of children. Back views of dingy public-houses make the scene more dismal; and wherever there is a butcher's shop it contrives to look like a cat's-meat warehouse. Chapel Street is the chief centre of business, and Sunday morning is its most busy period. It is very much like Shoreditch or Tottenham Court Road on a Saturday night, or the streets at the back of Clare market. There is a popular notion in the neighbourhood that things are sold a little cheaper on a Sunday morning, and many of the shopkeepers encourage this idea. The stall-keepers who crowd in the gutters with fish-stalls, vegetable-stalls, and hardware-stalls, are mostly residents of Agar Town; and when they have done their business for the day they go home to their huts like merchants to their villas.

Marylebone and the Outskirts

If large factories and centres of industry invariably attract a crowded, dependent population, terraces and squares of private mansions do the same. From Belgravia to Bloomsbury—from St Pancras to Bayswater—there is hardly a settlement of leading residences that has not its particular colony of ill-housed poor hanging on to its skirts. Behind the mansion there is generally a stable, and near the stable there is generally a maze of close streets, containing a small greengrocer's, a small dairy, a quiet coachman's public-house, and a number of houses let out in tenements. These houses shelter a large number of painters, bricklayers, carpenters, and similar labourers, with their families, and many laundresses, and charwomen. Each room, with a few exceptions, is the home of a different family, and the kitchens are often more crowded than any other parts of the house. This is particularly the case in old and faded neighbourhoods—as I stated in my chapter upon St James's, Westminster —and it is also the case in Marylebone, near the Regent's Park. Squares and terraces that are scarcely thirty years old are still surrounded by hopelessly faded streets—some of them builders' mistakes, and others designedly built for the class who now occupy them. They all bear a melancholy family likeness to each other. Their street doors are always open; a few trucks are generally standing in the gutter; a marine store-dealer's coloured placard sticks out prominently from one of the houses; and a flock of chickens are always strutting in the road. They often contain more uncomplaining poverty than some of the courts and alleys I have just been describing, or may be going to describe. Many of their inhabitants cherish a spirit of independence which a long course of intrusive visiting charity has not been able to crush.

In the district of St Paul's, Marylebone—a neighbourhood lying to the right of Lisson Grove, as you enter from the New Road—there are many streets that answer to this description. Byron Street, Brand Street, Bridport Street, are all filled with houses let out in tenements, each room fetching a rental of three shillings or three shillings and sixpence a week, and containing a large family. [Externally the two latter streets look like what are called 'genteel thoroughfares'.] Several families† will be gathered under one roof; most of these families will have six members of both sexes—some grown to the age of youth—and each house will thus contain a dense population†† of poor working people in a very small space. Many of these poor lodgers, when periodically pressed, will sell everything saleable, even to their clothes, rather than ask for a sixpence from the local charities. The Rev. Mr Keeling, who watches over the district, assures me that one half of his parishioners—or about five thousand people—have nearly all their garments in pawn at the present moment. * [Many have told the visiting clergyman that a year's constant work, with the greatest thrift on their part, will hardly raise them out of the distress into which they have fallen.]

Boston Place is an example of a lower class of settlement, lying

[* January, 1861.]

half-way between the position of a court and a street. The houses exhibit every stage of squalor and wretchedness: the rooms are let at about two shillings or two and sixpence a week; the huddling together is even more extreme and unwholesome, and the place is a harbour for a few thieves and prostitutes. A common mews let out to cabmen—very often a decayed collection of private or livery stables—is a very usual feature in such neighbourhoods as this; and Huntsworth Mews, in this district, is a fair sample of these places. The yard and stables are dirty and neglected, the stablehelps are brown with filth, and over each stable is a low, close room, containing a family more or less numerous. The stable population in this district numbers about one hundred families.

This is the side of Lisson Grove which is supposed to contain the decent poor; and on the other side, in the streets leading into the Edgeware Road, is a more densely crowded and even lower population. Bell Street, now famous in history as the spot where Turkish baths were first established, is the main stream of a low colony, with many tributary channels. There is no particular manufacture in the neighbourhood to call the population together; a great number are not dependent upon St John's Wood or the Regent's Park for a living; and they come together simply because they like the houses, the rents, the inhabitants, and the general tone of living in the settlement. Somers Town, Shoreditch, and the New Cut, Lambeth, are here repeated in their principal features, and the whole place looks like a flourishing branch of some great central bank of costermongers, dingy brokers' shops, and Irish labourers. The Irish have a marvellous power of lowering the standard of comfort and cleanliness in any court, street, or colony in which they appear; and certain sewer-like alleys near the Islington turnpike, certain back streets in the neighbourhood of Manchester Square—not to go 'over the water', or to the east of London—are exactly like certain 'gardens' or places in this part of Marylebone. Some of these 'gardens'—Smith's Gardens for example—contain dwarfed cottages, very battered and dirty, standing in black yards, and are the evident remains of Marylebone as a village. In such places you will generally find a sweep or a dustman, and the bit of ground in front of each hut is more convenient to receive saleable refuse than a kitchen or a back parlour. Some of the streets (I may mention George Street) are notorious haunts of thieves, prostitutes, and the lowest threepenny lodging-houses; and in this case, the blot upon the district is not made more foul by being the property of a parish officer. Rate collectors, registrars, and active vestrymen are too often the proprietors of these places, making an extra profit by their local knowledge. Sometimes the land such pest-houses stand upon is Crown or Church property, and the rent, and more, has to be expended in the work of counteracting their influence! There are no courts and alleys in this neighbourhood such as disgrace the east of London. The avenues are so broad that they may be almost classed as streets; the roadways are paved; there is no open drain trickling down the centre, and none that I saw were disfigured with public privies. The entrances, in one or two cases, were low archways, with pathways covered with various kinds of filth, but the interiors were open and fairly ventilated. I should prefer living in a hut in Smith's Gardens to living in a kitchen or back parlour in the St Paul's district.

The Christ Church division of Marylebone, in which Bell Street and all its ramifications stand, is watched over by the Rev. Llewellyn Davies.[1] The whole population of this crowded district is estimated at thirty thousand, and it embraces the worst part of the parish. The parochial work in such an area, which contains at least sixteen thousand idle and industrious poor, is necessarily very heavy, and, on the whole, it appears to be conducted sensibly and energetically. The principle of self-help—the only principle that tends to assist the poor without demoralizing them—is adopted in every practicable way; and the pure charities are numerous and well conducted. There are four classes of schools for boys, girls, and infants, where a small weekly payment is exacted; there is a special Sunday school for children not attending the day schools; there are free evening classes in connection with the Sunday school, and similar classes at another school for lads, men, and girls. A working party is held weekly to which mothers of families may bring work, and at which they will receive friendly advice and assistance as to household management. No healthy educational agency is neglected. Amongst the self-supporting institutions is a provident fund, which numbered one thousand two hundred and fifty depositors of small sums in 1860, and an amount deposited of 1,000*l*. No money paid into this fund is returned in any form except in tickets for necessaries. There is also a benefit club coming under this head, where members are entitled to receive certain payments during illness. Amongst the charities is a relief fund, the chief objects of which are to lend blankets, money (in small sums not exceeding 5*l*., without interest), to make allowances to the sick, and to supply linen and other comforts to women lying-in. [The number of in-door poor at the Marylebone Workhouse (January 18), amounting to two thousand and thirty-nine, would people a small town; whilst there are three thousand three hundred and thirty-two 'on the books' receiving out-door relief; and, in addition to these numbers, two thousand, eight hundred and fifty-one have had casual relief during the last week. The cost of the relief of the poor during the year has been 53,500*l*.

For all this such a public scandal as the death of an old woman from starvation on the workhouse steps on Christmas day, 1860, has not been avoided; and the following case presents even more painful features: I quote the newspaper report:— 'Some excitement was occasioned yesterday, December 25, 1860, in the neighbourhood of Lisson Grove, by the discovery of a poor deaf and dumb man in a dying state, from shocking neglect and destitution, in one of Hedge's Cottages, Chapel Street, Edgeware Road. The discovery was made, it appears, by Ann Dunn, a resident of No.3, Hedge's Cottages, who at once called the attention of the police to the unfortunate man. He was found in an almost naked state, frightfully dirty and emaciated, presenting the appearance of long-standing neglect, and of not having tasted food for days. He was removed in a helpless, but sensible condition, upon a stretcher to the St Marylebone Workhouse, where he was immediately admitted, and evinced much delight at the kind treatment and attention which was readily given him by the officers of the house. Mr Fuller, the resident surgeon, immediately attended him, and at first some hopes were entertained of his recovery, but he expired about two hours after his admission. His name, it has been ascertained, is Robert Hussey, aged forty-five; and his death is a melancholy instance of the shocking destitution of the metropolis even at Christmas.'

The Rev. Mr Davies, writing upon metropolitan distress in *Macmillan's Magazine* for February, 1861,[1] has the following remarks in defence of the parochial administration of this workhouse:—

'I admit, however, that notwithstanding the good intentions of the board, the results of their administration are by no means of a kind that would defy criticism. Not to speak of the insuperable difficulties of a constant weary struggle against vice, and idleness, and fraud, the management of so vast a business as that of the St Marylebone Workhouse requires great administrative capacity and constant vigilance; and a board of thirty perfectly equal members, elected every year, does not promise much eficiency in government.

*   *   *   *   *

'But even if such blots were more numerous and discreditable than they are, it is obvious—and no well-informed person could forget it—that the substantial relief of the poor is, and must be, the work of the guardians, and that *the better this work is done the less the public hear of it*. At the same time, the public have ample opportunities of knowing what is going on at the workhouse, through the meetings, open to ratepayers and reporters, at the workhouse and the vestry, and through the reports in the local newspapers. But the poor-law administration does not exterminate distress, nor pretend to do it. *No system of relief, however charitable, could possibly put an end to distress*. The causes of physical misery, whilst they remain, make that misery inevitable. In those instances of undoubted destitution which have been detailed before the magistrates and elsewhere, we do not know how much is due to drunkenness, that plague and curse of our poor. And how can you keep a drunkard out of want? Another cause of distress is scarcely less difficult to cope with—the imbecility and want of energy which infects some persons like a disease. Then there is the downright idleness of not a few, which keeps them from seeking work, and throws them out of occupation when they get it. The destitution which arises from sickness and misfortune—the character of the sufferers having been reasonably good—ought to be relieved humanely by the workhouse, if not more indulgently cared for, as one might surely hope it would be, by the kindness of friends and by Christian charity.']†

Passing out of Marylebone [and the north] proper, through the adjacent district of Paddington, on my road to a notorious western locality at Kensington called the Potteries,[1] I looked at some old almshouses standing opposite the Vestry Hall, near the Green. They belong to the parish, according to the inscription on the front, and are, to all appearance, in as low a sanitary condition as some of the worst huts in Clerkenwell. They lie below the level of the road, are small, ill-ventilated, and dirty, and afford a very poor shelter to their wrinkled inmates. A tall man can almost touch their roofs from the pavement; and their continuance in the present position and condition must arise from what Jeremy Bentham called an absurd regard for the directions of the dead.

The Potteries, at Kensington—a marshy district lying in the hollow behind the villas at Bayswater and Notting Hill—is in nearly the same condition now as it was some ten years ago, when attention was called to it in *Household Words*.[2] It is like nothing in and about London except Agar Town, and its interior and approaches are even worse than those of that house of call for the workhouse even in its worst days. Most of the roads into it must be what are known as 'undedicated roads'—highways not yet given up to or adopted by the public, and, consequently, dedicated to nothing but rivers of mud. The inhabitants are pig-trainers and brickmakers, keepers of ducks and fowls, 'fanciers' of spurring gamecocks, and red-jawed bull-terriers, and supporters of the very lowest forms of sporting. The pot-houses advertise 'Rat matches every Monday night', and the first sight I saw was that of two fowls which were combating in a dreary swamp of black manure-drainage, broken bottles, old bricks, and mud. The huts have grown a little the worse for wear, as all things do, and they hold together by some principle not yet discovered or laid down by theoretical builders. The settlement still retains its old proportions. It occupies about nine acres of ground, numbers nearly three hundred houses and hovels, including some of the neighbouring extensions, and contains at least a thousand of its original population. Refuse matter is still collected by the pig-trainers from club-houses and hotels, and boiled down in coppers, that the fat may be separated for sale. This business existed here long before the district rose around it, as it still exists in other outskirts of London; and the old inhabitants defend their right to the place, not only with legal parchments, but with energetic tongues. As a body they are happy and independent, and when sickness seizes one of them, a basin is carried round the huts, and a collection is made. They have a village Hampden,[1] who visits coffee-houses, reads newspapers, thinks for himself, speaks for others, and takes his stand upon the broad fact that pigs must be trained somewhere in a Christian land. He boasts that the pig-trainers have always paid twenty shillings in the pound, and is not at all disposed to sit down quietly under what he calls misrepresentation.

'We're not swine,' he said; 'we don't lie in that there mud. We train pigs and we train children. There's a hut yonder that doesn't look fit for a donkey to live in, according to the editor of the *Bayswater Chronicle*; but let me tell that man, or any man—let me tell you, sir—that the old woman as has lived in that hut for forty years has brought up as large a family of nice spoken boys as any woman in the Potteries. Let 'em come to me when they've got anything to say agen the place—let 'em meet me and talk it out at the temp'rance-hall, and I'll not shrink from 'em. There's ignorant people here, people as doesn't know a trough from a brickbat; who doesn't know the proper pronunciation of prudence, as I may say; but they ain't everybody. People as call theirselves Christians ain't got no right to come here and write books about us, calling us a lot of pigs; and I'll get that book as I've heerd on and tell Mrs Bayly a bit of my mind.'

This last remark applied to a work recently published about missionary work in the Potteries, called 'Ragged Homes, and how to Mend Them', which seems to have hurt the feelings of the village Hampden. The place, he considered, had never been fairly dealt with, either in illustrated journals, local newspapers, or volumes.

['Look at that brick-field,' he said, 'which we calls "the hocean"; there's nothing much the matter with that. A brick-field ain't a drawing-room. Well, a gent comes down here and takes a pictur' of that brick-field, and makes it look a hawful place. He puts in such a hut as I never see, and makes out that all the roofs of our cottages is covered with cow-dung. Now that ain't the way to go and talk about people, and show people up. We're sure to see these things now, because a working-man goes to his coffee-shop, reads his newspapers, and is not such a fool as he's often made out.']

Public discussion on the spot, he thought, was the only way of arriving at the truth, and he knew many who could stand up for their settlement. He looked upon the whole land as a grant from a former Bishop of London, and the brickmakers as interlopers and trespassers.

If settlers are wedded to a place like this, where, according to a sanitary report for 1856, the average age at death is under twelve years, and where there is nothing to look at but clay, pools of stagnant water, and the most wretched hovels, there is no help for them. The pig-trainers must be left in possession of their happy hunting-grounds, and what little pity we have may be bestowed upon the brickmakers. These hardworking people are huddled together on the borders of the swine preserves, in huts provided for them by their employer, at a rental of two and three shillings a week. They live here, for the old reason, to be 'near their bread', and they get nothing for their rental but the barest covering. The public privy, of course, does duty for a whole row of huts, and there is no more water now for this part of the settlement than there was some ten years ago. A school, with a service, is provided by their landlord, but this is hardly a substitute for the commonest necessaries, comforts, and conveniences. The same attempt to supply physical deficiencies by showy educational and spiritual stop-gaps, I noticed in Agar Town.

I should like to hear the village Hampden on this topic, at the local temperance hall, with the owner of the huts and brickfield in the chair.

THE SOUTH

Over the Water

It has long been the boast of moving panoramas that their chief aim is to convey instruction. They carry us across America, or from Southampton to India; they hop from city to city throughout Europe, or they glide past with certain pictures of Australia, but they avoid a sketch of London. No speculator has ever been bold enough to grapple with the back streets—the human warrens—on the south side of the metropolis; to start from Bermondsey, on the borders of Deptford, and wriggle through the existing miles of dirt, vice, and crime, as far as the Lambeth Marshes. Picturesque as poverty and wretchedness look upon canvas, free as pictures are from harsh voices and unpleasant smells, no attempt has ever been made to deal with the black-holes of London in this popular form, and the 'Special Correspondent' still remains in possession of the property.

A very vast and melancholy property it is. * Within the boundaries before mentioned, and down in the hollow of the water-side basin of London, lighted up at intervals with special markets of industry, or budding into short patches of honest trade, sinking every now and then into dark acres of crime, and covered everywhere with the vilest sores of prostitution, are something like four hundred thousand people, or one-seventh part of the whole metropolitan population. In many respects, its standard of civilization is lower than either that of Whitechapel or St George's in the East, especially in the Southwark and Waterloo Road districts. It has scores of streets that are rank and steaming with vice; streets where unwashed, drunken, fishy-eyed women hang by dozens out of the windows, beckoning to the passers-by. It has scores of streets filled with nothing but thieves, brown, unwholesome tramps' lodging-houses, and smoky receptacles for stolen goods. To look at such places—to know from experience that they have existed in this state for twenty years, and to learn from history that many have been notorious

[* The permanent poor in the district allotted to the Southwark police court alone, have been recently calculated at fifty thousand.]

for more than a century—makes me doubt whether the world has really such things as working vestries, inspectors of nuisances, police authorities, and local self-government. I am no advocate for routing out the industrious poor from an overcrowded district to make room for stucco temples or ornamental squares. Such metropolitan improvements are merely quieting doses for grumbling ratepayers, and schemes for benefiting one corner of London at the expense of another. The working-classes in most cases must live where their bread grows, and there are Acts of Parliament more than enough to exercise a control over the structure and arrangement of their dwellings. But the recognized haunts of vice and crime want no ventilation, no enlargement, no tinkering philanthropy. They ought to be ploughed up by the roots. The Mint, in Southwark, is still the dear old collection of dens which it was in the days of our grandfathers, and, if it has no murky cellars like old St Giles's, this virtue is due more to its geological formation than to its local self-government. The foundations are nothing but rotten muck. The whole district is far below the level of high-water mark in the river, and the sewage in many places bubbles up through the floors. The courts and alleys branch off on either side at every step, leading into endless mazes of low, sooty passages, squares, and 'rents'. Some of these holes and corners must have received their titles from the most bitter satirists, for they bear such names as White-hind Alley and Dove Court— emblems of purity—Rose Passage and Melior Street. In some cases a little learning and mystery are combined in the name, and one row of stunted dwellings is known as Pariatealia Place.[1] In another case the proprietor of the property is less ambitious, and is contented with the humble and appropriate name of Halfpenny Court. Considering the alarming fruitfulness of mothers in most of these wretched neighbourhoods, I should like to have some of the places christened Malthus Yard. This is a suggestion for the consideration of the Metropolitan Board of Works.

[A local correspondent, Mr Dexter,[2] writing January 30, 1860, gives this neighbourhood the same character as I do:—'Hundreds of the poor,' he says, 'living in Pariatealia Place and the courts, passages, squares and rents so thickly surrounding it, flock daily from eleven till one to the soup-kitchen. I am sorry I cannot give a better account of the neighbourhood than you do. Your statements are strictly true; and a more favourable relation would be wanting in accuracy. If any one will muster up courage sufficient for the task, and visit the people of the district, he will find more misery, wretchedness, and almost starvation than he would care to see often. I could point to Palmer's Rents—I think the next turning to Pariatealia Place; in one house would be found a blind girl, who, in the summer time, works at fancy knitting, in the City, but who, from illness and other causes, is so reduced that she cannot pursue her usual avocations. She has had no relief but the bread and soup the Melior Street soup-kitchen has supplied. Three doors nearer Snow's Fields may be found five or six families in a small house. On the ground-floor is a labourer with a wife and four small children. Nearly all the furniture and clothing they had has been disposed of, in order that the children, one of whom is ill, might not absolutely starve. At the top of the house may be found a self-reliant Irishwoman, who has struggled hard to keep herself, her brother and sister-in-law, and their children. But neighbours, as poor as herself, cannot find employment enough for her, and her brother has been several weeks out of employment, and unable to provide anything for his own family; while, to make the case still worse, his wife was last week confined. These cases are not isolated ones, but samples from very many hundreds, which lie together sickeningly close in these densely crowded courts and ill-ventilated houses. It will be long ere affairs can improve much among these people.'

The dreary zig-zag panorama of the south side of London— the part that is popularly known under the head of 'over the water'—might open at Lower Bermondsey, near Jacob's Island.[1] Here we begin with an old, dilapidated red-brick mansion, sunken, decayed, chipped, and neglected, let out in tenements, with rowing-sculls in its passage, a boat lying high and dry in its yard, and its old gardens covered with courts and huts of the most wretched character. Its over-hanging, hood-like porch is still full of the ancient mouldings, representing clusters of fruits and flowers, and containing the date, *in relievo*, of 1700. Near this place is a black, shattered wooden building, which looks in its outlines like those houses which children draw upon slates at the early age of three years. The courts at the back are crowded with hovels, whose rooms have not always got doors, and whose windows have not always got sashes. There are bare, black bits of ground occasionally containing one withered tree; and close courts with public yards, where the inhabitants have the usual privy in common. The rents are two shillings and three shillings a week by the room, or four shillings a week by the house. In one yard a ragged crippled man and a ragged child were spinning a rope, while a sooty woman, with an infant, looked on from one of the window-holes; and in another yard a decent old woman, whose room sent forth a gust of hot irons, was quarrelling with a bricklayer about the drain. 'I never see such people as you are,' said the man, 'you're never satisfied!'

Going towards London Bridge, you can branch off on either side, and visit numerous small courts and alleys, more or less dirty, neglected, and degraded, but you will find nothing, perhaps, worse than Magdalen Court, in Tooley Street. It is a blind alley of small two-storied houses—close, dwarfed, foul, and unwholesome; filled with the lowest order of people who prey upon sailors, and curtained at intervals with patched clothes, hanging across to dry from house to house. The rents are high, as an extra profit is always made out of such places, and the houses let for about seven shillings a week. There are hundreds of such courts at Wapping and Rotherhithe, on both sides of the river, filled with coarse drunken women, whose thick fingers are covered with showy rings. Sometimes a crew of Malay sailors are enticed into these traps; raw spirits are sent for in basins and quart pots from the neighbouring public-houses; robbery, quarrels, and madness follow, as a matter of course; knives are drawn, a 'muck'[1] is run, and the whole bleeding, riotous, drunken population roll out into the open thoroughfare.

Bermondsey Street will show you a few more holes and corners on your road to the back of St George's Church, in the Borough, every place being painfully like every other place, and every inhabitant, with a few struggling exceptions, painfully like every other inhabitant. [Here is an extract from the letter of another local correspondent written in January, 1861, about the Bermondsey Ragged Schools:—'I am sorry to say that the distress is still very great, as there are so many out of work. I have before me a list of cases filled up by the visitors, several of which I have also visited myself. This list consists of nineteen of these destitute families, containing a total of one hundred and fifteen human beings. Three of the fathers are unable to work through illness. Some have been out of work four and five months, some nine and ten weeks, and the rest are unable to get work at present. Most of these families occupy but one room. The following are some of the notes of the visitors:— "Not tasted food today",—"Very needy case",—"This case has not sought relief",—"The home very clean, but empty",—"The family is very much distressed",—"When visited, no food nor fire",—"One room, very wretched".']

When you arrive at the back of St George's Church, you may look up Kent Street, another nest of dirt, vice, and over-crowding, which is in much the same state as it was when Smollett called it 'a beggarly and ruinous suburb', and bemoaned the necessity for bringing visitors from the Continent through it on their road into London.[1] It was then the highway from Southwark to Dover—part of the Old Kent Road—and the French mail was often robbed while passing along it. The plan was to draw a rope across the entrance, over which the horse stumbled, and the post-boy had to return to the city and report the loss of his bags. Its character now is very slightly improved, and it is still the worthy companion of its neighbour, the Mint.

Passing over the Borough Road and down Mint Street, you will find yourself in the citadel of thieves. The low lodging-houses here—where beds are let at threepence a night—form the chief evidences of trade. At one of the doors of these saffron-coloured places I saw a half-drunken militiaman and a black sailor, but very few hulking men standing at the corners. There were few children in the muddy roads, and the silence was as noticeable as in Old Nichols Street, Shoreditch. Norfolk Street is the most notorious thoroughfare in this district—often figuring in the police reports; but every by-court and alley is choking with filth, vice, and crime.

Most people know, or have heard, something about the Mint, in Southwark, and I will not, therefore, dwell upon that, but pass down to the St Peter's district, near the river and Southwark Bridge. Here the inhabitants are chiefly labourers about the wharves, and dredgers, who get their living on the river by fishing for bits of old cord, iron, and fish. They seldom go lower than Deptford, and their gains are very precarious. Over-crowding is very common amongst them—six, eight, and ten people living in one room, and this long after the sons and daughters have grown up into young men and women. There are instances where the son or daughter will get married, and bring home the wife or husband to the same house or room, and thus two families are compelled to huddle together. This is very common in such neighbourhoods, as all delicacy of feeling, even when the inhabitants are not steeped in poverty, has been early destroyed in youth. Education means something more than merely learning lessons out of a book, and habits early implanted last longer even than leases, districts, or towns.[1]

Some of the houses in the courts about the Skin Market, although standing in an ancient neighbourhood—near the supposed site of the Globe Theatre and the old Bear Garden—have been built within the last twenty years. There is Pleasant Place, where the rooms are only about three yards wide, the back-yard about three feet square, and the windows not more than two feet and a half square. The court or passage in front is in exact proportion with these dimensions, and the houses stand in three parallel rows with their faces to each others' backs. I stood at the side of one of the end houses, and it seemed to me that I could almost span it with my arms. Each house lets for about four shillings a week, and contains two of these confined rooms. In White Hind Alley, near this place, there is a row of old black, rotten, wooden dwellings, chiefly rented by river thieves. This wretched district is watched over by the Rev. M. Mungeam (who kindly took me over it), the honorary secretary of the South London Visiting and Relief Association—a benevolent society which strives to do all the good it can in the vast expanse of London 'over the water', but whose funds are not equal to its work. It is a branch of the Metropolitan District Visiting Society at Charing Cross, and draws some part of its support from the parent source. Most of the local clergymen on the south side are on the committee.

Nearly the whole of the streets, courts, and alleys about Gravel Lane and Blackfriars are equally filthy, crowded, and faded. Crossing over the main road, we open up another channel of social degradation in the New Cut. The entrance to this thoroughfare in the Blackfriars Road is depressing enough, and the sight does not improve as you get further in. You begin with a closed block of houses, covered from garret to basement with fluttering rags of bills, and at every step you may glance right and left into wavy, smoky, damp, dismal side thoroughfares. No house to house visitation is necessary to show you the social condition of these places; they are either full of low prostitutes, with few children in the roads, or the roads are crowded with children and the houses are full of the working poor. Each street has got a dingy beer-shop, if not a public-house, and at least one small coal-shed, advertising 'an enormous fall in coals'. Such streets run at right angles into the Waterloo Road, cross over that very mangy thoroughfare, and continue into the heart of Lambeth, by the side of the South Western Railway. Granby Street is perhaps the worst sample of a prostitutes' street in this neighbourhood, and the vice it contains overflows in every house and oozes out on to the pavement.

The New Cut does not differ much from Shoreditch, or Chapel Street, Somers Town, and it may be shortly described as a succession of groves. There are groves of stiff cheap clothing, groves of hardware, groves of flabby-looking meat, groves of boots, and groves of haberdashery; with the stalls of coster-mongers, filled with fish and vegetables, lining the gutters. There are plenty of gin-shops and a few cheap bakers, and at one corner stands the Victoria Theatre, formerly called the Coburg. It is a large, well-built house, and has been celebrated, in its time, for good acting; but it is now one of the 'threepenny theatres', giving a very coarse kind of drama, suited to its audiences. The fittings are faded, the walls are smeared with greasy dirty, the pit floor is muddy and half covered with orange peel and broken bottles, and the whole place is a little cleaner than the courts and alleys at its back, but nothing more. The audience are worth looking at; and on the night of a popular drama, such as 'Oliver Twist', or 'Jack Sheppard', the gallery presents a most extraordinary picture. Half the evil, low-browed, lowering faces in London are wedged in, twelve-hundred deep, perspiring, watchful, silent. Every man is in his yellow shirt sleeves, every woman has her battered bonnet in her lap. The yell when Bill Sykes murders Nancy is like the roar of a thousand wild beasts, and they show their disapprobation of the act, and their approbation of the actor, by cursing him in no measured terms. I once heard an eminent performer say that he looked upon hisses as applause when he played Iago; and if he played it at the Victoria Theatre, earnestly and powerfully, he would stand a chance of being spit upon and pelted. The most daring 'star' never ventures to appear at this dramatic temple.

Not far from this place—towards the end of our panorama— nestling at the back of the Waterloo Road, immediately under the shadow of the large engineering premises of Messrs Maudslay, Sons, and Field, is a reproduction of the worst features of a back settlement in Manchester, Bolton, or Birmingham. In no part of the overcrowded parish of Lambeth —a parish that probably contains nearly one hundred and seventy thousand people—are there any streets more badly built, more neglected, or more hopelessly filthy and miserable than Jurston Street, Cooper Street, and their adjacent thoroughfares. Here is a sample of what a great manufactory may nourish— nearly always does nourish—under its lofty walls. The labourer receives his fair day's wages for his fair day's work, according to the market price; finds it necessary, like all other labourers, to be 'near his bread'; crowds upon a particular spot, and gets a wretched dwelling at a very high price. Six and seven shillings a week are paid for dwarfed houses in and about this London Bolton, and this for the privilege of living within the sound of the factory bell—of being surrounded by dust-heaps in the streets, and fronted by a yard, called Owen's Yard, let out as a winter refuge for showmen's vans. Most of the regular inhabitants here are employed at the engineering works, and the showmen—the vagrants as they would be called, squatting for a shilling a week in their yellow smoking boxes upon wheels—look down upon these toiling householders with pity and contempt. They have let out their giants, their fat women, their dwarfs, their spotted boys, and boa-constrictors, to different exhibitors about London, and they form a half-gipsy settlement in this public yard, free from bad drainage and overcrowded rooms.

Behind some of the houses at the end of Jurston Street, behind a cats'-meat shop, where the proprietors complained that they were not able 'to get their money in', are a few rows of stumpy, close cottages standing in very rotten yards. There is no gas-lamp to light this part of the settlement (this is the case with many similar places), and after dusk the inhabitants have to feel their way in and out of their houses. One of the male residents was looking at an overflowing drain, which was evidently faulty, and I asked him if he ever had a visit from the local inspector of nuisances.

'Inspector!' he said. 'We never see no inspector down here—no nothing, except the landlord for his rent.'

As I threaded my way out of this black, smoky, wretched Bolton-looking district I met two tallymen coming in to dun their debtors, with their oil-skin packs under their arms, [and a cabman clearing out, with what, I presume, were his worldly goods—an old round table, and a few battered chairs crammed inside a Hansom cab.]

POSTSCRIPT

A New Chamber of Horrors[1]

The time has now arrived for a new Chamber of Horrors; a room not veiled under the thin apologetic title of 'A Chamber of Comparative Physiognomy', but a fearful national apartment, supported out of the national taxation, and standing as a national monument of disgrace and shame. It shall not be filled with the sullen faces of murderers and regicides; it shall not be so broad in design that it may exhibit horrors of all countries; and it shall not be merely a wax-work holiday show for gaping rustics. It shall be a Poor-law Museum of men, women, and children starved to death [in England—in merry England—in wealthy England—in the country famed for nothing so much as its homely virtues;] it shall be set up on the waste ground usually devoted to heroic statues in Parliament Street, Westminster, and, [while it shall be a warning to reckless, breeding paupers,] it shall be the standing curse of the Poor-law Board, and every poor-law official throughout the country. The world is too busy, the newspapers are too universal in their aspirations, and our statesmen are thinking far too much of Europe, Asia, Africa, and America, to devote more than a passing glance to these most awful deaths, unless they are brought before them in a blunt, material shape. The dead man is hurried away in the parish coffin, the usual curt line is recorded in the registrar's book, the paragraph in the newspaper corner is read and forgotten, and the whole thing is buried in eternal night. This is not enough; and, for the sake of those strugglers who are left, we require more. Percentages, averages, and all the hocus-pocus of statistics are only mists, fogs, curtains, and sleeping-draughts, except to the official mind; and we, the public, require something more gross—and more palpable. The deaths from 'privation', 'deaths from want of breast-milk', 'deaths from neglect', 'deaths from cold'—or, in plain unsavoury words, from utter starvation—increase every year. They were two hundred and twenty-two (in London only) in 1848, they were five hundred and sixteen, within the same area, in 1857, and this, without questioning how many of the returns under the head of 'fever', ought to be classed as starvation. Here is a country that spends one hundred millions sterling a year in [universal] government, and yet allows hundreds of its children, in its metropolis alone, to be annually starved to death!

The first stone of the New Chamber of Horrors must be laid at once; its architecture must be in keeping with its contents; famished paupers must support its entablature, in the shape of caryatides, and the death's head must blossom on every column. The first full-length model that shall stand in its dark rooms shall be that of the poor old woman of seventy years of age, who was found dead at the Marylebone workhouse door, on Christmas night, 1860. The next grim model shall be that of the deaf and dumb man who was picked up, on the same day, in the same parish, cold and famished, and who died in the arms of the workhouse surgeon during the night. This shall form the basis of the show in the north transept.

In the south transept a full-length model shall be placed of the starved excavator who dropped dead in Manor Street, Clapham, on the 11th of January, 1861, while begging with some companions. He saved himself from being classed as a 'noisy impostor', but he lost his life.

In the east nave we shall have a full collection. We shall begin with a model of Thomas Bates, a melancholy suicide from work-house neglect. As every statue will have its story written under it, I give the newspaper story of poor Bates—a record doubt-less forgotten, although only written on the 2nd December, 1860:

'Mr Humphreys, the coroner for the eastern division of the county of Middlesex, held an inquest on Wednesday, at the Black Horse Tavern, Kingsland Road, upon the body of Thomas Bates, a cabinet-maker, aged sixty-two, who committed suicide by hanging himself in a public-house where he lodged. The evidence of the deceased's daughter and another witness was to the effect that he complained that he could not obtain admission to Shoreditch workhouse, and, in reply to an offer on the part of his daughter to accompany him there, he said, "they would bully the eyes out of her head if she went". He was very infirm and not able to work, although he did sometimes earn threepence or fourpence a day, and his children, who were all in poor circumstances, sometimes gave him a few halfpence. The deceased said several times that, if he were not admitted into the house, he should destroy himself. Upon the 14th of November he told the witness that he had applied, but had been refused admission, but was to have one shilling and sixpence a week and a four pound loaf of bread for three months. The relieving officer denied that the deceased had applied for admission into the workhouse. It appeared that the deceased was an inmate of the house from October, 1859, to the 4th of August last, during which time he was in the sick ward suffering from chronic bronchitis, but on the latter date he was discharged from the doctor's list as "relieved". He was then called before the board, who directed him to be discharged with an allowance of one shilling a week and a four pound loaf for two weeks. The clerk to the guardians said the deceased quitted the workhouse voluntarily, but afterwards qualified that statement by admitting that the man had not applied to be discharged, and that the board had ordered him to leave the house. Dr James Clark, surgeon to the Shoreditch workhouse, who attended him while he was an inmate, stated that deceased, when discharged by him "relieved", on the 4th of August, was not able-bodied, and was not in a fit condition to leave the house. After a lengthened inquiry, at which the Board of Guardians were represented by their solicitor, the jury returned a verdict that the deceased hung himself while in an unsound state of mind, through having been refused admission to the workhouse.'

By the side of Thomas Bates we shall place William Gurr, and tell his story as we find it recorded in the public journals of December 23, 1860:

'On Monday, December 17, an inquest was held before the coroner, at the Market-house Tavern, Finsbury Market, Shoreditch, on the body of William Gurr, aged sixty-seven years, a blacksmith, who died from starvation. Mary Gurr, of No. 2, King's Head Court, Long Alley, stated that she was the widow of the deceased, who had been very reduced and destitute. On Thursday fortnight he went into Shoreditch workhouse. Witness succeeded in obtaining a little work, and would not go into the establishment, as she could earn with her daughter about four shillings per week, and three persons had to subsist and pay rent out of that amount. Deceased came out on Monday, the 3rd instant, after being in the workhouse four days. He said to witness, "I would rather be at home, however much trouble I am in." The deceased left the workhouse and went before the Board of Guardians, who, after hearing the case, ordered him two shillings and sixpence and a loaf weekly. The deceased then came home and died in a few days afterwards. They never had meat for months. The only things they had to live upon were dry bread, treacle, dripping, with a little tea and sugar; and no beer. They were very deficient of wearing apparel and bedding. The deceased had not been able to work for the last eighteen months. The two shillings and sixpence per week from the parish, and the four shillings witness and her daughter earned, were all they had to subsist on and to pay rent, food, and firing. I believe that the deceased died from want of food and the necessaries of life. When the deceased went into the workhouse he was so ill from weakness and debility that he reeled and staggered as he walked. He had nothing at home but dry bread for days. While in the workhouse the deceased had one day tea for breakfast, one day meat, another day pudding, and meat again on Sunday. Deceased only had meat twice while in the workhouse, and no stimulants. After other evidence, Mr Thomas Pool Collier, surgeon, said that the deceased was dead when he was called. Had made a post-mortem examination. Several of the organs were healthy, but the stomach only contained a little water-gruel. There was not the slightest trace of fat inside or outside the body. The walls of the stomach were thin from want of nourishment, and the body was much emaciated. The coroner having commented on the case at some length, the jury returned a verdict of "Died from starvation through the want of the common necessaries of life." '

Our next full-length model will be that of Samuel Bailey, whose story is recorded in the public journals of January 30, 1861:

'On Monday evening, January 28, Mr Humphreys, coroner, held an adjourned inquest at the Prince of Wales, Bishop's Road,

Victoria Park, respecting the death of Samuel Bailey, aged forty-one, a widower.

'An emaciated boy, apparently about twelve years of age, said: "The deceased was my father. Previous to our removal to the workhouse, we lived at No.12, Weatherhead's Gardens, Crabtree Row, Bethnal Green. My father was a cabinet-maker, but had no work for the last three months, during which time he has been selling the furniture to procure us food, and for some time past we have had nothing to eat but bread. On Friday, the 4th instant, I went with my father to the workhouse, and on the way he told me he was going to ask for admission into the house, and I did not expect we should have gone home again, but we did return; and in the afternoon the relieving officer's assistant came and told my father to go again to the workhouse at four o'clock, and he did so, and they gave him two loaves of bread and an order to go before the board on Monday. We then returned home, and the bread which he received lasted us until Sunday. On Monday my father got up to go to the board at the workhouse, but he fell down immediately, and was unable to go. In the evening my aunt went to the workhouse to request them to send the chair used to convey those unable to walk; and, as her application was not immediately attended to, she swore at the person she saw, and because she did so, he refused to send the chair, and she returned without it, and said father must walk there; but he said he could not, and we remained at home until Wednesday night, when a policeman came and took father to the workhouse in a truck, and I walked by the side. When we got to the workhouse we were immediately admitted, and father died soon after."

'Dr Christie deposed to having made a post-mortem examination, the result of which was that he attributed death to exposure and want of nourishment.

'An immense mass of evidence was taken at the various sittings, which want of space compels us to omit, all tending to show the fearful state to which poverty had reduced the deceased.

'The jury returned the following verdict: "That the deceased died from exposure to cold and the want of food and other necessaries; and the said jurors do further say, the said death was accelerated by the great neglect of the relieving-officer of Bethnal Green parish; and the said jurors request the coroner to forward a copy of the same to the parish authorities, and also to the Poor Law Commissioners." '

This will form a group: The policeman wheeling the dying man to the workhouse in a truck, and the son walking by the side.

I can easily find a dozen more 'cases', even in London, and within the months of December, 1860, and January, 1861, to fill the new Chamber of Horrors, but my impression is that these will be enough. Before this museum of poor-law victims has been open a year, I believe that not a single instance of starvation will have to be recorded throughout the land.*

Our London Model Lodging-Houses[1]

After dwelling so long upon the 'horrors of London', I naturally turned to the other side of the account, and looked at what had been done or was doing to improve the homes of the poor. I knew that the 'Board of Health' had come and gone, and was now represented by the Government Local Management Act Office—a shadow of a shade.[2] I knew that a Common Lodging Houses Act, to prevent the huddling together of different families in one room had been in operation for some years, and that its provisions were enforced, or not enforced, according to the energy and conscientiousness of the local inspectors of nuisances.[3] I knew that many cellar-rooms, called 'kitchens', had been condemned in certain neighbourhoods; many ceilings had been compulsively whitewashed; many drains had been constructed; and many rotten dust-heaps had been removed.[4] I knew that there had been much talk, and much writing, about the

*Reprinted from *All the Year Round*.

social condition of the labouring classes, and that if I only held up my finger I might be deluged with pamphlets on this deathless subject. Although a writer by profession, I have a constitutional horror of English composition about any real work that requires to be done. Receiving certain reports, tracts, and prospectuses, more as a guide to places than to results, I went once more into the holes and corners of London to see what model lodging-houses we have really got.

The first place I arrived at was a block of buildings in St Pancras, lying between Agar Town and Chapel Street, Somers Town, the worst parts of the parish. They belong to a London society, started to some extent upon commercial principles, called the 'Metropolitan Association for improving the dwellings of the Industrious Classes'.[1] This society, I believe, was founded in 1842, and the St Pancras buildings were the first large block of model houses, or rooms in 'flats', erected in London. They are laid out to accommodate about one hundred and ten families, with about four hundred and twenty rooms, at a rental varying from three shilling and sixpence to seven shillings a week for each set of rooms. The highest prices give the command of three fair-sized rooms and a scullery, with every convenience. The plan of these rooms is very much like that of the 'flat' dwellings in Edinburgh. The outer door secures the family from intrusion, and locks in the household at night. The sitting-room is equal in size to the two bedrooms, and the latter are reached by two doors, one at each side of the sitting-room fireplace. The scullery is a narrow strip, about the length of the sitting-room. The fore-court is an enclosed playground for the children.

The height of the building is its chief structural defect, although, if the calculations have been carefully made, this ought to enable the association to lower their rents.[2] The tenure is leasehold; the building is apparently made to last for ages; and the nett dividend of the society from all their model houses is only about two per cent. The inference is, that too much money has been expended in building for posterity. The rents are grumbled at by many of the tenants, although they are under the market price of the neighbourhood, and too low to meet the expenses of the building, and make a fair return upon the capital sunk, according to the average yield of London house property. The winding well staircases, running up perhaps about sixty feet, with no protection at the sides or landings but an iron railing, reaching no higher than the waist of a man, are sad mistakes of the architect and builder. These staircases, at any hour of the day, are like Jacob's ladders swarming with children, and many accidents and deaths have occurred, so I was told, in the house, in consequence of these deep pits not being closed in. The necessary rail-guards should be fixed at once; such traps for careless, unwatched children, in a philanthropic building, are a disgrace that ought to be got rid of without an appeal to law.

The occupants are chiefly the higher class of labourers and artisans, and the regular payment of the different rents would show this, even if the friends of the association had not stated it in their reports.[1] This may seem a cheering fact to many people, but to me it bears a different aspect. I will state why I regard it unfavourably a little further on.

The other London buildings of the association are in different parts of the town. In Nelson Square, Bermondsey, there is accommodation in 'flats' for one hundred and eight families; at Queen's Place, Dockhead, ten dwellings have been taken and re-arranged for ten families; and in Albion Buildings, Bartholomew Close, some old houses have been taken, and fitted up so as to lodge decently about twenty-four families. In the east of London, in Albert Street, a block of family dwellings on the 'flat' system, has been built for sixty families; in Pelham Street, twelve houses have been built for twelve different families; and similar accommodation has been provided for nine families in cottages in Pleasant Row. In Albert Street, the society has also built a set of chambers for single men, with accommodation for two hundred and thirty-four tenants; and they have long held an old house in Compton Street, Soho, in the West, which will lodge one hundred and twenty-eight single men on the same plan. In St James's, Westminster—not far from this latter place—the association has also built another block of family buildings, capable of housing sixty families. Altogether, we may reckon the population in the society's model houses at the present time, as being nearly two thousand.

I have not visited all the houses belonging to this society, because they are not always open to inspection. The tenants, as before stated, belong to the best class of labourers and artisans, and they very properly object to be watched, counted, and inspected. Their wages are not lower than those of Hugh Miller, when he worked as a quarry-man, and they show a certain degree of independence.[1] The charity they receive through a sentimental standard of rent, is given to them in such a silent underground way, that they are not aware when they receive it. As long as they are allowed to remain in their rooms, and pay their rent punctually, they believe that they are under no obligation to a charitable body of ladies and gentlemen. It would be difficult to persuade them that a nett dividend of only two per cent upon the capital of their landlords, must prove that something is really given to them that they do not pay for.[2]

At the chambers for single men in Albert Street, Mile End, I found a large coffee-room, well lighted, well warmed, and fitted up with a due regard to cleanliness and comfort. There was also a kitchen, where a number of the lodgers were cooking and eating their dinners, and a rather dull heavy library, where one man was writing a letter. About one hundred and seventy-four lodgers were on the books (the place will house two hundred and thirty-four), principally clerks, labourers, and mechanics, with a few men living on small superannuations. The beds upstairs were in separate cupboards, very much like the baths at the public wash-houses, each lodger having a locker to himself, and a private key. The weekly rent for all this accommodation, which is substantially as good as what is generally given at a West-End club, is only two shillings and sixpence. This sum pays for gas, fire, newspapers, water, soap, towels, and books, as well as the rest of the lodging.

Looking at the building, and its low charges, I was not surprised to find that its lodgers came from all parts, and that while its nett profits had only been a little over one per cent upon the outlay, it had not benefited the neighbourhood in any perceptible degree. The Bethnal Green population—the low and really poor—are housed even more badly now than they were before the society started in philanthropic business. They have been pushed on one side, compelled to crowd closer together, because their huts have been pulled down for 'improvements' and new buildings, and are looked upon by the managers of model houses will ill-concealed contempt. Even in the family houses at the side of these club-chambers, no weaver or street hawker is to be found; the rents, although unremunerative, are pitched too high for such people, and there are standing rules to keep them out. The association is for improving the dwellings of the 'industrious classes'—a very loose and windy phrase—and, with one exception, hereafter to be noticed, these model buildings may be looked upon as intruders. At St Pancras, they have done nothing for the worst class in Somers Town and Agar Town, and they have wasted their means on a class who are well able to help themselves. I can find hundreds of tenants who are attracted to these houses from all sides by the low artificial rents, who have no more right to be pensioners of a half-benevolent society than I have. The costermongers—the street hawkers—the industrious poor, are still rotting up their filthy, ill-drained, ill-ventilated courts, while well-paid mechanics, clerks, and porters, willing to sacrifice a certain portion of their self-respect, are the constant tenants of all these model dwellings.*

* Earl Granville[1] made the following remarks in the House of Lords, February 28, 1861:—'He now came,' he said, 'to the third point, upon which he most entirely agreed—namely, the incalculable evil of the poorer classes being overcrowded to the extent which they had heard, and which account he believed to be perfectly true. The evil was great, but the difficulty was to find a remedy. The noble earl (Earl of Derby) made no suggestion, except that a committee should be appointed to inquire. The difficulty was enormous; and when they came to deal with the metropolis, with its three millions of inhabitants, it was impossible to deal satisfactorily with the question. He himself was a shareholder, in common with many of their lordships, in the Metropolitan Association for Improving the Dwellings of the Poor, and they received an interest of two per cent, and that was more than he had expected, though it was not an amount which would induce people to regard it as a profitable investment, and the question of interest had a most important bearing when they came to deal with the great question. He himself had spoken to one of the great contractors, and asked him whether it was possible to do what the Metropolitan Association was doing upon a large scale, and get such interest as would tempt persons into speculations of the sort; and after that gentleman had considered the subject in all its bearings, he thought that such a scheme must be fruitless. Another objection to such a scheme was that a great part of the people who went to such places to live were persons who could

The club-chambers for single men, I cannot help looking upon as a benevolent mistake. The Soho Chambers never presented any hopeful feature from their commencement, and they have long been a financial failure. The Albert Street Chambers, as I have just shown, are the next worst property on the society's books, and these are the only two establishments devoted to single men. Why charity—for charity it is, to a large extent—should lay itself out to help those who are best able to help themselves, I cannot possibly imagine. The tenants of the Soho Chambers have always largely consisted of the idle, not the industrious classes, and there is nearly as much dissipation in wasting whole days reading periodicals over a coffee-room fire, as in playing at skittles or drinking in a tap-room. Idleness is idleness whatever form it takes, and it may always be met with, in large quantities, at these club-chambers. Of all associations, the Society for Improving the Dwellings of the *Industrious Classes* is the least bound to help it in certain localities, at a considerable annual loss.

The family dwellings in Albert Street are carefully arranged; the staircase has no well, and the wash-house is in the playing-ground. The rents vary from four shillings a week, for two rooms and a scullery, to five shillings a week; the rooms in the area being the lowest in price, and the middle rooms the highest. The rooms at the top of the houses are the most difficult to let, and have been for the last ten years. A great demand exists for model cottages, containing two sets of rooms of three each, for two families; and those near the club-chambers, belonging to the society, are never unoccupied.

In another corner of Bethnal Green—in the worst and poorest part of this large and miserable district—Miss Burdett Coutts has partly built, and is now completing, a block of model lodging-houses.[1] They are light, cheerful, and somewhat ecclesiastical in appearance, and form, at present, three sides of a large quadrangle. They stand upon ground formerly occupied by

afford to pay for better lodgings. Even in the model lodging-houses a great many of the apartments had been taken by persons that were above the class whom it was the particular object to reach, and who were huddled up in small rooms.'

a notorious place called Nova Scotia Gardens, where the Italian boy was murdered, or 'burked', as it was called, some years ago, by Bishop and Williams.[1]

The east and west wings of these model houses are now filled with tenants. The rents in the east wing are four shillings a week for three rooms, three shillings and sixpence a week for two rooms and two shillings a week for one room. The rooms are small, but well ventilated; and there is every convenience throughout the house, even to baths. The laundry is at the top of the wing, well supplied with water, and the playing-ground for the children is in the quadrangle below. The staircases have two defects. There is a deep narrow well between the steps, which may lead to some serious accident, unless it be railed over; and the ventilation is too boisterous. Long, arched openings in the walls, running up nearly the whole length of the stairs, make the place too cold in the winter, although they are covered with thick blinds. Two hundred men, women, and children are in the east wing, and one hundred and fifty in the west wing—making a population of three hundred and fifty. When the place is finished this will be more than doubled, and the workmen are now busily employed in building the back row of rooms. The rooms in the east wing number about one hundred and eighteen, and in the west wing one hundred and five. The rents in the west wing are a little higher than those in the east wing; being five shillings a week for three rooms, four shillings a week for two rooms, and two shillings and sixpence a week for one room.

I feel a delicacy in criticising the charitable designs of an estimable lady, who has a perfect right to do what she likes with her own. Miss Coutts may have no intention of calling these buildings model lodging-houses, in the popular acceptation of the term, but the public will doubtless so name them for her, and look upon them as improved dwellings for the local poor. This they are not, and never will be, and the sooner the truth is told about them the better. The industrious poor of Bethnal Green are very sparingly represented in them, and then only on the east side. A weaver, who can only earn about seven or ten shillings a week in the present condition of his trade, would not be able to pay the rents of such rooms, even if they were large enough for his shuttle, which they are not, and even if the manager thought proper to admit him. Street hawkers and the old inhabitants of Nova Scotia Gardens are never found in such places, and the court and alley population are left exactly where they were.[1] The clearance, like all clearances, must have raised their rents, and caused them to huddle more closely together.

An analysis of the population in the west wing of these new buildings would show something like the following:—A clerk, employed in the city, who came here from Hoxton; a warehouseman, employed in the city, who came here from Clerkenwell; a workman, employed at Woolwich, who runs up and down by the Eastern Counties' Railway; a compositor, employed in the neighbourhood, who came here from the city; a railway guard employed at the railway; the family belonging to the mate of a ship who is in the East Indies; a working cooper, who came here from St Luke's parish; two or three more warehousemen and clerks, who came here from the city; a printer who came here from the country; a labourer who works some distance out of London; with a few working mechanics, perhaps not more than half-a-dozen out of fifty tenants who really sprung from the district. Whatever good such buildings may do, they can never improve the neighbourhood they stand in. They fly over the heads of those who are most in want of improvement, instead of burrowing under their feet. They attract a crowd of sharp-sighted tenants from outside districts who are a little more advanced in cleanliness and civilization, and are quick to see where ten shillings' worth of comfort is selling at less than half-price.

The other building belonging to the Association for Improving the Dwellings of the Industrious Classes, which I have spoken of as an exception to the general rule of misappropriation, is the model lodging-house in St James's, Westminster. Here, the sixty families are chiefly working tailors—the staple poor of the district; and although the site is not very cheerful, every room is occupied. Three rooms, on the 'flat' plan, let here for seven shillings and sixpence a week; and a second class of rooms, let in blocks of three, at six shillings and twopence a week.

The 'Healthy Houses', a small private speculation near here, in Husband Street, are very dark and badly constructed, the bedrooms having no chimneys or fireplaces. Eight families are housed in this block, paying five shillings and sixpence a week for three rooms on the ground floor, and six shillings and sixpence a week for similar rooms at the top. The best feature about them is the glazed bricks in the passages and staircases, which present a surface that rejects the dirt, and is easily kept clean.

Passing by the parochial model lodging-houses which exist in St James's, Westminster, Marylebone, and other parishes, I come to the buildings belonging to the Society for Improving the Condition of the Labouring Classes.[1] There are nine establishments; one in George Street, Bloomsbury, for one hundred and four single men; another in Hatton Garden for fifty-four single men; a 'renovated lodging-house' in Charles Street, Drury Lane, for eighty-two single men; and a similar house in King Street, Drury Lane, for twenty-two single men. There are also the renovated dwellings for families in Wild Court, Drury Lane, with one hundred and six rooms;[2] a similar building in Clark's Buildings, Broad Street, St Giles's, containing eighty-two rooms; the Thanksgiving Model Buildings in Portpool Lane, Gray's Inn Lane, for twenty families, and one hundred and twenty-eight single women, with a public wash-house; the renovated dwellings for families and single men in Tyndall's Buildings, Gray's Inn Lane, containing eighty-seven family rooms, and forty beds for men; and the building in Streatham Street, Bloomsbury, for fifty-four families.[3]

The society is supported by donations, subscriptions, and loans borrowed at interest, and it has now been in existence for nearly twenty years. It has doubtless done much good in improving the habits of many of the dirty poor, but it has also met with the same bitter experiences as the other leading association. The people it has gathered under its wing are not often the class it ought to have started to benefit. In the Streatham Street houses, I saw indications of comfort in those dwellings I could look into which told me that certain well-paid workmen were accepting a lodging partly paid for by charity. One of the warm friends of the association has recently said that 'they find no reluctance on the part of the working classes to accept this kind of benevolence'. I can only say, I am sorry for it. The standard of morals must be very low where men with health, strength, and skilled hands, are content to accept anything that they do not fully pay for.

The building in Streatham Street is rather gloomy, built in a very heavy style to last for centuries, and disfigured by galleries with broad flat brick columns, when iron would have been so much lighter. These columns make the entrances dark, and throw a gloom into the bedrooms in front. The rents are about six or seven shillings a week for three rooms, and five shillings a week for two rooms. The rent-book shows the superior class of tenants who have been sucked into these houses. In the week ending February 2, hard as the times are supposed to be, there were only two gaps of a few shillings each in a rental of fourteen pounds sterling. One of these gaps was caused by a death, the other by a want of work. Can any house-agent, dealing with working people in London, show an equally clear rent-book at the present moment?

The single men's lodging-houses are very similar to many established by private individuals in different parts of London, particularly those opened by Mr Sartoris in Commercial Street, Whitechapel.

I went to the one in Charles Street, Drury Lane, where beds are made up for eighty-two men at fourpence a night each, or two shillings a week for each lodger. The beds are clean, and not too close together, and the house has seldom many vacant. In the kitchen, about a dozen men were standing about the room, some cooking at the fire, others talking and idling. One old man was writing in one of the boxes, which are like the compartments in common coffee-rooms; and another was asleep, with his head and arms lying amongst some broken potatoes on one of the tables. They looked to me all greasy, faded men—men difficult to keep clean, who smelt of onions, and were mostly out of employment. The old lady, who regarded herself as the mother of them all, told me that many were lawyers' clerks, linendrapers' assistants, and mechanics. One lodger, a compositor, not then in the house, she had had for years. Some stopped a night only, some a month, some came from the country; and occasionally a few thieves crept in as lodgers, and stole a few of the other lodgers' clothes. She had never had but one costermonger—a most superior man of his kind, who lived there for two years, until he got married, when he left, most probably to live up a court.

Nearly all the kitchens of these places reminded me very much of a low ward in a debtors' prison, particularly the kitchen in Charles Street.

The society claims to be instituted for improving the condition of the labouring classes. Here, I am sorry to say, we have another loose phrase adopted as the watchword, or key-note of an association, which is well-intentioned, and royally supported in its operations. It would be rather difficult to define who the 'labouring classes' really are, and I am afraid that many lodgers sheltered by this society would hardly bear a strict examination into their claims as labourers. Without any wordy flourishes, the society is a clean, wholesome lodging-house company, providing decent accommodation for any one who knocks at their doors, if he is not a costermonger, or a confirmed dweller in courts. No one seems to touch the lowest of the low, or their putrid hiding-places, and the depths in education reached by ragged schools are not yet reached by philanthropists in providing model dwellings.[1]

Our benevolent societies are all either too large-minded, or tied to the log of a rumbling title. [We want a division of labour,—a large association of real workers, not talkers and givers—and a body of home missionaries who will tuck up their shirt-sleeves, and go out with brooms, shovels, pails and whitewashing brushes. We want creeds of all kinds put on the shelf, for a short period, and a few years of 'soap and water societies'; 'scrubbing-brush societies', and such like combinations.] We have heard a good deal lately about muscular Christianity, and if it is anything more than a mere name, a splendid field of action is open before it.[2] In no part of the world,—not even in the remotest dens of savage wildernesses,— is there such a field for labour as in our London courts and alleys. Peel off the stucco at any point, and there is the mass of dirt, vice, and social degradation festering beneath. I have lived in it and amongst it ever since I could walk and talk, and I speak with some authority when I say that I know what it is. No one has ever properly grappled with it, has ever thoroughly understood it, or perhaps tried to understand it. The attempts at reform have been mere pickings at the surface,— feeble, half-supported efforts to do good. [The man only preached at, goes back to his den and rubs the lesson off his mind in a few minutes. The child only preached at, goes out of the school, puts its tongue in its cheek, throws a 'handspring' in the mud, and forgets all it ever learnt in its domestic hell. Education, as I have said before, is something more than merely 'sitting under' a preacher, or learning lessons out of a book.] We all know what home influence is for good or evil, and here are one hundred and fifty thousand families living in dens that are worse than sewers. The most awful thing in connexion with these people, is to find them utterly blind to their dirt and misery. Their senses are blunted by long familiarity, they cannot see the over-crowding, the mass of rotten filth that surrounds them; they cannot smell the stench; they are choked with dirt, and yet feel clean; and they slink up the foul back streets, and are satisfied with their condition. The six thousand dwellers in London model lodging-houses * look down upon them with contempt, the very porters spurn them from the model doors, and they sink back a million of hopeless lepers, that no man will touch.**

* *Population in Model Houses in London, Estimated.*

	Persons.
Metropolitan Association's Buildings	2,200
Society for improving the condition of the Labouring Classes, in all buildings	1,900
The Strand Building Company, Eagle Court, Strand	125
Mr Hilliard's Houses at Shadwell	560
Parochial and Private Houses on the Model Plan	1,000
	5,785
Miss Coutts's Houses, Bethnal Green	400
	6,185[1]

** Reprinted from *Good Words*.

Mistaken Charity[1]

No art is so difficult as the art of charity. To give a man a some-thing (except in money) that he really wants, or to organize a home for him that he will really prize, are things that are not done once in a hundred years. The rudest idea of the charitable refuge is the almshouse. It existed at the time when waggons did the journey to York in a week or ten days, and when it was not safe to wander towards Charing Cross after dusk. There is a wonderful sameness about all buildings of the kind. They have a central hall with a clock and a bell; a number of small brick tenements projecting to the right; an equal number projecting to the left; a pump, a cabbage-garden at the back, an ornamental grass-plot (where the charity is rich) laid out in front; a statue of the founder, or a tablet to his memory; a dull uniformity; and an awful silence. Every room is like every other room, and every door is opposite some other door. How can the inmates of such a place be happy? Neither broken-down haberdashers, decayed Turkey merchants, nor needy frame-knitters are grateful for such refuges. They go to them, because beggars have no power to be choosers. They walk about, reflecting each other's pauper-ism; they constantly revolve round the same old ideas, and they moodily watch each other's decay. No matter how picturesque the general view of their building may appear; no matter how healthy or delightful may be the locality in which they are placed; no matter whether you call their institution by the name of college or almshouse; there is a mixture of the workhouse and the penitentiary in its constitution which it will never lose while a single inmate remains. *

If almshouses that are almost rural in their aspect are felt to be prisons, how much less attractive those dwarfed, dark, cottage-looking dens must be, that, through the changes of time, are now in the very heart of the City? You may meet with them at every turn;—in Moorgate, Cripplegate, Bishopsgate, and Southwark.

* This paragraph is taken mainly from an old article of mine in the *Daily News*.

Their founders never had any politico-economical idea of making them repulsive in order to check the growth of the poor. Their design and position were supposed to be faultless by those who founded them. From the day on which they were raised, to the present hour—a period perhaps, of more than three hundred years,—their low rooms have never been without inmates. Sometimes they shelter a few stooping old men who creep about the paved yards, or peer through the railings at the gate; and sometimes a few withered old women who clean their cottage windows, brush their doorsteps, and fetch water from the pump. These pensioners exist, like strange animals in a cage, and are placed at the roadside for idle, thoughtless passengers to gape at. The field or country lane of the sixteenth, seventeenth, or even eighteenth century, in which their original hermitages were built, has become a close street of busy warehouses, if not an alley of dirty hovels. The old pensioners find themselves in everybody's way; and everybody is in their way. Their air, and their light, are half blocked out by a law of metropolitan progress, and their poor lives are doubtless shortened by the accidents of their position. They live daily and hourly in a way that their benefactors never meant they should live in; and the boards and corporations who manage their funds are as well aware of this as most people. Too much respect is paid to the assumed, not the real, wishes of the dead; and no one has courage enough to ask Parliament to remove these unfortunate almshouses.

In London and the outskirts there are at least a hundred of these charitable refuges, and more than one-third of this number are jammed up in and about the city. There is one row for the deserving poor—re-built in 1789—up a court in Moorgate Street. The houses are clean and comfortable, and the situation is not very confined, but the ground must be wasting away under such an unproductive class of buildings.* The deserving poor in each of

---

* VALUE OF LAND IN THE CITY.—In consequence of improvements being made in Newgate Street, Great Tower Street, and two other places within the City, land to the amount of 2,670*l*.—of which sum 890*l*. (one-third) has been contributed by the Metropolitan Board of Works—will be given up to the public. From the quantity so applied, we find the average rate per acre to be 180,000*l*. sterling.— *City Press*, 1860.

these six houses, receive now about six or seven shillings a week each; but if the freehold was sold, offices and warehouses would rise upon the spot, and every dependant of this charity would be benefited for ever and ever. In Great St Helen's, Bishopsgate, there is another asylum, known as Judd's, founded in 1555, and rebuilt in 1729. It shelters six poor men who have each two rooms and ten shillings a week, and who are doubtless very happy. Neither of these places can be strictly called almshouses; the first being an ordinary row of small dwellings, and the last a large, old-fashioned mansion. The rooms now occupied by each of these six poor men, would fetch about thirty pounds a year if let out as offices, and a building might be raised on the ground occupied by this old refuge, that would pay a much higher rental.

It is not necessary to describe even half-a-dozen of these places, nor to look into each deed under which they were founded, to know that their removal would benefit the charities they represent, and the people at present living in them. Let any one, in passing over London Bridge, towards Southwark, look down upon a squat row of cottages lying between St Saviour's Church and the wharf warehouses of Messrs Humphrey and others. These almshouses were built in the last century by Mrs Shaw Overman, for eight poor women. Each house contains only one room on the ground floor, and the residents have five shillings a week each. New London Bridge and its approaches from the south have raised a noisy, ever-crowded roadway high above their heads, and the wharf buildings, Bridge House hotel, and other places have towered up round them, until they seem now to live at the bottom of a deep brick well. They are evidently standing in the way of business very much against their will, for they have no particular associations with Southwark at the waterside. They are called the 'witches', by costermongers and boatmen, and would doubtless be very glad if they were able to choose another lodging. Their cottages look like mushrooms by the side of the lofty, yellow warehouses; and huge packages seems always hanging over them at the end of cranes, threatening to fall and crush them. If the ground these ill-placed refuges stand upon were sold to the building genii of the neighbourhood, the eight old ladies who depend upon Mrs Overman's charity now, and those who may have to depend upon it in the future, might retire to any lodging coming within their means, secure in an income doubled if not trebled.

This is the case with many London almshouses; and every hour that is lost in altering it according to the dictates of business, common sense, and humanity, is so much wrong inflicted upon the poor, helpless inmates, in opposition to the real wishes of those who founded these charities. Let each knot of dependants be boldly pensioned off, with liberty to go where they like, to live where they like, and to spend their money as they like. This is real charity, and while it will reform old almshouses—the gifts of past philanthropists—it will set a healthy example before the philanthropists of the future.

Conclusion[1]

[Weeks spent in Westminster, near the Abbey, would only multiply these experiences; and weeks spent in and about Whitechapel, St George's in the East, Bethnal Green and Shoreditch, Clerkenwell, St Pancras, Bermondsey, Southwark, Lambeth, 'over the water' generally, and Marylebone, would certainly produce a like result. Wherever you sink a shaft—whether in the centre or the outskirts—and penetrate with a good guide, perseverance, and fair local knowledge, you will find endless veins of social degradation. In all my journeys through the holes and corners of London I have found a terrible sameness—little more than one thing—a dead level of misery, crime, vice, dirt, and rags. I have had but one story to tell, and I have told it as faithfully as it could well be told. The scale upon which my chapters have been unavoidably planned has imposed a treatment rather broad and superficial, and a rather arbitrary arrangement of districts. I have kept to certain distinct patches of London whose titles were familiar to the public, and by this means, when

a strict description of parochial boundaries was out of the
question, I have laboured to show upon what locality I stood. I
have passed by many holes and corners in Fleet Street, the Strand,
Chancery Lane, Holborn,* Gray's-inn Lane, and other quarters
that are dirty, ill-constructed, and overcrowded enough to merit a
place in the catalogue. At present the melancholy list is full. I shall
now endeavour to deal with a few of the social questions arising
out of my survey, and shall then hold my peace.][1]

Setting aside the criminal population of London, and that small
number of the London industrious poor who struggle against the
degrading influences of the neighbourhoods in which they are
mostly compelled to live, we shall find at least one-third[2] of our
three millions of human beings in the metropolis housed in filthy,
ill-constructed courts and alleys, or crowding in unwholesome
layers, one over the other, in old houses and confined rooms. The
life they lead daily and hourly is full of debasing lessons. Decency
is lost where large families of all ages and of both sexes are
accustomed to live in one apartment, and habits are engendered
which last for generations. This carelessness about comforts and
conveniences acts upon landlords. There is little demand for pure,
wholesome, well-constructed dwellings, and they are not supplied. The court and alley property in and about London, which is
a disgrace to a city of enterprise and civilization, is in most cases
up to the level of its consumers. A low, wretched standard of

---

* The Earl of Shaftesbury made the following remarks in the House of Lords,
February 28, 1861—:'In eight small courts,' he said, 'off Holborn Hill, he found
sixty-two houses, three hundred and fourteen rooms, of the average size of eight
feet by three and seven by nine. In these rooms lived one thousand four hundred
and seventy-nine persons. It was impossible to imagine the physical and moral evil
which resulted from these circumstances, or to describe the fearful effects on the
population. But he might say that there were adults of both sexes living together in
the same room, in which every social necessity, every domestic act, must be
performed; that there were not only adults of both sexes living in the same room,
but adult sons sleeping with their mothers, and brothers and sisters very
commonly sleeping in the same bed. He was stating what he knew to be the truth
when he said that incestuous crime was frightfully common—common to the
greatest possible extent within the range of these courts.'[3]

living makes the poor huddle together in such places, without any general desire to improve them. Model lodging-houses, if built in advance of a general demand for such superior dwellings, would not raise the tenants to the level of the building, but would drag the building down to the level of the tenants. I think it was the Duke of Bedford who built a number of superior three-roomed cottages on his estate, because he disliked to see his labourers huddled together in one room. The habit of living in one room, however, was too strong for the reformer, and in a few months each cottage was filled with three separate families, the original tenant having sub-let what he considered his spare space. The records of philanthropy could supply many more discouraging anecdotes, but there is too much reservation on such points. No country in the world spends so much money in charity as England—no country is taxed for benevolent purposes to anything like the same extent.* In London alone there is every conceivable form of institution for the relief of the sick, the infirm, and the specially afflicted. Squat rows of almshouses meet us, as I have just said, at every turn, nestling in the very heart of the city and its outlets. Nearly a million of 'cases' receive free medical advice and assistance in London alone every year. The hat is always going round. The first stone of some benevolent building is always being laid. We dine, we sing, we act, we make speeches in aid of the funds of a thousand institutions; we are never tired of doing what we consider good. Casinos, harmonious pot-houses, and pugilistic exhibitions,** catch the benevolent infection and work like mill-

[* Our national poor-rate is estimated at six millions sterling per annum. It has also been calculated that another million a year is devoted to charitable purposes, and about an equal amount of benevolent permanent resources is derived from the liberality of former generations. Our national paupers are estimated at one million.

A parliamentary return, moved for by Mr Villiers, and published February 12, 1861, shows that in England and Wales there are 7,432,587 persons rated to the poor rate; the gross estimated rental at Lady Day, 1856, was 31,315,595l.; the rateable value at Lady Day, 1856, was 25,737,056l.; and the number of houses rated to the relief of the poor, was 1,400,237.]

[** 'PUGILISTIC BENEFIT FOR THE DISTRESSED COVENTRY WEAVERS.—The announced pugilistic demonstration in aid of the funds for this charitable purpose took place on Monday evening, January 28, 1861, at the National horses to aid noisy soup-kitchens.[1] [I can only wonder that prostitution is not moved to be charitable, and that the mangy Haymarket does not give up a few nights' earnings every winter for the benefit of the poor.] The impulsive virtues flourish even upon dunghills, and people bestow with one hand while they are compelled to receive with the other. Paupers unite in teapot testimonials to matrons and overseers, which they purchase out of the money saved from tobacco and snuff. The hard-hearted man, the cold-blooded political economist, the hunks, the gripe-all, are empty dreams. Business is business in every hole and corner, and no trade will ever be conducted upon sentimental

baths, Westminster Road. The benefit was to all intents and purposes "a bumper", and this must be highly gratifying to those members of the P.R. who had taken so much interest in carrying out this charitable gathering. The spacious building was crowded in every part. Phil Benjamins was the M.C., and was assisted in the discharge of his duties by Jemmy Shaw, with the most praiseworthy zeal. The sports opened with the performance of Professor Thomas, and then came the sparring, the bouts, which followed in admirable time, being between the following men, viz:—Dillon and Plantagenet Green, George Crockett and Dan Collins, Job Cobley and Travers, Ben Caunt and Jem Ward, Bos Tyler and Harry Brunton, Bob Brettle (who came expressly from Birmingham, with his belt and cups,) and Mike Madden, Jerry Noon and Alec Keeene, W. Shaw and Young Reed, Tom Paddock and Tom King. Sam Hurst, the champion, who, from lameness, was unable to spar, came on the stage and exhibited the belt for which he and Tom Paddock had contended. Then followed Harry Broome, the ex-champion of England, and Harry Orme; but, before the bout between these distinguished members of the ring took place, Broome, in a neat speech, returned thanks on behalf of the committee for the liberal manner in which they had been supported in their charitable undertaking. Then came a spar between George Brown and Jemmy Welsh, Harris and Hicks being the next exhibitors, and last, though not least, was the wind-up between Nat Langham and Jem Mace, the last-named man exhibiting his belt. In addition to these leading men there were many others present who were anxious to set-to, but had not the opportunity. Tom Sayers was unable to attend, nor did Lynch, the American, put in an appearance to spar with Harrington. Broome, in his speech, announced that 197*l*. had been taken in money at the doors, this being irrespective of money that will have to be accounted for by tickets sold, so that the whole affair, in a pecuniary view, was eminently successful.

* * * * *

'A donation of 50*l*.—the result of a musical performance—was presented to the Bow Street Police Court poor-box, on 31st January, 1861, by Mr Weston, the proprietor, and Mr Corri, the musical director, of Weston's music-hall, Holborn.

'A donation of 10*l*.for the same poor-box was received by Mr Corrie from the proprietor of the Argyll Rooms, a casino in Windmill Street, Haymarket.']

principles; but, after the shop shutters are put up, the ledger is posted, and the till money is counted, the large heart begins to do its work. We are certainly not suffering from too little heart in our social system, but perhaps from too much. The head, after all, is not the worst guide in works of charity, as those men find who have to analyse results. Benevolent people who act from impulse rather than reflection—warm-hearted, open-handed givers—are hourly pained by seeing their gifts misapplied, or their institutions fattening the class whom they were never intended to benefit. Model lodging-houses, designed to work good, but planted in uncongenial soil, become occupied by tenants, as I have just shown, who require no assistance from a sentimental standard of rent, and the 'swinish multitude' are still left wallowing in their blind alleys. Soup-kitchens, like free theatres, attract the wandering tribes of London—open their doors without any effectual check or inquiry, dispense food, as in Spitalfields, to the extent of thirty thousand pounds sterling, and find, after all, that they have fed the wrong men. Hospitals, asylums, charity schools, and other forms of permanent out-door relief, are worm-eaten by imposition, and yet they flourish. They stand up as monuments for foreigners to gaze at, and are, at the same time, our glory and our shame. They show a class on one hand always ready to give, and they show another class—low, wanting in self-reliance and self-respect, demoralized by much charity—always ready to receive. The seeds of the old lavish poor-law have borne bitter fruit, and a working-class has grown up who look to a parish pension as the honourable reward of age. The simplest and cheapest forms of insurance are neglected; the usurious loan offices, whose thousands of branches spread into every district, are welcomed as friends; early reckless marriages are contracted—[marriages, as I have said before, that are as much a 'dissipation' as gin-drinking, or any other abomination,—] children are produced without thought, set upon their feet without clothing, taught to walk, turned into the street without food or education, and left to the ragged school, the charitable public, or the devil. Homes for such outcasts spring up on all sides; large-hearted men and women rush forward to help the neglected; and the class is sometimes unfortunately increased by the very efforts made to relieve it.

I am grieved to have to write like this of honest labourers—of men who ought to do their work, keep homes over their heads that are something better than dog-kennels or pigsties, and shrink from a gift as if it were a wound. [They increase and multiply, and all for what? To become paupers; to glut the labour market; to keep their wages down at starvation point, to swell the profits of capital. They look to everyone to relieve them, but make few efforts to relieve themselves. The most perfect poor-law; the most perfect administration of that poor-law; the most lavish charity can do nothing for them compared to the wonders of self-help. Let them defer their marriages for six or seven years, and they will turn their backs on strikes and starvation.] My sympathies are with them in any well-considered scheme to benefit their condition. I have lived amongst them and know their ways; I willingly acknowledge their many virtues, their generosity, their endurance under suffering, but I want to see them with a little more pride. They may not always beg themselves, but they make their wives and families beg for them. The disgrace is theirs where the poor, pinched women in scanty clothes are sent to crowd round the parsonage-door, or to hold out the well-thumbed, creased petitions in their thin, bloodless hands.

The labour thrown upon the working clergy in the lowest districts by this want of self-reliance on the part of the industrious poor is something enormous. Their houses become tailors'-shops, eating-houses, dispensaries, banks, schools, sanitary committee-rooms—everything but clerical sanctuaries. The old classic, the pet divine, are thrown on one side or forgotten; and to walk all day in muddy boots, to give out tickets and read letters, to return home at uncertain hours with grubby hands, and to spend the evening in making up parochial accounts is their daily and hourly task. They see distress that they cannot relieve; they know its cause, and yet they have not the heart to reprove it; they toil and beg for their local charities, often with little effect, and sometimes eat into their own scanty incomes rather than neglect their dependants. The poor-law, which, if properly constructed, ought to relieve them of this ceaseless, disheartening drudgery, is only a millstone round their necks. It starts with a proper determination to check pauperism in every possible way, but it never succeeds in carrying out its object. It breaks down, as it has broken down this winter—not so much from glaring faults in its individual administrators, as from the make-believe character of its system. Its plan is to get rid of the poor—to pass them on—to toss them from hand to hand, and not to grapple with them. It makes all the show, spends much of the money, and leaves other people to do the work. A pauper is often disposed of by being told to go farther; but he sometimes dies in the streets, and creates a public scandal.* The workhouse doors may be closed, the lights may be put out, the master may be in bed; but other doors are open, other lights are burning, other people are stirring. The workhouse—the rate-payers themselves—become receivers of out-door relief when the starving poor are thus thrown upon stray charity.

The question of an equalization of poor-rates generally springs up when the condition of the poor is examined; and those who have advocated this change in the plan of rating with the greatest care and ability have sometimes mistaken the effect it would produce upon the pauper population; it would not reform their condition; it would not remedy the evils under which they suffer; it would not make them more decent, more moral, more independent; it would not drain off superabundant labour from overstocked markets. It would make one portion of the poor—the great majority—more comfortable; and it would make another portion, the minority, less comfortable. As a measure of justice it would deal principally with property, and would not check pauperism in the slightest degree. We should

[* On Friday morning, January 11, 1861, Mr Carter received information of the awfully sudden death of a man in Manor Street, Clapham. The deceased, with four other men, were walking through the streets, in consequence of the frost stopping their work as navigators, soliciting the contributions of the charitable to relieve their destitution. The dead man, who was singing in the road with the others, suddenly staggered and fell. A surgeon stated that death was caused by cold and hunger, and the poor man's co-mates said that they had been two days without food.]

get rid of glaring inequalities in assessment, and all landlords would be reduced to one level of taxation. Companies that have sucked up a parish—like the Bank of England, which stands, I believe, on the whole of St Christopher-le-Stock—would not be their own assessors, their own guardians, their own relieving officers, paying sums that are ridiculously small when contrasted with other assessments. [We should get rid of one notorious difficulty in the way of 'metropolitan improvements'. New streets might then be cut without any fear that capitalists would hesitate to provide houses for the working classes in other districts, because checked by the poor-rates.] The pauper in the west, with his five shillings a week and his loaf of bread, would have to divide his dole with the pauper in the east, who gets nothing but a loaf and a shilling a week, but that would be all. The great problem of how to check pauperism without cruelty or neglect would still be unsolved.

[Attempts have been made to improve the physical condition of the poor by what is called 'sanitary reform'. Like all meddling legislation this may do as much harm as good.[1] If certain kitchens are condemned as not being fit for human dwelling-places, the rents in that particular district are raised, and this practically by the order of the local officer of health. If certain rooms in a house are closed according to law, and the dwelling accommodation of the district is not stretched in another direction, the rooms that are left have the same value as all the rooms in the house had before. The tenants, not the landlord, are the sufferers by this enforced change, and they are compelled to huddle more closely together, and to pay an increased rent. It seems an awful thing that a felon in prison should have one thousand cubic feet of breathing space, while many poor working-people in the most overcrowded districts have not more than two hundred cubic feet of air in their rooms for each person; but the first is paid for and given out of the taxes, and the second has to be worked for and bought. If the Metropolis Local Management Acts, or any other sanatory Acts, compel the poor, by inspection, to purchase five hundred cubic feet of air for each member of their families, they either compel them to better their condition, or to pinch their half-empty stomachs for the sake of the public health.[1] I am afraid that this attempt to improve the poor by Act of Parliament is as unsound in principle as it is often mischievous in effect.]

The educational agencies at work upon the rising generation may do something to raise the moral tone and habits of those who will be men and women in ten or fifteen years' time; but the present generation, the idle and industrious poor who have passed the age of manhood, I am afraid must be given up. Their habits are formed; they are beyond the influence of schools or classes, and their ambition can only be excited on behalf of their children. Philanthropy can do no harm and much good by devoting all its energies to the young, and the more it improves their minds and morals the more chance is there that they will aim at a higher standard of living.*

This is the only road out of the slough of pauperism, dirt, and overcrowding which exists in London, and if that fails us there is no hope.

[*The London ragged schools, I believe, number one hundred and fifty, containing twenty thousand children. The unpaid teachers at these schools amount to two thousand.][2]

APPENDIX

Appendix

TABLES OF POPULATION AND STANDING ROOM

The following tables give precise information about huddling together in London, &c., according to the census of 1851, though they tell us nothing about huddling in houses. Twenty per cent, or one-fifth more, must now be added to the whole population. In the low districts this percentage will scarcely represent the increase of numbers grown on the spot, or received from 'improved' neighbourhoods. The tables take the broad areas of districts and sub-districts, and are, therefore, no guide to the overcrowding in particular corners of those districts.

Districts of London.	Population in 1851.		Number of Persons to an Acre.
Lewisham . . . . } Plumstead . . . . }	34,835	...	2
Wandsworth . . .	50,764	...	4
Hampstead . . .	11,986	...	5
Fulham . . .	29,646	...	7
Camberwell . . .	54,667	...	13
Hackney . . .	58,429	...	15
Poplar . . . . } Bow . . . . }	47,162	...	16
Greenwich . . . } Woolwich . . . }	99,365	...	19
Rotherhithe . . .	17,805	...	21
Kensington . . .	44,053	...	23
Islington . . .	95,329	...	30
Lambeth . . .	139,325	...	35
Paddington . . .	46,305	...	36
St. Pancras . . .	166,965	...	61
St. George, Hanover-square .	73,230	...	63
Chelsea . . .	56,538	...	65
Bermondsey . . .	48,128	...	70
Westminster . . .	65,609	...	72
St. Martin's-in-the-Fields .	24,640	...	81
Newington . . .	64,816	...	104
Marylebone . . .	157,696	...	105
St. Olave, Southwark .	19,375	...	115
Bethnal Green . .	90,193	...	119
St. Saviour, Southwark .	35,731	...	143
Shoreditch . . .	109,257	...	169
Clerkenwell . . .	64,778	...	170
St. George, Southwark .	51,824	...	180
Whitechapel . . .	79,759	...	196
St. George's-in-the-East .	48,376	...	199
City of London . .	129,128	...	210
St. Giles's . . .	54,214	...	221
St. James's . . .	36,406	...	222
Holborn . . .	46,621	...	238
St. Luke, Old-street .	54,055	...	246
Strand . . .	45,000	...	316

No.	Registrars' Sub-Districts.	Population, 1851.
	LONDON	2,362,236
1-6	WEST DISTRICTS	376,427
7-11	NORTH DISTRICTS	490,396
12-19	CENTRAL DISTRICTS	393,256
20-25	EAST DISTRICTS	485,522
26-36	SOUTH DISTRICTS	616,635

WEST DISTRICTS.

No.		
1	St. Mary, Paddington	17,252
	St. John, Paddington	29,053
	Kensington Town	29,183
	Brompton	14,870
	St. Peter, Hammersmith	4,467
	St. Paul, Hammersmith	13,293
	Fulham	11,886
2	Chelsea, South	19,050
	Chelsea, North-west	17,669
	Chelsea, North-east	19,819
3	Hanover-square	20,216
	May Fair	12,980
	Belgrave	40,034
4	St. John, Westminster	34,295
	St. Margaret, Westminster	31,314
5	Charing Cross	12,587
	Long Acre	12,053
6	Berwick-street	10,798
	St. James's-square	11,469
	Golden-square	14,139

NORTH DISTRICTS.

No.		
7	All Souls, Marylebone	28,841
	Cavendish-square	14,687
	Rectory, Marylebone	27,633
	St. Mary, Marylebone	22,814
	Christchurch, Marylebone	33,895
	St. John, Marylebone	29,826
8	Hampstead	11,986
9	Regent's Park, Pancras	31,918
	Tottenham-court	28,433
	Gray's-inn-lane	26,523
	Somers-town	35,641
	Camden-town	21,115
	Kentish-town	23,326
10	Islington, West	47,881
	Islington, East	47,448
11	Stoke Newington	4,840
	Stamford-hill	5,549
	West Hackney	18,732
	Hackney	20,850
	South Hackney	8,458

CENTRAL DISTRICTS.

No.		
12	St. George, Bloomsbury	16,807
	St. Giles, South	19,951
	St. Giles, North	17,456
13	St. Ann, Soho	17,335
	St. Mary-le-Strand	11,615

No.	Registrars' Sub-Districts.	Population, 1851.
	St. Clement Danes	15,467
14	St. George-the-Martyr	18,813
	St. Andrew, East Holborn	13,971
	Saffron-hill	13,837
15	St. James, Clerkenwell	21,529
	Amwell, Clerkenwell	15,720
	Pentonville	11,904
	Goswell-street	15,625
16	Old-street	10,617
	City-road	16,840
	Whitecross-street	13,657
	Finsbury	12,941
17	St. Botolph, East London	23,824
	Cripplegate	20,582
18	West London, North	12,946
	West London, South	15,887
19	London City, South-west	9,204
	London City, North-west	11,847
	London City, South	11,461
	London City, South-east	10,594
	London City, North-east	12,826

EAST DISTRICTS.

No.		
20	Holywell, Shoreditch	17,245
	St. Leonard, Shoreditch	19,449
	Hoxton New Town	23,505
	Hoxton Old Town	17,431
	Haggerston, West	20,276
	Haggerstone, East	11,351
21	Hackney-road	23,910
	Green, Bethnal Green	23,555
	Church, Bethnal Green	21,787
	Town, Bethnal Green	20,941
22	Artillery, Whitechapel	6,769
	Spitalfields	15,336
	Mile End, New Town	14,543
	Whitechapel, North	12,530
	Whitechapel Church	7,818
	Goodman's Fields	12,069
	Aldgate	10,694
23	St. Mary, St. George's East	18,067
	St. Paul, St. George's East	20,319
	St. John, St. George's East	9,990
24a	Shadwell	16,179
	Ratcliff	15,212
	Limehouse	22,782
24b	Mile End, Old Town, West	29,582
	Mile End, Old Town, East	27,020
25	Bow	18,778
	Poplar	28,384

SOUTH DISTRICTS.

No.		
26	Christchurch, Southwark	16,022
	St. Saviour, Southwark	19,709
27	St. Olave, Southwark	8,015
	St. John, Horsleydown	11,360
28	St. James, Bermondsey	18,899
	St. Mary Magdalen	13,934
	Leather Market	15,295

No.	Registrars' Sub-Districts.	Population 1851.
29	Kent Road	18,126
	Borough Road	15,862
	London Road	17,836
30	Trinity, Newington	20,922
	St. Peter, Walworth	29,861
	St. Mary, Newington	14,033
31	Waterloo-road, 1st	14,088
	Waterloo-road, 2nd	18,348
	Lambeth Church, 1st	18,409
	Lambeth Church, 2nd	26,784
	Kennington, 1st	24,261
	Kennington, 2nd	18,848
	Brixton	14,610
	Norwood	3,977
32	Clapham	16,290
	Battersea	10,560
	Wandsworth	9,611
	Putney	5,280

No.	Registrars' Sub-Districts.	Population, 1851.
	Streatham	9,023
33	Dulwich	1,632
	Camberwell	17,742
	Peckham	19,444
	St. George, Camberwell	15,849
34	Rotherhithe	17,805
35	St. Paul, Deptford	24,899
	St. Nicholas, Deptford	7,071
	Greenwich, West	18,800
	Greenwich, East	16,228
	Woolwich Dockyard	17,140
	Woolwich Arsenal	15,227
36	Plumstead	13,191
	Eltham	2,568
	Lee	8,478
	Lewisham Village	6,097
	Sydenham	4,501

A MEDICAL OPINION

*Dr Conway Evans's Reports on the Strand District,
London. 1858.*[1]

'The manner in which parts of the district are crammed with people is one of the greatest of its evils which have to be mitigated. The importance of this matter was dwelt upon in my first annual report, in which it was shown that in one of the parishes of this district *at least 581 persons are packed upon every acre of its surface.** The evil consequences of this overcrowding are manifold; into a discussion of all of them the limits of this report do not permit me to enter: some of them, however, must be briefly adverted to.

'By this state of overcrowding the duration of life generally is shortened and health impaired; and these effects, though manifest when looked for, as will be presently shown, in persons of adult age, are far more readily discoverable in the case of infants and young children, to the high death-rate of which class your attention was directed on a former occasion. But it is not merely that so many of the children born in the district die at an early age—66 infants of the age of one year and under, having died out of every 10,000 persons residing in the district during the past year—but it is that very many of those children, who do not speedily fall victims to the circumstances by which they are surrounded, grow up weakly and scrofulous, and sooner or later throng the out-patient rooms of the public hospitals and dispensaries, or come under the care of the private medical practitioner, or the parochial surgeon, suffering from one or other forms of *tubercular* disease. The loss of health thus induced is in the case of adults in some respects more costly to the community at large than that resulting from *fever*, as it sooner or later involves, not a *temporary*, but a *permanent* inability to labour, until at length death steps in and relieves the public of the expense thus thrown upon it. . . .

'But the evil consequences of overcrowding are not limited to the impairment of health, or even to the destruction of life, either in the manner referred to or by favouring the occurrence and spread of disease; but by its action not only are the bodily powers prostrated and sapped, but the moral life is also degraded and debased; and ignorance, indecency, immorality, intemperance, prostitution, and crime, are directly or indirectly fostered and induced. The mode in which prostitution originates in overcrowding is but too frequently illustrated in this densely peopled district; indeed, cases occasionally come under

* St Clement Danes.

my observation in which this vice cannot but be regarded as the necessary and inevitable result of the indiscriminate manner in which the sexes are huddled together. . . .

'To this subject of overcrowding your earnest attention is solicited, for it is without doubt the most important, and at the same time the most dificult, with which you are called upon to deal; and sooner or later it must be dealt with. Houses and streets may be drained most perfectly; the district may be paved and lighted in such a manner as to excite the jealous envy of other local authorities; new thoroughfares may be constructed, and every house in the district furnished with a constant supply of pure water; the Thames may be embanked, and all entrance of sewage into that river intercepted; but so long as twenty, thirty, or even forty individuals are permitted—it might almost be said compelled—to reside in houses originally built for the accommodation of a single family or at most of two families, so long will the evils pointed out in regard of health, of ignorance, of indecency, immorality, intemperance, prostitution, and crime continue to exist unchecked. So long as no kind of privacy whatever can be obtained even by the individual members of a single family; so long as brothers and sisters, as well children as adults, are obliged to live, sleep, and perform the offices of nature in the same room with their parents, and it may be with other relatives, or possibly with strangers; and so long as the amount of air* which each person has to breathe is less than *half* or even *one-third* the quantity which nature requires: so long will the pious zeal and virtuous

---

'* In the Pentonville Prison the inmate of each cell is supplied with between 800 and 900 cubic feet of air, and means are employed for renewing this every sixteen or twenty minutes. The *minimum* amount of space in barracks allowed to each soldier by the Ordnance Rules of 1851 is 450 cubic feet. In the rooms of the crowded courts and alleys of the Strand district, the amount of breathing-space to each person frequently falls much below the Ordnance minimum. In one court, in which I caused measurements to be made of four rooms (taken without selection), the following were the results:—

	Amount of Breathing-space to each person.
Top-floor, back room, tenanted by a single family consisting of 3 persons	191 cubic feet.
First-floor, tenanted by a single family consisting of 5 persons	310 „
Second-floor, back room, tenanted by a single family consisting of 4 persons	251 „
Back-parlour, tenanted by a single family consisting of 4 persons	164 „

indignation of public declaimers against prostitution be a libellous satire upon themselves, and so long will all efforts at improving the health and elevating the social condition of the poorer classes of the district be comparatively unavailing.'

A CHARITABLE ACCOUNT

FIFTEENTH REPORT of the ASSOCIATION for Promoting the RELIEF of DESTITUTION in the METROPOLIS, and for Improving the Condition of the Poor, by means of Parochial and District Visiting, under the superintendence and direction of the Bishop and Clergy, through the agency of Unpaid Visitors, and without reference to religious persuasion. (4, St Martin's-place, Charing Cross.)—For 1859 and to July 1, 1860.

Extract from a letter of the Rev. Cornelius Hart, late of Old St Pancras Church, Camden Town.

'Our population has increased to nearly 10,000, and I regret to say that some of my private friends, who were accustomed to give their half-crowns at our annual collections at the church, have been removed from us by death; and now we have no one residing in the district but those who, out of their deep poverty, cast in their mites into the treasury. Our houses are, for the most part, let out in lodgings, and several families reside in one house.

'Our visitors have sought out and found many a deserving family reduced to the lowest extremity of want, and yet, with the good old English feeling—ashamed to beg, and considering it degrading to ask parochial relief.'

From the Rev. Theophilus Saulez, of All Saints, Islington.

'I beg to acknowledge the receipt of your letter, enclosing a cheque for 50*l.*, for which I am exceeding obliged, as the poverty of my district at this moment is most deplorable. The terrible distress occasioned by want of work, and the refusal of the parish authorities to give any out-door relief, is great; indeed, beyond the conception of English hearts. There are instances, in my district, of families having parted with every piece of furniture, and almost every rag of clothes, to enable them to pay their rent, and thus not break up the family circle by going into the workhouse. It is quite impossible for us to maintain these families, and the parish will not relieve them, and therefore their sufferings from hunger and cold are most distressing.

'All those with whom we are acquainted, whether Roman Catholics, Dissenters, or Churchmen, if in distress, we assist so far as our means will allow.'

From the Rev. W.R. Wroth, of St Philip, Clerkenwell.

'The population of the parish is 9,000, and of this number at least 5,000 are poor; the rest are far from wealthy—the greater number being clerks in offices, &c. with very limited incomes. There is no endowment for any purpose whatever; and when I mention that we have to raise in the parish (to say nothing of the support of the incumbent) the annual expenses of public worship, support of schools (a heavy rent having to be paid for school-buildings), Mother and Infant Society, Provident Fund, Clothing Club, and other charitable purposes, the Committee will readily understand how valuable is their grant, and how much our means of usefulness would be diminished by its withdrawal.'

From the Rev. W. Hinson, of St Mark, Old-street.

'I sincerely thank you for the cheque for 50*l.* which your Committee was good enough to vote towards the funds of the District Visiting Society of my parish. It has come in most opportunely, for I grieve to say that I hear of fresh cases of great poverty daily. This wretched strike among the builders and carpenters has brought much distress into many families. I find its influence *everywhere*. And what should I do without such assistance as that so cheerfully afforded by your excellent society? In fact, had I not bread to give, I might remain at home; for it would, indeed, be a mockery to speak of spiritual things, unless the hand were first of all stretched out to relieve the fainting body.'

From the Rev. C.M. Christie, of St Simon, Bethnal-green.

'I am much obliged to the Metropolitan Society for the help afforded me, and have now to ask the favour of a special grant for the two under-mentioned purposes (for the relief of lying-in women, and to supply needlework to poor women attending a Mothers' Meeting, held weekly in the district). I have no means of procuring money on the spot—a sermon only produces about twenty-five shillings, and my congregation cannot even pay the current expenses of the church. All the ordinary grants allowed me are required almost *to save life*. One death is reported from starvation, and of one who would not complain; and there are now several women, known to me, recently confined, and without the necessary food.'

From the Rev. T.J. Rowsell, of St Peter, Stepney.

'This season has been a trying one to our poor. We have been much called upon, and obliged to work very hard. In the first place, the results of the strike were felt; for as soon as the cold weather came, we found that the women and children were thinly and poorly clad, and they had saved nothing. Also we have had a large amount of sickness, and more deaths than I have witnesssed for many years. But amidst all this distress and woe, our visitors have done good and Christian work; and I may say, that the troubles of our poor have been cheered and hallowed to them, and to ourselves, by the mercy and help conveyed, and the happiness derived, from the sacred interchange of kindness and gratitude. If these poor districts were left unassisted, there would be a frightful amount of suffering.'

The above letters are corroborated by many others of similar import received from the parochial clergy during the past year (1859); and they help to show that the metropolitan distress of 1860-61 was not so very 'exceptional'.

I give the schedule of grants of this association, not because the amount it distributes is very large, compared with the whole charities of London, but because the details of distribution show the wide extent of ragged London.

A. No. 1.—Schedule of Grants to Visiting Societies.—1859.

Names of Parishes and Districts.	No. of Grants.	Amount Granted.	
		£	£
St. Andrew, Holborn:—			
St. Peter, Saffron-hill	1	40	
Trinity, Gray's-inn-road	3	100	
			140
Aldgate, St. Botolph	2	...	60
Bethnal Green:—			
St. Matthew	1	30	
St. Bartholomew	2	55	
St. James the Less	2	50	
St. Jude	2	60	
St. Matthias	4	110	
St. Peter	1	20	
St. Philip	3	80	
St. Simon	3	70	
St. Thomas	1	25	
St. John	3	70	
St. Andrew	3	65	
			635
S. Bartholomew the Great, Smithfield	1	...	20
Chelsea:—			
Old Church	1	20	
St. Luke	1	40	
Chelsea Upper, St. Jude	1	20	
			80
Clerkenwell:—			
St. James	2	60	
St. John	2	60	
St. Mark	1	20	
St. Philip	1	40	
			180
St. George's-in-the-East:—			
Christ Church	2	70	
St. Matthew	1	25	
			95
Islington, All Saints	2	...	75
St. Philip	1	...	20
Isle of Dogs, Christ Church	1	...	30
Kensal Green, St. John	1	...	15
Carried forward	...	...	1,350

Names of Parishes and Districts.	No. of Grants.	Amount Granted.	
		£	£
Brought forward . .	...	...	1,350
Limehouse:—			
St. Anne	1	25	
St. John	2	60	
			85
St. Luke, Old-street:—			
St. Mark, Old-street-road .	2	60	
St. Barnabas, Goswell-street .	1	30	
			90
Marylebone:—			
St. Paul, Lisson-grove . .	2	...	50
Moorfields, St. Bartholomew's .	1	...	20
Newington:—			
St. Mary	2	65	
Trinity	2	70	
St. Peter, Walworth . .	1	50	
			185
Pentonville, St. James . .	2	...	40
St. Pancras:—			
Somers' Town District . .	1	30	
St. Jude	2	60	
Old Church District . .	1	40	
St. Bartholomew, Gray's-inn-road . . .	1	30	
Trinity District . . .	1	30	
St. John, Charlotte-street .	2	60	
Fitzroy Chapel . . .	1	20	
St. James District . .	1	30	
St. Thomas, Agar Town .	1	30	
			330
Ratcliff Cross, St. James . .	2	...	70
Shadwell, St. Paul . . .	1	...	40
Shoreditch:—			
St. John, Hoxton . . .	2	80	
St. Mary, Haggerstone . .	2	60	
All Saints, Kingsland . .	2	45	
St. James, Curtain-road .	1	50	
St. Stephen, Old Ford . .	1	20	
			255
Soho, St. Anne	1	...	40
Carried forward . .	...	...	2,555

Names of Parishes and Districts.	No. of Grants.	Amount Granted.	
		£	£
Brought forward . .	...	...	2,555
Stepney:—			
St. Dunstan	1	40	
St. Peter	2	65	
St. Thomas	1	25	
Trinity	1	25	
			155
Spitalfields, St. Mary . . .	1	...	25
Westminster, St. John . .	1	...	60
Whitechapel:—			
St. Mary	2	100	
St. Jude	3	70	
			170
Total . .	...	...	2,965

A. No. 2.—Schedule of Grants to Visiting Societies, from the 31st December, 1859, to 30th June, 1860.

Names of Parishes and Districts.	No. of Grants.	Amount Granted.	
		£	£
St. Andrew, Holborn :—			
St. Peter, Saffron-hill . .	1	30	
Trinity, Gray's-inn-road .	3	85	
			115
Aldgate, St. Botolph . . .	1	...	20
Bethnal Green:—			
St. Bartholomew . . .	2	70	
St. James the Less . .	1	30	
St. Jude	1	40	
St. Matthias . . .	1	50	
St. Peter	2	50	
St. Philip	1	30	
St. Simon	2	75	
St. John	1	30	
St. Andrew	1	20	
			395
Carried forward . .	...	...	530

Names of Parishes and Districts.	No. of Grants.	Amount Granted.	
		£	£
Brought forward . .	...	...	530
S. Bartholomew the Great, Smithfield	1	...	25
Bloomsbury, St. George . .	1	...	40
Chelsea:—			
Old Church	1	20	
St. Luke	1	40	
Chelsea, Upper, St. Jude .	1	20	
			80
Clerkenwell:—			
St. James	2	90	
St. John	2	40	
St. Mark	1	20	
St. Philip	—	—	
			150
St. George's-in-the-East:—			
Christ Church . . .	2	...	75
Islington, All Saints . . .	2	...	50
Kensal Green, St. John . .	1	...	15
Limehouse:—			
St. Anne	1	30	
St. John	2	70	
			100
St. Luke, Old-street:—			
St. Mark, Old-street-road .	1	35	
St. Thomas, Charterhouse .	2	60	
			95
Newington:—			
St. Mary	1	35	
Trinity	1	30	
			65
Pentonville, St. James . . .	2	...	45
St. Pancras:—			
Somers' Town District .	1	30	
Old Church District . .	1	40	
St. Bartholomew, Gray's-inn-rd.	1	40	
St. John, Charlotte-street .	1	30	
Fitzroy Chapel . . .	—	—	
St. Luke	2	50	
St. Thomas, Agar-town .	1	20	
			210
Shadwell, St. Paul . . .	1	...	50
Carried forward . .	...	...	1,530

Names of Parishes and Districts.	No. of Grants.	Amount Granted.	
		£	£
Brought forward . .	...	...	1,530
Shoreditch:—			
St. John, Hoxton . . .	1	50	
St. Mary, Haggerstone . .	2	50	
St. Andrew, Kingsland . .	1	40	
St. James, Curtain-road .	1	50	
St. Paul, Bow-common .	1	10	
St. Stephen, Old Ford . .	1	20	
			220
Stepney:—			
St. Dunstan . .	2	70	
St. Peter	1	50	
St. Thomas	1	25	
Trinity	1	30	
			175
Spitalfields, St. Mary . .	1	...	25
Strand, St. Clement Danes .	1	...	50
Westminster, St. John .	1	...	60
Whitechapel:—			
St. Mary . . .	2	75	
St. Jude	1	30	
St. Mark	1	40	
			145
Total . .	...	...	2,205

B.—Schedule of Grants to Provident Societies.
1859.

	No. of Depositors.	Amnt. Deposited.	Grants for Prem.
		£	£ s.
To the Rev. J. M. Andrews, of St. Jude, St. Pancras	947	639	16 0
„ Rev. T. R. Redwar, of St. Thomas, Liberty of Rolls	179	127	3 4
„ Rev. W. Kerry, of St. Thomas, Bethnal Gr.	794	433	10 17
„ Rev. F. Statham, of St. Peter, Walworth	2,383	752	18 16
„ Rev. D. A. Moullin, of Trinity, Newington	1,383	772	19 6
„ Rev. J. T. Smith, of St. Mary, Newington	2,058	672	'16 16
„ Rev. C. Hart, of Old Church, St. Pancras	654	398	9 19
„ J. S. Altmann, of St. Andrew, Islington	1,008	407	10 4
„ Rev. R. Maguire, of St. James, Clerkenwell	2,052	654	16 7
„ Rev. E. Garbett, of St. Bartholomew, Gray's Inn	325	215	5 8
„ Rev. J. Jennings, of St. John, Westminster	5,090	2,548	63 14
„ Rev. E. R. Jones, of St. Anne, Limehouse	1,836	613	15 7
„ Rev. T. Bazeley, of All Saints, Poplar	1,623	348	8 14
„ Rev. W. Scott, of Christ Church, Hoxton	838	331	8 6
„ Rev. E. Spooner, of Trinity, St. Pancras	1,274	891	22 5
„ Rev. N. Wade, of St. Anne, Soho	394	194	4 17
„ Rev. T. Saulez, of All Saints, Islington	1,055	665	16 13
„ Rev. H. Hutton, of St. Paul, Covent-garden	395	316	7 18
„ Rev. J. Keeling, of St. Paul, Lisson-grove	700	311	7 16
„ Rev. Dr. Courtenay, of St. James, Pentonville	202	67	1 14
„ Rev. T. J. Rowsell, of St. Peter, Stepney	1,315	1,281	32 1
„ Rev. T. J. Rowsell, of the School Church, Stepney	859	503	12 12
„ Rev. W. Valentine, of St. Thomas, Stepney	223	129	3 5
„ Rev. W. Gill, of St. John, Charlotte-street	320	178	4 9
„ Rev. F. H. Vivian, of St. Bartholomew, Bethnal Green	..	335	8 8
„ Rev. R. Lee, of St. Dunstan, Stepney	475	285	7 3
„ Rev. Dr. Spencer, of St. Matthew, Marylebone	111	101	2 11
„ Rev. J. E. Keane, of St. Jude, Bethnal Gr.	870	220	5 10
„ Rev. C. M. Christie, of St. Simon, Bethnal Green	288	87	2 4
„ Rev. J. Saunders, of St. Luke, Old-street	2,000	876	21 18
„ Rev. J. Chambers, of St. Mary, Soho	139	86	2 3
„ Rev. C. H. Carr, of St. John, Limehouse	460	180	4 10
„ Rev. W. J. Grundy, of St. James the Less, Bethnal Green	73	29	0 15
„ Rev. J. Tagg, of St. John, Bethnal Green	454	162	4 1
„ Rev. W. J. Finch, of St. Peter, Hackney	176	52	1 6
„ Rev. J. G. Maul, of St. John, Drury-lane	274	176	4 8
„ Rev. H. Ward, of St. Barnabas, King's-sqr.	389	56	1 8
„ Rev. A. Myers, of All Saints, Kingsland	471	167	4 4
	34,087	16,256	406 17

MODEL LODGING-HOUSE ACCONTS. [sic]

Report (July 31st, 1860) of the Society for Improving
the Condition of the Labouring Classes.

Hatton-garden: Single Men.—In the tabular statement appended to
the report, it appears that the sum of 308*l*.10*s*. has been received at the
Hatton-garden Chambers, for the year ending the 31st December, 1859,
and deducting therefrom 271*l*. 6*s*. 4*d*. for expenses, there remains a
profit of 37*l*. 3*s*. 8*d*. There has been one death, out of an average
population of 182.

Charles-street: Single Men.—The sum of 398*l*. 15*s*. 2*d*. has been
received at Charles-street Men's Lodging-house, Drury-lane, and the
expenses have been 264*l*. 11*s*. 10*d*., leaving a profit of 134*l*. 3*s*. 4*d*.
There has been no death in these buildings, out of an average
population of 80.

King-street: Single Men.—The sum of 79*l*. 4*s*. 4*d*. has been received
at King-street Men's Lodging-house, Drury-lane, and the expenses have
been 93*l*. 8*s*. 8*d*., leaving a deficiency of 14*l*. 4*s*. 4*d*. There has been no
death in these houses out of an average population of 21.

George-street: Single Men.—The sum of 626*l*. has been received at
George-street Men's Lodging-house, St Giles', and the expenses have
been 371*l*. 8*s*. 3*d*., leaving a profit of 254*l*. 11*s*. 9*d*. There has been no
death in these buildings, out of an average population of 98.

Portpool-lane: Dwellings.—The sum of 444*l*. 8*s*. has been received
from the tenants of the Thanksgiving Model Buildings, Portpool-lane,
Gray's-inn-lane, and deducting therefrom 306*l*. 16*s*. 7*d*. for expenses,
there remains a profit of 137*l*. 11*s*. 5*d*. In the family houses there has
been no death; average population 78. In the single women's rooms
there have been three deaths (all above 60 years); average number of
inmates, 52.

The Laundry, Portpool-lane.—From the wash-house and laundry
adjoining the Model Buildings, Portpool-lane, the receipts have been
394*l*. 2*s*. 1*d*., and the expenses 516*l*. 2*s*. 4½*d*., leaving a deficiency of
122*l*. 0*s*. 3½*d*. This deficit is caused by extensive alterations and
repairs.

Streatham-street: Family Dwellings.—The sum of 735*l*. 15*s*. has been received from the dwellings for families in Streatham-street, Blooms-bury; the expenses have been 350*l*. 17*s*., leaving a profit of 384*l*. 18*s*. There have been five deaths out of an average population of 221: these were all of children under ten years of age.

Wild-court: Family houses.—The sum of 598*l*. 14*s*. 3*d*. has been received from the renovated dwellings at Wild-court, Drury-lane, and the expenses have been 507*l*. 12*s*. 8*d*., leaving a profit of 91*l*. 1*s*. 7*d*. There have been nine deaths in these houses, out of an average population of 340, six of which were of children under ten years of age.

Tyndall's-buildings: Family Dwellings.—The sum of 515*l*. 18*s*. has been received from the tenants of Tyndall's-buildings, Gray's-inn-lane: the expenses have been 580*l*. 3*s*. 10*d*.; leaving a deficiency of 64*l*. 5*s*. 10*d*. The expenses of this year include a considerable sum paid for furniture, bedding, &c., which is due to capital account. There have been ten deaths in the family dwellings and single men's lodging-house; with an average population of 294, six of which were of children under ten years.

Clark's-buildings: Family Houses.—The sum of 504*l*. 17*s*. has been received from the tenants at Clark's-buildings, Broad-street, Blooms-bury: the expenses have been 439*l*. 12*s*. 7½*d*., leaving a profit of 65*l*. 4*s*. 4½*d*. There have been two deaths in these buildings (both above eighty years of age), out of an average population of 220. The mortality in the entire property of the society has this year been 30, out of an average population of 1,585, being less than at the rate of 20 per 1,000. Seventeen of the deaths were of children under ten years of age; seven of persons above sixty. Several adults, and the greater number of the children, died from epidemic diseases.

SOCIETY for IMPROVING the CONDITION of the LABOURING CLASSES.
BALANCE SHEET, Dec. 31, 1859.

Dr.

	£ s. d.	£ s. d.
To Sundry Creditors	788 9 0	
Rent and Salaries	357 0 0	
Interest due to date	342 5 11	1,487 14 11
To Loans advanced to the Society, viz.:— _Per ct._		
Thos. Twining, Esq., at 4½	420 0 0	
Miss E. Sperling ... at 4½	5,000 0 0	
Ditto ... at 5	1,500 0 0	
Miss F. A. Marris ... at 4½	700 0 0	
John Sperling, Esq., ... at 4	500 0 0	
Ditto ... at 5	1,500 0 0	
Miss Jacob ... at 4	800 0 0	
Miss Unwin ... at 3½	400 0 0	
F. Pitman, Esq. ... at 4	250 0 0	
Colonel Fenning ... at 5	200 0 0	
Mrs. Somes ... at 4	100 0 0	
Edmund Jeffrey, Esq. at 4	688 0 0	
John Bridges, Esq. ... at 5	1,000 0 0	
H. Holland, Esq. J. G. Hildyard, Esq. } at 5	1,000 0 0	
G. Arbuthnot, Esq. ... at 4	500 0 0	14,558 0 0
To Surplus:— Being excess of Assets, taken at Cost, over Liabilities.		20,447 7 8
Total		**36,493 2 7**

Cr.

	£ s. d.	£ s. d.
By Cash at Bankers and in hand		275 6 0½
By Cash at Bankers, the gift of Miss Turner, to be laid out in the erection of Model Lodging-houses in Hull, inclusive of Interest accrued		5,225 0 0
By Stock on hand		137 0 0
By arrears of Rent ... 89 12 5		
Deduct bad ... 57 14 5		31 18 0
By Properties, taken at Cost, viz.:—		
George-street, Men's Lodging-house		
Streatham-street, ditto	8,916 15 11	
Deduct Amount advanced by Mr. Bull on mortgage at 5 per cent.	3,500 0 0	6,426 14 2
Thanksgiving Model Buildings	12,315 17 11	
Deduct Amount advanced by Colonel Passy, on Mortgage at 4 per cent.	4,500 0 0	5,416 15 11
Charles-street Model Lodging-house		7,815 17 11
Hatton-garden, ditto		1,163 14 2
King-street, ditto		1,077 14 7
Laundry, Portpool-lane		135 0 0
Wild-court Lodging-houses		811 11 3
Clark's-buildings, ditto		3,364 19 1
Tyndall-buildings, ditto		1,161 10 5½
Freehold Property, Tunbridge Wells		2,699 11 0
Deduct Amount advanced by Mrs. Turner, on Mortgage at 5 per cent. 1,100 0 0		
Ditto, Rev. W. J. M. Ruxton, at 5 per cent. 850 0 0		
Ditto, J. Sperling, Esq., at 5 cent. 800 0 0	3,500 10 0	750 0 0
Total	2,750 0 0	**36,493 2 7**

We have examined these Accounts with the Books and Vouchers, and find them correct,

QUILTER, BALL, JAY AND CO.

February 4, 1860.

Dr.   ABSTRACT of CASH ACCOUNT from December 1858 to December 1859.   **Cr.**

Dr.	£	s.	d.	£	s.	d.
To Balance on the 31st Dec., 1858:						
At Bankers'	90	4	5			
Bill of Exchange	65	8	7			
Cash in hand	15	0	8¼			
Ditto for Wages	6	6	0			
Loans				176	19	8¼
Income-tax on Interest				700	0	0
Rents received from,—				32	2	11
Hatton-garden	308	10	0			
Charles-street	398	15	2			
King-street	79	4	4			
George-street	626	0	0			
Portpool-lane	444	8	0			
Ditto, Laundry	394	2	1			
Streatham-street	735	15	0			
Wild-court	598	14	3			
Tyndall's-buildings	515	18	0			
Clark's-buildings	504	17	0			
Legacies				4,606	3	10
General Donations				1,129	8	0
Annual Subscriptions				512	5	6
Sale of Publications				34	11	7¾
Gift from Miss Turner, to be laid out in the erection of Model Lodging-houses in Hull	5,000	0	0			
Interest on ditto	250	0	0			
				5,250	0	0
Total				12,868	4	1

Cr.	£	s.	d.	£	s.	d.
By Loans repaid				1,400	0	0
Interest on Loans				1,067	4	1
Current Expenses of,—						
Hatton-garden, Men's Lodging-house	271	6	4			
Charles-street, ditto	264	11	10			
King-street, ditto	93	8	8			
George-street, ditto	371	8	3			
Portpool-lane Family and Single Women	306	16	7			
Portpool lane Laundry	516	2	4½			
Streatham-st. Family Houses	350	17	0			
Wild-court, ditto	507	12	8			
Tyndall's-buildings, Family and Men's	580	3	10½			
Clark's-buildings, Family	439	12	7½			
				3,702	0	2
Printing, Stationery, Salaries, Advertisements and Office Expenses				1,054	4	11½
Allotments for Balance of Amount paid in respect thereof				89	14	4
Collector's Poundage				29	14	6
Preliminary Expenses at Hull				25	0	0
Balance at Messrs. Williams, Deacon and Co., Hull Improvement Fund				5,225	0	0
Balance at Bankers				273	17	5
Cash in hand				1	8	7½
Total				12,868	4	1

We have examined these Accounts with the Books and Vouchers, and find them correct,

QUILTER, BALL, JAY, AND CO.

February 4, 1860.

TABULAR STATEMENT, showing the Rates, Taxes, Repairs, and other Expenses of each Establishment for the Year ending December 31, 1859.

Payments.	Hatton Garden £	s.	d.	Charles Street £	s.	d.	King Street £	s.	d.	George Street £	s.	d.	Portpool Lane Dwellings £	s.	d.	Portpool Lane Laundry £	s.	d.
Rent	82	6	4	43	6	4	14	4	0									
Poor and Police Rates	12	13	4	7	17	6	1	16	0	16	17	6	37	10	6	17	4	0
General Rate	4	13	4	3	10	0	0	16	0	7	10	0	15	3	6	8	3	8
Sewers Rate	0	0	0	0	11	8	0	2	8	1	5	0	2	0	8	1	8	8
Metropolitan Rate	0	16	8	1	3	4	0	5	4	2	10	0	3	6	0	2	8	0
House Duty	3	15	0	2	12	6				8	8	9	7	0	0	1	5	0
Land Tax				4	5	0	1	2	8	12	15	0				3	4	9
Property and Income Tax	2	1	8	1	9	2	0	6	8	10	6	9	19	6	9	2	4	9
Ground Rent													7	3	9			
Tithe	1	0	0										0	18	0			
Water	3	12	0	6	15	6	2	3	6	9	2	0	15	0	0	45	0	0
Soap, soda, and cleaning materials	32	18	0	4	9	0	2	10	3	4	6	8	3	5	0	21	3	3
Coal, coke, and wood	17	16	5	29	15	0	12	16	3	33	16	0	33	16	8	108	5	10
Gas	1	13	9	19	16	0	13	7	6	50	10	0	22	4	8	67	13	10
Insurance	65	0	0	3	10	0							11	16	0			
Superintendants' and servants' salaries	20	16	1	67	12	0	20	16	0	123	10	0	19	18	0	143	0	0
Washing lodging-house linen	2	5	5	26	0	0	7	7	7	30	6	0				36	8	0
Sundries	5	2	5	9	16	2	7	9	5	10	0	11	9	19	0	13	15	8
House furniture, linen, &c.	4	10	0	14	1	2	6	17	10	27	16	5	60	10	0			
Materials for repairs	5	18	4	6	5	0	2	7	0	9	0	0	20	3	4	9	8	5
Labourers' wages				11	17	0	3	0	0	13	7	3	17	16	11	35	13	10½
Total charges	271	6	4	264	11	10	93	8	8	371	8	3	306	16	7	516	2	4½
Net rents, balance of {Profit / Loss	37	3	8	134	3	4	14	4	4	254	11	9	137	11	5	122	0	3¼
Gross rents	308	10	0	398	15	2	79	4	4	626	0	0	444	8	0	394	2	1
Cost	1,077	14	7	1,163	14	2	135	0	0	6,426	14	2	12,315	17	11	811	11	3

TABULAR STATEMENT—*continued.*

Payments.	Streatham Street. £ s. d.	Wild Court. £ s. d.	Tyndall's Buildings. £ s. d.	Clark's Buildings. £ s. d.	£ s. d.	Total. £ s. d.
Rent	…	238 10 10	231 6 8	271 4 8	…	880 18 10
Poor and Police Rates	56 5 0	28 7 0	34 18 0	30 18 9	…	244 7 7
General Rate	25 3 0	12 12 0	9 18 8	7 10 0	…	94 17 2
Sewers Rate	4 3 4	2 2 0	2 0 8	1 5 0	…	15 4 4
Metropolitan Rate	8 6 8	4 4 0	3 11 2	4 12 0	…	31 4 6
House Duty	…	5 6 6	1 16 0	14 17 0	…	45 4 9
Land Tax	26 11 3	11 15 2	…	4 10 8	…	83 9 9
Property and Income Tax	9 13 9	5 16 0	6 5 0	15 5 3	…	60 11 9
Ground Rent	72 12 11	…	…	…	…	72 12 11
Tithe	…	…	…	…	…	1 18 0
Water	20 0 0	21 18 0	13 6 0	25 0 7	…	161 16 6
Soap, soda, and cleaning materials	3 3 0	2 12 0	2 7 0	1 3 0	…	48 17 9
Coal, coke, and wood	18 2 11½	10 11 9	25 2 6	1 2 6	…	306 5 11½
Gas	15 10 9	18 11 0	17 19 3	12 7 0	…	245 1 11
Insurance	4 19 0	5 8 6	78 0 0	13 0 0	…	39 14 9
Superintendants' and servants' salaries	31 4 0	31 4 0	7 6 0	…	…	593 14 0
Washing lodging-house linen	…	…	8 19 10	5 10 6	…	128 3 7
Sundries	12 5 8½	9 0 4	77 10 5	7 13 4½	…	85 2 7½
House furniture, linen, &c.	7 12 3	23 13 4	27 3 9	10 6 0	…	230 17 2½
Materials for repairs	12 3 0	30 0 0	32 12 11	11 19 0	…	131 0 6
Labourers' Wages	23 4 3	46 0 3	…	…	…	201 10 7½
Total charges	350 17 0	507 12 8	580 3 10	439 12 7½	…	3,702 0 2
Net rents, balance of { Profit / Loss	384 18 0	91 1 7	64 5 10	65 4 4½	104 14 11½ / 200 10 5½	904 3 8
Gross Rents	735 15 0	598 14 3	515 18 0	504 17 0	…	4,606 3 10
Cost	8,916 15 11	3,364 19 11	2,699 11 0	1,161 10 5	…	38,073 8 6

We have examined these Accounts with the Books and Vouchers, and find them correct.

QUILTER, BALL, JAY and CO.

February 4, 1860.

MONTHLY REPORT OF THE SOCIETY'S ESTABLISHMENTS.

December 31, 1860.

Buildings.	Description.	Amount of Accommodation.	Average Number of Occupants.
Hatton-garden . . .	Single men's lodging-house .	54 beds . .	49 persons.
Charles-street, Drury-lane .	„ „ „ .	82 „ . .	77 „
King-street, Drury-lane .	„ „ „ .	22 „ . .	18 „
George-street, St. Giles' .	„ „ „ .	104 „ . .	97 „
Portpool-lane, Gray's-inn-lane .	Family houses . .	20 houses . .	18 families.
„ „ Streatham-street, Bloomsbury .	Single women's rooms .	64 rooms . .	55 persons.
„ „ Wild-court, Drury-lane .	Family houses . .	54 houses . .	54 families.
Tyndall's-buildings, Gray's-inn-lane .	Rooms for families . .	106 rooms . .	102 „
„ „ „ .	Single men's lodging-house .	87 „ . .	66 „
Clark's-buildings, Bloomsbury .	Rooms for families . .	40 beds . .	35 persons.
		82 rooms . .	78 families.

The number of washers at the public washhouse, Portpool-lane, has been 2,632, and the amount received 50*l*. 17*s*. 1*d*.

The SIXTEENTH REPORT (abridged) of the DIRECTORS of the METROPOLI-TAN ASSOCIATION for Improving the DWELLINGS of the INDUSTRIOUS CLASSES, presented to the Shareholders at the Annual Meeting held on the 22nd day of June, 1860.

FAMILY DWELLINGS.

Albert-street.—In the statement No. 4 it appears that the sum of 801*l*. 0*s*. 4*d*. has been received from the dwellings for families in Albert-street, Mile-end New Town, during the year ending the 31st March, 1860, and deducting therefrom 374*l*. 10*s*. 3*d*. for expenses, there remains a profit of 426*l*. 10*s*. 1*d*. There have been seven deaths out of an average population of 285; two of the deaths were of children under ten years of age.

Albert Cottages.—The sum of 466*l*. 1*s*. has been received from the tenants of the Albert Cottages, Pelham-street, Mile-end New Town, and the expenses have been 165*l*. 10*s*. 5*d*., leaving a profit of 300*l*. 10*s*. 7*d*. There have been two deaths, both of which were of children under ten years of age, out of an average population of 110.

Albion-buildings.—The sum of 259*l*. 16*s*. has been received from the tenants in Albion-buildings, Bartholomew-close, and the expenses have been 101*l*. 18*s*. 8*d*., leaving a profit of 157*l*. 17*s*. 4*d*. There have been three deaths in these buildings, all of which were of children under ten years of age, out of an average population of 93.

Ingestre-buildings.—The sum of 1,145*l*. 6*s*. 7*d*. has been received from the tenants in Ingestre-buildings, New-Street, Golden-square, and, deducting therefrom the sum of 762*l*. 13*s*. 10*d*. for expenses, there remains a profit of 382*l*. 12*s*. 9*d*. Out of an average population of 342 at these buildings, there have been six deaths, four of which were of children under ten years of age.

Nelson-square.—The sum of 1,357*l*. 6*s*. 3*d*. has been received from the tenants in Nelson-square, Snows-fields, Bermondsey, and deducting therefrom 578*l*. 8*s*. 8*d*. for expenses, there remains a profit of 778*l*. 17*s*. 7*d*. There have been fifteen deaths in these dwellings, out of an average population of 505; eleven of which deaths were of children under ten years of age.

Pancras-square.—The sum of 1,388*l*. 4*s*. 4*d*. has been received from the tenants in Pancras-square, Old Pancras-road, and the expenses have been 747*l*. 8*s*. 4*d*.; leaving a profit of 640*l*. 16*s*. There have been eleven deaths in these buildings, out of an average population of 487; five were of children under ten years of age. It will be seen that there is an increase of upwards of 200*l*. in the receipts from these buildings during last year.

Pleasant-row.—The sum of 183*l*. 1*s*. 6*d*. has been received from the tenants in Pleasant-row, Mile-end New Town, and the expenses have been 86*l*. 3*s*. 2*d*.; leaving a profit of 96*l*. 18*s*. 4*d*. There has been no death in these buildings, out of an average population of 55.

Queen's-place.—The sum of 93*l*. 9*s*. has been received in respect of the property in Queen's-place, Dockhead; and the expenses have been 101*l*. 7*s*. 2*d*.; leaving a deficiency of 7*l*. 18*s*. 2*d*. There has been no death in these buildings, out of an average population of 51.

DWELLINGS FOR SINGLE MEN

Metropolitan Chambers.—The sum of 1,152*l*. 3*s*. has been received at the Metropolitan Chambers, Albert-street, Mile-end New Town, and the expenses have been 990*l*. 8*s*. 6*d*.; leaving a surplus of 161*l*. 14*s*. 6*d*. There has been one death at these chambers, out of an average population of 171.

Soho Chambers.—The sum of 701*l*. 10*s*. 6*d*. has been received at the Soho Chambers, 36, Old Compton-street, and the expenses have been 841*l*. 10*s*. 1*d*.; leaving a deficiency of 139*l*. 19*s*. 7*d*. There has been no death at these chambers, out of an average population of 77. As suggested at the last annual meeting, the sinking-fund for these chambers has been increased, with a view to terminating the lease at the first opportunity, viz. in March, 1870.

Mortality.—The mortality in the entire property of the Association has this year been 45, out of an average population of 2,186, being at the rate of 21 per 1,000; 27 of the deaths were of children under ten years of age.

The balance of the profits of the year ending 31st March, 1859, after providing for the dividend then declared, and carrying, as then suggested, 82*l*. additional to the sinking-fund account of the Soho Chambers, for the year ending 31st March, 1859, and also deducting 6*l*. for a sinking-fund for Queen's-place, has been carried to the guarantee-fund account, increasing that fund to 1,151*l*. 15*s*. 7*d*.

Dividend.—The profits for this year, notwithstanding the heavy repairs, amounting to 396*l*. 5*s*. 10*d*. more than those of last year, and, after deducting the sum of 100*l*. carried to the sinking-fund account of the Soho Chambers for the year ending 31st March, 1860, amount to the sum of 2,146*l*. 1*s*. 1*d*. The directors, therefore, recommend that a dividend of 2*l*. per cent., clear of income-tax, should be declared; which, when deducted from the net profit, 2,146*l*. 1*s*. 1*d*., will leave a balance of about 330*l*. to be carried to the guarantee fund.

No. 1.—Share Account, March 31, 1860.

—	Amount Received.			Unpaid thereon.			Total.		
	£	s.	d.	£	s.	d.	£	s.	d.
Metropolitan Shares	90,647	10	0	652	10	0	91,300	0	0
Ramsgate District Branch Shares .	1,675	0	0	...			1,675	0	0
Torquay District Branch Shares .	1,957	0	6	617	19	6	2,575	0	0
Bristol District Branch Shares .	5,835	0	0	40	0	0	5,875	0	0
Total . .	100,114	10	6	1,310	9	6	101,425	0	0

Examined the annexed account, and find the same correct,

> T. Baker,
> Edward Vansittart Neale, } *Auditors.*

No. 2.—CAPITAL ACCOUNT, March 31, 1860.

DR.

	£	s.	d.	Increase since last Report. £	s.	d.
To Amount received on Shares	90,647	10	0	600	0	0
Ramsgate District Branch	18	8	2			
Sinking Fund to redeem Pancras Square Leasehold	496	14	0	48	9	0
Ditto, Soho Chambers Leasehold	349	7	0	189	5	2
Ditto, Ingestre-buildings ditto	109	19	5	19	14	2
Ditto, Queen's-place ditto	8	0	0	8	0	0
Unclaimed Dividends	382	18	11	36	11	9
Guarantee Fund	1,151	15	7	373	17	10
Donations (to be returned when Donors found)	12	2	0			
Profit, as per Revenue Account	2,146	1	1			
Total	**95,322**	**16**	**4**			

CR.

	£	s.	d.	Increase since last Report. £	s.	d.
By Preliminary Expenses	3,233	16	7			
Albert-street Family Dwellings	11,365	11	8	954	19	11
Ditto Cottages	6,371	4	1			
Albion-buildings	2,381	1	3			
Ingestre-buildings	9,852	6	3			
Nelson-square	23,051	18	2			
Pancras-square	18,306	1	3			
Pleasant-row	2,979	9	4			
Queen's-place	111	8	2	55	0	0
Albert-street Chambers	13,772	7	3			
Soho Chambers	1,422	7	7			
Investment in New 3 per Cents.	732	7	4			
Cash in hands of Messrs. Barclay, Bevan and Co.	1,724	18	7	148	18	3
Cash—Balance	17	19	0			
Total	**95,322**	**16**	**4**			

Examined the annexed Account, and find the same correct.

T. BAKER,
EDWARD VANSITTART NEALE, } *Auditors.*

No. 3.—REVENUE ACCOUNT, March 31, 1860.

Dr.

	£	s.	d.
To Dividend of 2 per cent. on 90,047l. 10s .	1,800	19	0
Amount carried to Soho Chambers Sinking Fund Account .	82	0	0
Ditto Queen's-place ditto .	6	0	0
Balance carried to Guarantee Fund .	373	17	10
	2,262	**16**	**10**
Advertising .	8	13	0
Printing .	19	0	6
Rent of Offices, Coals, Gas, Cleaning, &c. .	120	0	0
Auditors .	10	10	0
Salaries .	420	11	4
Petty Cash .	36	5	8
Interest on Sinking Fund .	23	8	4
Loss by Soho Chambers .	139	19	7
Amount further to Soho Chambers Sinking Fund .	82	0	0
Loss by Queen's-place .	7	18	2
Balance .	2,146	1	1
	3,014	**7**	**8**

Cr.

	£	s.	d.	£	s.	d.
By Divisible Balance, March, 1859 .	2,262	16	10	2,262	16	10
Balance of Rents :—						
Albert-st. Family Dwellings	426	10	1			
Albert Cottages .	300	10	7			
Albion-buildings .	157	17	4			
Ingestre-buildings .	392	12	9			
Nelson-square .	778	17	7			
Pancras-square .	640	16	0			
Pleasant-row .	96	18	4			
Albert-street Chambers .	161	14	6			
Fees on Transfer of Shares .	1	10	0			
Interest on Investment in New 3 per Cents. .	21	3	0			
Bristol Branch, per Centage .	20	0	0			
Brighton do., balance ditto .	10	0	0			
Ramsgate do., ditto .	8	7	6			
Torquay do., ditto .	7	10	0			
				3,014	**7**	**8**

Examined the annexed Account, and find the same correct.

T. BAKER,   } Auditors.
EDWARD VANSITTART NEALE,

No. 4.—TABULAR STATEMENT, showing the Rates, Taxes, Repairs, and other Expenses of each Establishment, for the Year ending March 31, 1860.

(Values given as £ s. d.)

	Albert Street, 60 Families	Albert Cottages, 33 Families	Albion Buildings, 24 Families	Ingestre Buildings, 60 Families	Nelson Square, 108 Families	Pancras Square, 110 Families
Rent			18 14 2	288 15 0		89 13 2
Poor and Police Rate	54 13 4	31 10 8		80 12 6	104 13 0	108 2 0
Lighting Rate					11 16 7	22 0 0
House Duty	13 2 6					37 10 0
Land Tax						
Property Tax	15 2 1	8 17 6	5 12 6	26 15 6	23 18 6	37 10 0
Sewers and Main Drainage	10 5 0	5 18 4	3 2 6	19 9 3	29 18 0	28 0 0
General Rate	44 8 4	25 12 6		26 15 6	28 13 1	58 0 0
Church Rate			2 13 4	15 9 0	3 14 9	
Consolidated Rate			5 16 8	32 18 6		
Ward Rate			0 8 4			
Repairs of building	93 5 0	39 5 7	27 11 1	89 0 5	190 3 3	129 9 5
Repairs of house linen, utensils, &c.				17 0 0		35 0 0
Sinking fund to redeem leaseholds						
Water	27 0 0	18 18 0	5 4 0	30 13 6	50 0 0	45 19 0
Gas	18 9 11	5 0 0	4 3 3	28 13 8	26 15 0	40 19 0
Superintendents' and servants' wages	82 9 0	23 9 4	14 11 8	87 11 0	79 14 6	79 10 9
Cleaning materials, soap, &c.	15 15 1	3 8 10	6 3 8	8 8 8	15 12 0	21 5 0
Washing house linen						
Coals, coke, and wood						
Insurance		3 9 8	2 5 0	11 5 0	13 10 0	15 11 0
Newspapers and periodicals						
Total charges	374 10 3	165 10 5	101 18 8	762 13 10	578 8 8	747 8 4
Net rents, balance of { Profit / Loss }	426 10 1	300 10 7	157 17 4	382 12 9	778 17 7	640 16 0
Gross Rents	801 0 4	466 1 0	259 16 0	1,145 6 7	1,357 6 3	1,388 4 4
Cost	11,365 11 8	6,371 4 1	2,381 1 1	9,852 6 3	23,051 18 2	18,306 1 3

TABULAR STATEMENT—continued.

	Pleasant Row 9 Families. £ s. d.	Queen's Place, 10 Families. £ s. d.	Albert Street Chambers, 234 Single Men. £ s. d.	Soho Chambers, 128 Single Men. £ s. d.	£ s. d.	Total. £ s. d.
Rent	...	48 2 5	57 3 11	288 15 0	...	715 5 7
Poor and Police Rate	11 9 4	7 17 6	...	31 10 0	...	506 4 5
Lighting Rate	...	0 18 9	12 6 9	...	...	34 15 4
House Duty	...	...	...	...	...	106 12 3
Land Tax	...	...	...	11 5 0	...	39 14 0
Property Tax	3 14 9	2 8 9	14 17 9	14 1 3	...	148 6 7
Sewers and Main Drainage	3 9 0	0 18 8	10 19 10	11 5 0	...	116 4 2
General Rate	2 3 0	2 5 5	47 6 10	8 3 4	...	260 1 0
Church Rate	9 6 4	2 2 3	...	11 13 4	...	6 13 8
Consolidated Rate	...	0 5 7	...	...	...	5 16 8
Ward Rate	...	...	...	...	...	0 8 4
Repairs of building	36 7 3	23 2 7	92 18 2	60 18 8	...	782 1 5
Repairs of house linen, utensils, &c.	...	...	43 13 6	16 17 1	...	60 10 7
Sinking fund to redeem leaseholds	...	...	...	18 0 0	...	72 0 0
Water	8 18 0	2 0 0	23 0 0	16 16 0	...	229 16 0
Gas	...	5 0 0	88 0 8	46 18 6	...	259 7 10
Superintendents' and servants' wages	9 3 0	4 12 5	357 18 6	211 5 0	...	950 4 5
Cleaning materials, soap, &c.	0 2 6	0 6 2	49 4 5	15 3 10	...	135 10 11
Washing house linen	...	...	44 9 1	41 17 1	...	86 6 2
Coals, coke, and wood	1 10 0	...	82 8 0	11 9 6	...	93 17 6
Insurance	...	1 7 0	52 10 0	6 0 0	...	107 7 8
Newspapers and Periodicals	...	...	13 3 1	19 11 6	...	32 14 7
Total charges	86 3 2	101 7 2	990 8 6	841 10 1	2,945 17 2 }	4,749 19 1
Net rents, balance of { Profit / Loss }	96 18 4	7 18 2	161 14 6	139 19 7	147 17 9 }	2,797 19 5
Gross rents	183 1 6	93 9 0	1,152 3 0	701 10 6	...	7,547 18 6
Cost	2,979 9 4	111 8 2	13,772 7 3	1,422 7 7	...	89,613 14 10

LETTERS[1]

To the Editor of 'The Penny Newsman'

SIR,—As one of the working-class I beg to offer my thanks to 'Scrutinizer', for his sympathy and able reply to the charge of improvidence which has been made against us; and I hope I shall not presume too much by offering a few remarks thereon. That many of us indulge in strong drink must be admitted, but there are also many who take it in moderation, as a necessary article of support during the hours of toil; and I would advise all who cannot use it as a blessing to abstain from making it a curse. In reference to our friend's expenditure of 18s. per week for three persons, I think all must admit there is no extravagance in it. But I cannot take 18s. a week as an average for the labouring class. If we look at the docks we find that 15s. is the price for extra men, in Government yards 13s., and some others still less. Now, the number of working-men having *no* children to provide for is indeed extremely limited; on the other hand, I think the average number in family given by your correspondent is too low. I think *four* children might be set down, on which to base the calculation of cost; therefore there will be six to provide for now. I think I may say without fear of contradiction that to lay out 18s. in the best way for that number, parents will find that they are not so well fed as the inmates of a poorhouse, but they have liberty, and are free born Englishmen, which is our boast. I will now glance at the mechanic—to which class I belong—and having reared a family in London, always found some difficulty in providing by the produce of my labour for the necessaries requisite to produce comfort. From my experience I believe the wages paid in London to the working class generally is quite equal to any town in the kingdom, and I know it is better than in some. Now we must take it for granted that all mechanics in London do not receive the large wages spoken of, for I should say the majority receive less, and some much less; therefore I will suppose that 1l. 10s. will be something like an average, and I will endeavour to provide for a man, his wife, and four children, great and small, as they may be, in what I consider a plain way, without much luxury. Beer is said by some to be a luxury, and a ruinous one; so it is, when taken in excess, but I think it useful, and I would ask anyone who knows anything of a smith's shop, a shipyard, and many other trades, if two pints of beer per day during the hours of toil is not very acceptable. Some trades, perhaps, may do with half that quantity; I will, therefore, take the half quantity in my reckoning of expenditure, as follows:—

Weekly Expenditure for Six Persons.

	£	s.	d.
Rent for two rooms	0	4	0
Bread and flour	0	5	4
Meat and suet	0	5	0
Butter and cheese	0	2	8
Tea, sugar, and milk	0	2	4
Vegetables	0	2	0
Coal and wood	0	1	4
Candles, soap, &c.	0	0	9
Children's schooling	0	1	3
Sick club	0	0	9
Beer for the man at work . .	0	1	0
Beer at supper for man and wife .	0	1	2
Tobacco	0	0	3
"Newsman"	0	0	1
Halfpenny for each child as a treat .	0	0	2
Total	£1	8	1

Such, sir, is what I think necessary for comfort in a working man's home. I shall then have a balance of 1s. 11d. per week, or 4l. 19s. 8d. annually, to supply clothing, wear and tear of all articles in the house, doctoring, &c.—for where there is a family we are compelled to have medical assistance at times, and as the sum in question is not sufficient for the clothing, &c., we must of necessity curtail the victualling department to meet the expense. I have provided in my expenditure for sickness quite as much, I think, as I ought, with my income; and I think the 9d. weekly will produce 15s. per week in sickness, so if I lose time by sickness I must go back 15s. each week (without counting any additional expense which is sure to be incurred in such cases), and if I lose time from any other cause it cannot be recovered. This, sir, is the saving I have been able to effect during my life.

I am, sir, yours respectfully,

WORKING MAN.

THE WORKING MAN AND HIS 'EXTRAVAGANCE'

To the Editor of 'The Penny Newsman'

SIR,—The liberal tone of feeling expressed in the leaders of the *Penny Newsman* induces me to hope a few plain, simple expressions of my opinion may meet with insertion in the next number. My position for the past thirty years has been that of a superintendent and manager of works in various parts of the kingdom, and in the metropolis as well; and I have in that time had ample opportunities of seeing and studying the habits, wants, and feelings of some thousands of mechanics and labourers with whom I have been mixed up, and no man can (I humbly, but firmly, state) know more of their real points and bearings than myself; but I have heard and read so many statements of late (particularly in the past severe winter) as to the 'improvidence, waste, and extravagance of the working men and labourers in the disposal of their large wages', that I felt myself bound to say the charge is generally false and groundless as a whole; and I assert that some of those statements have been made by clergymen and others, who evidently wrote for mere writing sake, and they have done a serious injury to themselves as clergymen by misstating the causes of the depression of the working classes. I will endeavour to point out what is the real and positive facts of the case. In the first place, the working men are not receiving large wages, but just barely sufficient, with the most scraping and rigid economy, to make their wages last out the week—that is, if they have, as is mostly the case, a wife and children to support besides themselves. That single men, who are prudent and cautious, may put by a something in the 'savings'-bank', whilst others may patronize the beer-house and gin-shop, whose tastes are depraved, I will admit; but, as a general rule, the husband and father will be always (or nearly so) found in his home, where every penny of his hard earnings will be best spent; but there are many cases where the family of children are large, and the pressure for maintenance of them is so heavy, that the wife is often obliged to leave her own home to go out charing—that is, cleaning other persons' homes—whilst her own home and her children are neglected and filthy. Husband and wife return home together at night tired out with the day's work, and often several miles' walk after it, and, perhaps, wet through. A cheerless, cold, and uncomfortable home presents itself; that home, in most cases a single room, but at the best two rooms, are all they have. The children are hastily fed on a few scrap victuals, and put to bed, whilst the husband, and sometimes the wife as well, adjourn to a well-warmed and lighted tap-room, where they seek together a little temporary enjoyment or comfort which cannot be found in their own cheerless home; for it is not sufficiently considered that the working men, especially in the metropolis, have not a large range of rooms to choose for residence in, but are positively obliged to settle down and nestle in such localities as will suit their slender means. Let me ask the question—how many hundreds of mechanics and labourers, with their wives and families, are huddled together within an area of less than a quarter of a mile of the printing-offices of the *Penny Newsman*, whose homes are sickening to look on, much worse, then, must it be to be compelled, as the occupants are, to exist in them from year's end to year's end? That, and no other, is their choice at present, for they must be within a reasonable distance of their workshops or factories, and if they are too far off from their work their pockets must be affected by the increased expenditure of getting to and from their work. Give the poor working-men a fair chance of having a decent home, and the generality of them will avail themselves of its comforts, and society be benefited by their having a cheaper supply of room, fresh air, and good water for their homes. It is a positive mockery to expect a labouring man to be what is called provident under his present circumstances. I will take a labouring man obtaining eighteen shillings per week all the year round, with no sickness, or loss of work, or stoppage of work. Now, I know he may possibly, with a wife and child, contrive to make his money last out on the following scale,* and no luxury is here shown. The list I have enclosed shows bare necessaries; and it must be borne in mind that eighteen shillings per week is in London the labourer's standing wages; fifteen shillings and sixteen shillings are taken by hundreds and thousands, but the pinch and

* Expenditure calculated for a labouring man with wife and child :—

	For Three Persons per Day.			For Three Persons per Week of Seven Days.	
	s.	d.		s.	d.
Bread . . .	0	7	......	4	0
Beer . . .	0	2	......	1	2
Meat and potatoes .	0	6	......	3	6
Butter and cheese .	0	2½	......	1	6
Tea and milk .	0	1¾	......	1	0
Candles and firewood .	0	1	......	0	6
Coals . . .	0	1¾	......	1	0
Clothes and shoes .	0	4¼	......	2	6
Rent . . .	0	3½	......	2	0
Soap and Cleansing materials .	0	1¼		0	10
Total . .	2	7		18	0

Luxuries or amusements are in no way to be recognized in the above.

privation is all the greater, for it is certain that the markets for provisions are considerably higher than they were, and God alone knows what the calamitous results would have been had free trade not been enforced.

I am, &c.,

Feb. 2, 1861
SCRUTINIZER.

'PHILANTHROPY THAT PAYS'

To the Editor of 'Lloyd's Newspaper'

SIR,—In a leading article, with the above heading, in your paper last week, you appeal to capitalists to employ some portion of their money in creating joint-stock companies to erect habitable dwellings for the poor. With the general tenor of your remarks I most cordially agree, but I think that the appeal will be much more readily answered, and the beneficial effects derivable therefrom incalculably superior, were it directed to the poor. The skilled artisan, the ordinary mechanic, and the common labourer are the men to whom I would apply for the funds to build decent homes for themselves and their class, and who will most readily do it. Startling as the proposition may seem that the poor shall become the bankers of the poor; unsound in theory and impossible in practice as, at first sight, many may consider it to be, attention to the following statement will show them that such is by no means the case.

About the year 1844 an *outré* idea entered the heads of some dozen unemployed, half-starved Lancashire weavers: they resolved to improve their condition; without money and without friends, with no helping hand stretched out to them, not even a kindly word to cheer them on, but with perseverance and honesty as their guide, they would start a business on entirely new principles, and become the pioneers in a new science. 'We will find our own money, and stand our own friends,' said they, and most nobly they did so.

By subscribing 2*d*. a week, they raised, in shares of 1*l*. each, about 20*l*.; with this they commenced business. Their premises were so humble, and the stock inside so limited, that no one had moral courage enough to take down the shutters when at last the opening day came—they cast lots for it. A tradesman in the town having heard of the threatened opposition, came to see what kind of an appearance they put in to commence with, and went away joyfully declaring that he could 'wheel all the lot away in a barrow', and prognosticating a speedy 'shut up'. However, the Rochdale Equitable Pioneers' Society (such was its name) is in existence at the present moment, and the balance-sheet for the September quarter, 1860 (the account for the quarter just ended has not come to hand at the time I write), shows the following results:—The receipts are 37,816*l.* (exceeding 140,000*l.* a year); capital in hand, 34,525*l.*; profit, after paying all expenses, setting aside 107*l.* for educational purposes, giving 20*l.* to the town infirmary, and 5*l.* to the surgeon, is 4,342*l.* Out of the profits five per cent goes to the shareholders on their paid-up capital, and the residue is divided among the customers in proportion to the amount they have spent at the shop during the quarter—an exact account of which is kept.* They commenced as general dealers only—they now sell everything that is wanted to eat, drink, wear, or use in any station of life. The works are rapidly increasing, and the advantage to the town is incalculable. Impelled by their example, and encouraged by their success, 200 co-operative stores have sprung into existence in the north, representing capital amounting to 5,000,000*l.* Verily, this is 'Philanthropy that Pays'.

Some short time back I called attention to these facts in the columns of a morning contemporary (*Daily Telegraph*), and asked how it was that London was so much behind the north; the *Era*, referring to my remarks, said I was in error in asserting that this movement was not progressing here, and instanced the National Co-operative store in the Euston-road, with several branches in London. I have not had time to inquire much about it yet, but have seen their balance-sheet for the last quarter, and affairs stand thus:— Number of shareholders, 2,400; capital in hand, 2,953*l.*; business done, 4,978*l.*; which, considering the society did not open until March last, is most astonishing.

Then why not form co-operative building societies?[1] I believe this would find more favour among the people, when it once came to be understood. It would teach the poor a valuable lesson, that if they want to improve their condition it must be by their own organized exertions. If they want anything done they must do it themselves, for other help there is none. It would leave no room for the cant of the professional philanthropist, and save the working classes from the ostentatious parade and humiliating patronage of their 'kind friends'.

Should you deem this worthy of notice I shall be happy to forward you some further particulars respecting the management and working of co-operative societies generally.

I remain, yours, &c.,

Feb. 2, 1861.   HENRY H. WILTSHIRE.

---

* Contrast these profits with those of the benevolent lodging-house societies.

A Model District Census.

*Statistics of the District of Christ Church, St. George's East,
Rev. G. H. McGill.—Area,* 43 *acres.—(Made Feb.* 6, 1861.)

Number of streets and courts						52
„	houses					1,888
„	poor families				about	4,575
„	respectable families				„	512
„	persons				„	13,300
„	poor among them				„	11,000

Places of Worship.

	Accommodation for
Christ Church, Church of England	2,000
School Church, „ „	200
Beulah Chapel	600
Ragged School Church, Church of England	120
Trinity, Methodist	500
Primitive Methodist	120
Watney-street ditto	50
Workhouse, Church of England	500

Day Schools.

	On Books.
Christ Church, Boys	350
„ „ Girls	200
„ „ Infants	400
Middlesex, Boys	120
„ Girls	115
Adult School (Evening, at Christ Church)	60
School of Art	50
Methodist Day-school, Back-road	about 150

Sunday Schools.

Christ Church, Boys	200
„ „ Girls	275
„ „ Bible Class	25
Beulah Chapel	150
Trinity, Methodist	100
Watney street	30
Ranters	100

Benevolent Societies.

Penny Bank	3,000 depositors.
Dorcas Society	70 members.
Blanket and Rug Society	100 „
Christ Church Institute	120 „
District Visitors	21 „
Provident Society and Sick Club	100 „
Mothers' Meeting	100 „
East London Savings Bank, with a very large number of depositors.	
Deposits now invested, about	£90,000

CENSUS and other Particulars of the District of Christ Church, in the Parish of St. George's East, the Rev. G. H. McGILL, M.A., Incumbent.

	Number of Houses in each Street or Court.	Average Number of Families in each House.	Number of Rooms in each House.	Number of Poor Families in each Street.	Average size of the Rooms in each Street. Height (Ft. In.)	Length (Ft. In.)	Width (Ft. In.)	Average Rental of each Room per Week. (s. d.)	REMARKS.
Albion-place	16	1	2	16	7 6	10 0	9 4	0 6	Costermongers, labourers, slop-workers, &c.
Ann-street	44	4	4	176	7 3	9 4	8 7	1 9	Labourers and sailors.
Anthony-street	48	3		144	6 11	9 10	8 9	1 10	Little tradesmen and lodging-houses.
Buross-street	47	3	4 to 6	141	7 2	8 7	9 1	2 0	Employed on the docks and on the river.
Browning's-court	4	2	4	16	6 6	8 0	9 4	1 6	Very poor.
Cannon-st.-road (east side)	60	2	6 to 8	..	8 8	10 7	10 6	..	The principal street.
Catherine-street and court	68	3	4 to 6	150	9 0	9 6	9 0	2 0	Tradesmen and dock servants.
Chapel-street	65	3	4	195	9 7	10 0	10 0	1 10	Small shops and labourers.
Charles-street	44	4	4 to 6	176	7 8	10 0	9 5	1 10	Tradesmen, &c.
Church-road (west side) to Spencer-street	62	2	4	124	8 0	9 7	8 10	1 10	Small shops, sailors, and dock labourers.
Chapman-place	11	2	4	22	7 3	9 3	8 4	1 0	Lodging-houses and sailors.
Chapman-street, Lower	89	3	4 to 6	267	7 0	9 10	9 0	1 9	Dock servants and small shops.
Chapman-street, Upper	46	3	4	150	7 6	10 0	9 5	..	Labourers and lodging-houses.
Coburgh-court	4	3	4	12	6 6	7 9	8 0	..	Very low.
Commercial-road (south side) from Cannon-street East to Sutton-street	93	2	8	..	8 8	11 3	12 2	..	Respectable tradesmen, &c.
Cornwall-street, Upper	61	3	4 to 6	183	8 6	10 0	9 0	1 9	Very poor.
Cross-street (part)	29	2	4	58	6 11	9 9	8 5	1 9	Small shops.
Dean-street	24	2	6	48	7 5	9 6	8 7	3 6	Clerks and persons employed in city.

> In this street and Star-street there are living in 123 houses about 1,500 persons, including 300 children, many without shoes or stockings.

Street	60	4	4	240	8	0	8	4	8	2	8 1 9	Remarks
Duke-street	38	4	4	140	7	3	9	0	7	9	1	Very low and poor.
Fenton-street	29	3	5 to 6	87	8	2	10	0	6	0	2	Sailors and dock labourers.
Fenton-street, Lower	13	2	4	26	7	6	9	11	10	10	1	Ditto ditto.
Friendly-place	5	1	2	10	7	2	8	1	8	3	1	Low.
Hungerford-street and court	41	4	4	164	7	2	9	7	9	9	1	Very poor.
John-street, Lower	33	2	6	..	7	8	8	7	8	6	3	Clerks and middle class.
John-street, Upper	25	2	6	..	7	6	9	10	7	6	3	Very poor and miserable.
Jones-row	6	2	2	12	8	0	9	0	5	8	1	The worst street in the district morally.
Joseph-st., Cannon-st.-road	33	2	4	76	7	3	10	0	9	9	1	Very low and immoral.
Kinder-street	46	2	4	92	7	0	9	11	3	9	1	Labourers, sailors, and families.
Little Ann-street	8	4	4	32	7	6	9	2	7	9	1	Labourers.
Little Turner-street	29	4	4 to 6	116	7	8	8	8	3	10	2	Sailors and warehousemen.
Mary-street and place	30	4	4	120	7	3	10	0	5	3	2	Tradesmen and sailors.
New-road (north side)	79	3	4 to 6	79	8	1	8	7	10	6	2	Warehousemen, &c.
Richard-street	71	3	4 to 6	142	8	6	10	0	4	6	3	Lodging-houses.
St. George's-place	20	2	8	..	8	8	10	0	11	6	1	Very low and poor.
Salter-street	10	3	4	30	8	10	10	11	8	10	1	Very poor.
Smith's-place	10	2	4	30	6	0	9	9	10	10	1	Labourers in gas-works.
Short-street	3	3	4	6	8	0	10	9	10	10	1	Sailors, labourers, and sugar refiners.
Spencer-street (north side)	81	3	4	243	8	2	10	5	4	10	1	Very low and miserable.
Star-street	63	3	4	252	7	5	9	9	11	0	1	A few respectable inhabitants and lodgers.
Sutton-street	29	9	4 to 6	58	7	9	8	10	5	11	4	Labourers, sailors, and their families.
Tarling-street	89	3	4	267	8	0	9	9	3	10	1	Hawkers, fishmongers, &c.
Union-street and passage	24	3	4	72	8	0	10	0	4	8	1	Clerks and respectable inhabitants.
Upper John-street	21	3	6	63	8	7	9	9	5	10	1	Very poor.
Virginia-court	3	3	4	12	8	1	9	9	5	6	1	Persons engaged in slop work.
Walburgh-street	42	3	4 to 6	126	8	6	14	0	0	0	2	Respectable inhabitants.
Watney-street	45	2	6	..	8	2	9	6	6	6	..	Low and poor.
White's-gardens	6	2	4	12	8	2	9	11	6	9	1	Poor but decent labourers.
York-place	6	3	4	..	7	4	11	..	..	9	1	
Totals	**1,888**	..	..	**4,575**	—	—	—	—	—	—	—	

THE EAST END INCUMBENT ON LONDON
POOR RATES

This is an abridgement of the Rev. G.H. McGill's forcible pamphlet upon London Poor Rates, published in 1858. With a few alterations it might have been published in 1861. The evil it was written against has grown rather than diminished.

It has been carefully computed by those well able to form a correct opinion, that the total number of indoor poor in the Metropolitan Unions, amounts to, on an average given day, about 27,000; on the 1st of January, 1858, it was 30,098: and this number, multiplied by 3, will give the total number of indoor poor in one year, thus, 27,000 x 3 = 81,000. The total number of outdoor poor, on a given day, is about 72,000; on the 1st of January, 1858, it was 73,000. This number, multiplied by 3½, will give the total number of outdoor poor receiving relief in the course of a year, 72,000 x 3½ = 252,000. Add to this the 81,000 indoor, and we have an annual aggregate of recipients of poor-law relief amounting to the enormous number of 324,000.

The cost of this vast multitude amounts, on the average, to about 750,000*l.* annually. And, if the rates were equally spread over the real property of the metropolis, it would not be a very heavy burden to bear. The total property tax value of the metropolitan districts is nearly 14,000,000*l.* a year. If this enormous rental were equally burdened with the poor rate, it would amount to little more than one shilling in the pound per annum. But the grievance is, that it is not equally burdened. A few examples will prove the case better than a thousand arguments. A few facts will substantiate the injustice of the present distribution of the poor rate better than whole pages of declamation.

The parish of St Nicholas, Deptford, paid in the year 1857 (omitting fractions) 10*s.* in the pound poor rate. St Nicholas, Olave, in the city, paid 8*s.* in the pound. St Ann, Blackfriars, paid 6*s.* St Mary Mounthaw, 5*s.* 6*d.* Shadwell, 4*s.* 6*d.* St George's-in-the-East, 3*s.* 9*d.*, Whitechapel, Bethnal Green, Shoreditch, Ratcliff, St George's, Southwark, St Saviour's, Bermondsey, Rotherhithe, Woolwich, Fulham, and some others, over 3*s.* in the pound; while, on the other hand, the rich parishes of St George's, Hanover-square, paid about 7*d.* in the pound; Paddington about 4*d.* in the pound; St James's, Westminster, about 10*d.* And it is worthy of remark, that the assessments are generally much higher in the poor parishes than in the wealthy ones. Many of the former are rated at the full value, while many of the latter do not exceed three-fifths of the property tax valuation. This increases the disproportion very materially.

The following Table will show, at a glance, that the inequality of the poor rate is not confined to a few isolated parishes, districts, or unions in the metropolis, but that about one-fourth of the whole is grievously oppressed with pauperism; while another fourth is almost entirely exempted from contributing towards the support of the poor. The remaining half, not included in the following Tables, will not be much affected by a general equalization of the rates over the whole metropolis, except so far that they will benefit by the general contentment among the poor which such an equalization would inevitably produce.

RICH UNIONS.

	Property Value.	Poor Rate, 1856 *	Indoor Poor, Dec. 25, 1857.	Outdoor Poor, Dec. 25, 1857.	Total.
	£	£			
St. George's, Hanover-sq.	1,097,580	21,315	587	abt. 861	1,448
Paddington . . .	534,763	11,823	287	608	895
St. James's, Westminster	494,660	18,620	786	610	1,396
City of London Union .	953,357	51,754	896	abt. 1,800	2,696
Totals . . .	3,080,360	103,512	2,556	3,879	6,435

This is the bright side of the picture. These are rich unions: three of them individual parishes as well as unions; the City Union is a conglomeration of ninety-eight parishes, some paying 6s., and it is stated even 8s. in the pound, others not more than a penny. The contribution which the parish of St Christopher-le-Stock is called upon to pay for the next six months being only 2l., while that of St Nicholas Olave is at least 2s. per annum in every pound value. Three millions of the favoured property pays 103,000l. a year poor rate, and keeps about 6,435, poor. Let us look at other unions very differently circumstanced.

* The Parliamentary Returns for 1857, as yet published, do not give in these unions the exact amount spent in the maintenance of the poor; it is on this account that the Returns for 1856 are of necessity made use of. The probable expenditure for St George's, Hanover-square, in 1857 was about 23,000l., for Paddington 13,000l., and St James's 20,000l. All have increased a little, but the increase has been, as far as property is concerned, fully compensated for by the increase in the value; and, as far as the poor is concerned, it only makes the disproportion more palpable and the expenditure per head greater; the more money expended on the 6,435 poor, of course the greater the cost per head.

POOR UNIONS.

	Property Value.	Poor Rate, 1856.*	Indoor Poor, Dec. 25, 1857.	Outdoor Poor, Dec. 25, 1857.	Total.
	£	£			
St. George's, East . .	180,000	25,691	1,205	2,161	3,366
Fulham . . .	138,168	16,007	abt. 1,000	2,000	3,000
Bethnal Green .	128,927	20,461	1,110	2,200	3,310
Whitechapel . . .	223,987	29,438	1,044	2,311	3,355
Shoreditch . .	331,450	38,711	1,060	3,183	4,243
Bermondsey . .	128,014	17,538	636	1,001	1,637
Newington . . .	249,867	24,652	837	1,387	2,224
St. George's, Southwark	176,956	17,213	734	2,541	3,275
St. Saviour's, ditto .	174,383	15,461	407	1,061	1,468
Greenwich . . .	344,850	30,709	1,237	8,853	5,070
Stepney . . .	331,108	36,713	1,006	2,523	3,529
Lambeth . . .	664,226	49,995	3,106	6,956	10,062
Totals . . .	3,069,936	322,589	13,382	31,157	44,539

Here we have the reverse side of the picture. Poverty, squalor, wretchedness, destitution, starvation. Property of a less value than the four rich unions paying 322,000*l.* a year poor rates, in lieu of 103,000*l.*, and supporting 44,539 poor in lieu of 6,435. It will be seen that this is not the case of an isolated parish, or an exceptional union, but the case of twelve unions, all in the same sad predicament; and to them might be added the equally distressed districts of Rotherhithe, St Olave, Southwark, St Luke, Old-street, Chelsea, and the East and West London Unions. Each and all of these are burdened with an overwhelming amount of pauperism, depreciating the property, and driving away every respectable inhabitant who can possibly reside elsewhere. The evil, then, is most extensive. It is daily and hourly increasing. The rich unions are gradually paying less, and the poor ones gradually increasing their expenditure in an equal ratio. The four rich unions paid 107,186*l.* in 1855, or 3,674*l.* more than in 1856, while the twelve poor unions paid 304,048*l.*, or 18,541*l.* less than in the succeeding year. And this is the inevitable tendency of the present operation of the law. The rich districts will gradually become richer, and the poor ones poorer.

No doubt a poor man prefers spontaneously to live in a poor locality. He does not like his poverty to be remarked by others; and he knows that it will not be remarked by those who are equally destitute with

* See previous note.

himself. It is evident to common sense that it contradicts the fitness of things for the nobleman and the beggar to jostle against each other day after day, and to live close to each other in the same town. It is the instinctive desire for a separation of classes which causes the large landowner of the West End to stipulate for the erection of good houses only on the property which he lets out to lease,—houses which the rich only are able to pay for, houses in which the poor cannot possibly hope to live. Hence in parishes like St George's, Hanover-square, the poor, even if they wished it, are utterly unable to find houseroom. They may sweep the streets, may work as bricklayers, smiths, carpenters, painters, paviours, lamplighters, cabmen, butlers, footmen, cooks, housemaids, and so on in the aristocratic parishes of the West End, but it is impossible for them to live in houses of their own, or in the places where they work. There are no lodgings to be had suitable to their means, and so they go away to other neighbourhoods that are compelled to keep them when out of work, or prostrated by sickness, or by any other visitation of Divine Providence. The alteration of the Law of Settlement in 1834, by which hired servants ceased to gain a settlement in the parishes where their employers lived, has been one chief cause of the grievous inequality which has been pointed out. Before that law came into operation the parish of St George, Hanover-square, paid 2s. 6d. in the pound per annum, and other wealthy parishes in like proportion, but since it became the law of the land, the rates of the West End parishes, whose only poor are almost all livery servants—32 per cent of the entire population of St George, Hanover-square, being so employed—have gradually dwindled down to the present insignificant sum of sixpence or sevenpence in the pound per annum. Now, there is no intention of charging the influential inhabitants of the aristocratic parishes with the desire of wronging the poor by that enactment, but it is very certain that it has had that effect. While the servant is strong and healthy, his master in Belgravia has the benefit of his services, when he can no longer discharge his duties, he is turned adrift to seek relief in such parish as he may be able to obtain a lodging in.

But besides the alteration in the Law of Settlement above alluded to, great changes in the incidence of the poor rate have been caused by the various improvements that have been made from time to time in the Metropolis. The houses of the poorer classes have been pulled down for the widening of thoroughfares and the formation of new streets. The parish of St Giles affords a remarkable instance of this. Large companies, too, by the purchase of such houses for the purpose of extending their business, have been instrumental in effecting such changes. One of the most palpable instances of this is the contrast which exists between the poor rate paid by the St Katharine and the London Docks. At the time that the St Katharine Docks were formed, upwards of one thousand poor men's houses were pulled down, and their places occupied by the warehouses and quays of that powerful company. No provision was made for the ejected tenants of those houses who were driven at one swoop from the parish where they were born, and where they were before chargeable, to the adjacent parishes of Whitechapel, Aldgate, St George's-in-the-East, and Shadwell.

The pauperism of St Katharine's became at once a vanishing quantity, while that of the neighbouring districts was simultaneously increased in an equal ratio. After five years' residence the poor became irremovable, and the St Katharine's Dock Company now pay about 700*l.* a year in poor rates, while the adjoining London Dock paid last year upwards of 19,000*l.* The two companies employ the same class of labourers, their docks are close together, but the one had the good fortune to occupy the whole of a parish, while the other only occupies portions of the four parishes of St George's East, Shadwell, Wapping, and Aldgate. But the question arises at once, is it fair that this enormous disproportion should exist between two companies employing the same labourers, and being situate in such near proximity as these are? Is it fair that the one should escape from contributing to the relief of the pauperism which their labour draws around them, and that the other should be compelled, not only to pay their own share, but the share of both?

The causes, then, of the inequality which at present notoriously exists in the incidence of the metropolitan poor rates, are these, 1st, The tendency which all men, more or less have, to consort with their equals in life—that tendency which induces the man of wealth to live at the West End, and the poor man at the East—that tendency which has its material manifestation in the class of houses which are erected in those respective localities, and which tendency no legislation can remedy. 2ndly, The alteration of the Law of Settlement which deprived the servant living in the rich man's family of his claim upon the rich man's parish; and, 3rdly, The various improvements which have of late years destroyed many of the poor men's dwellings that were scattered here and there in the richer localities, and have driven them to take refuge in places already overcrowded with the poor, generating disease and misery and vice of the most fearful and alarming character. These are the chief causes of the evil whereof so many thousands of the ratepayers of the metropolis complain, and for which they ask, at the hands of an enlightened Legislature, a speedy and effectual remedy.

But it will be well to glance at the evils which result from this state of things. It is not the intention of the author of this pamphlet to lay much stress upon the deterioration of property in the overburdened parishes. The landlords and ratepayers, though they have valid reasons for complaint, are yet competent to defend their own interests, and make themselves heard through their representatives in Parliament. It may, however, be remarked, by the way, that almost all the inequality which has now grown to such an extravagant height has arisen within the last twenty-five years; and that the present owners are suffering from a burden which, when the property was purchased, they had no right to anticipate. Twenty-five years ago St George's, Hanover-square, paid as high a rate as St George's-in-the-East, but now it does not pay more than ⅛th as much. It has dwindled down from 2s. 6d. in the pound to 7d., while St George's-in-the-East has risen from 2s. 6d. to nearly 4s. in the pound.

The following statement will show the gradual increase of the burden in an Eastern parish, which is only a sample of the rest of its poor neighbours.

St. George's-in-the-East.

Quarter.	Indoor Poor.	Outdoor Poor.	Poor Rate Collected.	Medical relief Indoor.	Medical relief Outdoor.
			£		
Michaelmas, 1836	813	1,297	3,250	109	228
Midsummer, 1837	941	1,388	3,940	110	224
Michaelmas, 1837	661	1,219	4,294	100	184
Midsummer, 1841	1,145	1,211	6,241	132	416
Michaelmas, 1841	1,003	1,096	4,594	118	441
Midsummer, 1846	948	1,830	5,120	292	725
Michaelmas, 1846	844	1,692	5,014	281	913
Midsummer, 1851 } Michaelmas, 1851 }	1,114	2,405	{ 6,728 { 5,551	} 575	2,495
Midsummer, 1856 } Michaelmas, 1856 }	1,414	3,698	{ 7,974 { 8,456	} 588	2,789

From the foregoing figures it will be seen that an enormous increase of pauperism has taken place during the last twenty years. That the rates paid are nearly trebled, the number of persons relieved by the rates trebled, and the medical cases relieved more than quintupled. Indeed it is a startling fact that the meat given per week to the sick poor in 1836 was about 6 or 7 lb., and that it now amounts to 300 lbs. per week. And this is the normal state of most of the poorer unions in the metropolis.

Fulham, with its 138,000*l.* value, relieved more poor on the 1st of January, 1858, than Paddington and St George's, Hanover-square, with their 1,600,000*l.* of value. Meanwhile the wealthy parishes at the West End have been gradually diminishing their expenditure, or at all events not increasing it. In 1847, St George's, Hanover-square, paid 21,363*l.*; in 1852, 14,516*l.*; in 1856, 21,315*l.*; and in 1857, about 23,000*l.* This statement shows the inevitable tendency of the present law, which is to make the rich parish richer, and the poor parish poorer. It tends to impoverish the ratepayers and to reduce the poor man to the very verge of starvation. It will be found on a careful calculation that the 44,539 paupers in the poorer unions above alluded to, are relieved at an expense of 322,589*l.* per annum, and that this gives about 7*l.* 5*s.* per head, or 2*s.* 9*d.* per week. Of course this sum includes every item of expense, relieving officers, medical officers, and all the charges incidental to the relief of the poor. Now, it must be very evident that the great body of the outdoor poor are the chief sufferers from the inadequacy of the relief afforded by such a sum as this. The indoor poor are all fed on the same dietary principles, or at all events there is not much variation in this respect in the different metropolitan unions; nor is it supposed that the salaries of union officials vary very much, though their duties are ten times more arduous in some parishes than in others. The hardship then falls chiefly on the outdoor poor. They, in fact, as a general rule in the poorer parishes are *got rid of*—not *relieved*, for it would be a mockery to call it relief—at the expense of a shilling and a loaf per week.

Now what is done in the richer unions, in Paddington and St George's, Hanover Square? The poor-rates in 1857 amounted in the former of these parishes to about 13,000*l.*, and in the latter to about 23,000*l.* The total amount of their poor on the 1st of January, 1858, was 2,343. Now this gives an average of 15*l.* 7*s.* expended on each poor person relieved, against 7*l.* 5*s.*; or nearly 6*s.* per week, instead of 2*s.* 9*d.* Every reflecting person will ask whether this is fair to the poor man. Is he, because he belongs to the City Union, to receive out-door relief to the amount of 5*s.* and a loaf per week, with a new suit of clothes at Christmas; or, because he belongs to Paddington, to be amply supported in his distress; and is he, on the other hand, because he belongs to St George's-in-the-East or Bethnal Green, to be reduced to starvation? The law ought to be equal for all. But it is not equal, nor will it ever be equal till the whole of the Metropolitan area is subjected to an equalized rate, on a fair and just basis of assessment.

But some may say that the condition of the poor in London is after all not so very bad, that we do not hear of any outbreaks of starving people, or any resistance to the laws as at present administered. Those who have a stake in the welfare of this great city ought not to be left in ignorance of the fact that almost every winter some of the bakers' shops are stripped of their contents by the starving multitudes, assisted, of course, by persons of bad character who make the prevailing distress the excuse for robbery. Instances of this have occurred within the last two months, and large bodies of the unemployed have been marching about terrifying the timid, and creating feelings of alarm even among the boldest. Perhaps it may be objected, that these men were not in distress, but have only made distress an excuse for their lawlessness. This is not the case, for such exhibitions are never seen except in seasons of distress. It is a remarkable fact, for which the writer appeals to personal experience, that when work is scarce, or unattainable, there will be upwards of one hundred applications for assistance, in one day at the church vestry, after week-day service, and this will continue as long as the distress continues; but as soon as employment is obtainable, the applications drop off from one hundred to less than ten in the course of a single week. This is a strong proof that the London poor are not mendicants from choice, that they only apply for assistance when they stand absolutely in need of it. And doubtless there are many whom even the pressure of the most urgent distress will not drive from their seclusion to seek the aid of the charitable, much less of the relieving officer. During the last winter the writer relieved on the same day the daughter of a rector, and grand-daughter of an Irish bishop, and one who had been the chief constable in one of the largest parishes in London. Nor are such cases as uncommon as many would suppose. What would the weekly shilling and the weekly loaf do for such as these! These are the people, and such as these that are ranged under the head of 'deaths by privation', which forms so fearful an item in the Registrar-General's periodical report.

Let the rich men of London read the following extract from that report, and ponder well upon it while they enjoy the temporal blessings which God has given them with no unsparing hand:—

Deaths from	1848	1849	1850	1851	1852	1853	1854	1855	1856	1857	Total.
Privation	39	46	23	28	23	34	32	35	28	29	317
Want of Breast Milk	171	176	180	252	267	302	325	358	366	363	2760
Neglect	8	7	5	6	2	10	1	13	8	11	71
Cold . . . , .	4	6	3	6	12	12	22	54	12	13	144
Totals . . .	222	235	211	292	304	358	380	460	414	416	3,292

These four classes of deaths are all more or less the result of inadequate food; the first absolutely so; and the second generally arises from the nursing mother not obtaining such nourishment as is necessary for her at such a time. And it will be observed that as the poor rates have diminished in the richer, and increased in the poorer parishes of the metropolis, so these deaths have increased in an equal ratio. In the short space of ten years they have nearly doubled: they have risen from 222 in 1848, to 416 in 1857. Three thousand two hundred and ninety-two victims of want in ten years!

Some people say that if the rates be equalized over London extravagance will be the result. But what extravagance can possibly be so extravagant as the extravagance of human life which the present state of things encourages and keeps up! What money-extravagance is worthy to be compared with that which the telltale record of the Registrar-General here discloses to our view!

It can be neither politic nor economical to permit the wanton waste both of property and of human life which the present operation of the poor-law undoubtedly causes in the metropolis. It is not politic, because the large amounts of relief given in the rich parishes of the City and West End, tend only to increase idleness and sloth; to make the poor depend more upon parochial assistance than upon their own exertions: and at the same time the miserable pittance doled out to the suffering poor of the destitute parishes only tends to make them discontented and even dangerous; leading sometimes to suicide and despair, and at other times to the commission of wilful and deliberate crime.

The suicides by hanging in London in 1857, were 106; by poison, 107; by drowning, 371: making a total of 584. There can be no moral doubt whatever that if the circumstances of each were known, destitution would prove to be the cause of a very large percentage of these deaths.

The cases of privation which occurred in the first six weeks of the present year (1858), were all without exception in poor and oppressively rated parishes, in Shadwell, in Chelsea, in St Margaret's, Westminster, in Bethnal Green, in Poplar and in Lambeth; every one of which complains of the unfair distribution of the poor rate in the metropolis. The clergy of Shoreditch, Bethnal Green, Chelsea, Poplar and Lambeth have petitioned for an alteration in the present law; and have they not a cause? shall they suffer their poor to be starved to death and raise no cry in their behalf?

They are of opinion that private charity will never be able to supply an adequate cure for the disease. It has done much, and doubtless without its aid the number of persons perishing annually from destitution would have been much greater than they are at present. But all the charity of all the societies established in London for the relief of the distressed, will be found to amount to less than a farthing in the pound on property tax value of the metropolis. There are two societies which take the lead in ministering to the urgent wants of the necessitous in the winter season, these are the Metropolitan District Visiting and Relief Association, whose offices are in St Martin's-place, Trafalgar-square, and the Philanthropic Society. Now the total income of both these societies does not amount to more than 5,000*l.* per annum. The income of the former is a little over 3,000*l.* a year, and of the latter somewhat more than 1,000*l.* These sums are very judiciously expended, and have saved many valuable lives every year; but what are they when compared with the expenditure of the poor rates, which amounts to 800,000*l.* per annum?

It is calculated that 1*d.* in the pound on the whole value of the metropolis would give 50,000*l.*, or ten times the amount of the sum expended by both the associations alluded to. And is it likely that the benevolent donations of the rich will ever reach a sum like this? If private charity then be utterly inadequate to meet the difficulty, no other plan remains but an equal rate over the whole of the Metropolitan Districts.

Notwithstanding the multitudes of returns made to parliament in the statistics of poor-law relief, there is yet a considerable amount of difficulty in ascertaining the exact sums spent for the relief of the poor. And this difficulty is very much increased by the want of explicit information from the lightly rated parishes. They usually return the police and county rate with the poor rate, and then say that the inequality is not so great as it really is. Now police and county rates do not vary much, and the former would probably be higher in the West than in the East, because of the greater amount of property to be protected; they therefore ought to be discarded from the computation altogether as having nothing whatever to do with the relief and maintenance of the poor. But St George's, Hanover-square, includes poor, police, county, baths and washhouses, and burial board, in one item, amounting, in the aggregate, to 1*s.* 10*d.* in the pound. Probably the poor relief is not more than 7*d.* or 8*d.* For the police cost 6*d.* in the pound, and the county rate 4*d.*, so that there is only 1*s.* left for baths, washhouses, burial board, and poor. Again, the return from Paddington includes the same items under one head, and the amount is only 1*s.* 1*d.* Now it would not only be much fairer, but much more in accordance with the form of the required return, that the items should be stated separately, as in Shoreditch, where it stands thus,—county rate, 4*d.*; |

police rate, 6*d.*; poor rate, 3*s.* 10*d.*; baths and washhouse, *nil.* Or in St George's-in-the-East, where the items are,—county rate, 3*d.*; police rate, 6*d.*; poor rate, 3*s.* 9*d.*

The difficulty of ascertaining the exact amount of inequality was fully admitted by the assistant secretary to the Poor Law Board, Mr Lumley, in the able paper read by him before the Statistical Society, on the 20th of April last, which paper it may be well to offer a few remarks upon in this place. Mr Lumley, as the groundwork of his observations, divides the whole of the metropolitan unions into five districts, the Western, Central, Eastern, Surrey, and the Kentish. After giving the comparative amounts raised in each of these districts in 1803, and showing that the rate per pound then varied very little indeed, the Western being 2*s.* 8*d.*, the Central, 2*s.* 9*d.*, the Eastern, 2*s.* 8*d.*, the Surrey, 2*s.* 9*d.*, and the Kentish portion, 3*s.* 5*d.*, he went on to show that a great alteration had taken place of late years, the return for 1857 making the Western only 1*s.*, the Central about 1*s.* 3*d.*, the Surrey and Kentish about 1*s.* 6*d.*, while the Eastern district has risen to 2*s.* 4*d.*, proving that in the last half century the separation of the richer from the poorer classes has mainly taken place.

Perhaps some persons may be inclined to say that the difference between the western portion and the eastern is not so very great, only 1*s.* 4*d.* in the pound, it is hardly worth the outcry that is made on the subject; the inequality is not so extensive after all. But if the subject is examined a little more carefully, it will be seen that Mr Lumley's statements are no criteria whatever as to the inequalities of the existing rates. In every one of the districts averaged by Mr Lumley there are poor parishes thrown in with rich ones, and the small rates of some make amends in the average for the large rates of others. For example, the Western average is 1*s.* in the pound, but Fulham, which is a component part of the average, paid last year 3*s.* 6*d.* against Paddington's 4*d.*; Chelsea paid 2*s.* 5*d.* against St George's 7*d.* It is true that the average may be 1*s.*, but does Fulham only pay 1*s.*? does Chelsea, does Hammersmith? The central portion again was shown to average 1*s.* 3*d.* How is this average made up? Of such glaring facts as this: St Christopher-le-Stock, rated at 9,000*l.* a year, paying 2*l.* for the next six months, and St Mary Mounthaw, rated at 900*l.*, paying over 600*l.* for the same period. The one a sum too small to calculate, the other 13*s.* 4*d.* in the pound for the six months. The average therefore is an utter fallacy, as far as the inequality of the parochial poor rates are concerned. Mr Lumley admitted, and it was a great admission to make, that an union rate might be very well applied to the whole of the ninety-eight City parishes. And if so, why not to the whole metropolis? Again, with regard to the Kentish district the same observation is applicable. The average is about 1s. 6d. But the utmost disparity exists in the component elements of that average. It will be enough to say that Kidbrook pays only ½d. in the pound per annum, and St Nicholas, Deptford, over 6s. And in the Surrey division, inequalities of the same kind, though perhaps not so glaring, undoubtedly exist. The average is about 1s. 6d. But St George, Southwark, paid 3s. 1d., Rotherhithe, 3s. 2d., Bermondsey, 3s. 2d., St Saviour's and Christ Church about 3s., while Putney, Battersea, Clapham, and Streatham paid comparatively little in the shape of poor rates. And in the Eastern district also, the average of which was shown to be 2s. 4d., the same remarks may be made. Shoreditch, paying 3s. 10d., and St George's-in-the East, 3s. 9d., are placed by the side of St Katharine, where the poor rates are merely nominal. It is no consolation whatever to the struggling ratepayers to assure them that the *average* is but light, when they pay not according to the average, but according to the arbitrary demands made for the starving poor, dwelling in the limited area of their own parish. 2 + 10 would give an average of 6, but that average does not destroy the original inequality between 2 and 10. It still remains 5 to 1. Though Mr Lumley admits that an equal rate would be a blessing to the City, and that the Eastern district pays 2⅓ times as much for the poor as the Western, and that this disparity is on the increase, Shoreditch having increased its expenditure for the poor, 10,418l. in the last year, and St George's-in-the-East, 9,508l. during the same period, yet he refuses to decide for or against the proposal which has been made to equalize the rates over the whole area. He states that this has been done in Oxford, Liverpool, Bristol, Exeter, and other places, and therefore there is his official authority for the fact that the measure which this pamphlet is intended to support, involves no novelty, but is recommended for adoption, not only by the sympathies of the humane, but by the practical deductions of the experienced.

The increase of the poor rate in the distressed Eastern districts during the last five years has been enormous, and is still going on. The six unions of Bethnal Green, Whitechapel, St George's-in-the-East, Shoreditch, Stepney, and Poplar, though their annual value is under a million and a half, have increased 90,000l. per annum in the last five years, *i.e.* from 1852 to 1857. It would startle any of the respectable ratepayers of the richer parishes to be informed of the number of summonses that are issued every quarter for the rates: they amount to upwards of 4,000 in the parish of George's-in-the East alone. And, of course, many of the poor persons summonsed are unable to pay.

THE POOR LAW AND THE POLICE COURTS

'For some time past* monthly returns of the number of persons in receipt of relief in England and Wales have shown a decrease in comparison with the corresponding months of the previous year, but at length in December the scale has been turned, and whereas at the close of 1859 the number was 827,461, it was 835,129 at the close of 1860, an increase of 7,668, not far from 1 per cent. This increase is chiefly due to the midland counties and the metropolis, Wales and the eastern counties adding in a less degree to it; but the manufacturing districts in the north continued to show a considerable decrease in the number of paupers relieved. Thus far as to the comparison between December, 1859, and December, 1860; but another comparison may be made— namely, between the beginning and the end of December last, to show to what extent the poor law had then met the distress caused by the severe weather which set in in the middle of that month. Now, these returns show that the numbers relieved at the end of the first week of last December were 807,187, and at the end of the fourth week 835,129, an increase of only 27,942, or 3·46 per cent. In fact, the increase of relief in that extraordinary weather was not so very much more than always takes place in December. In December, 1858, the numbers relieved at the end of the fourth week were 13,146 more than at end of the first week; in December, 1859, 22,051 more; in December, 1860, 27,942 more. Taking all England, fewer persons by 23,533 were receiving relief at the end of December, 1860, than at the end of December, 1858, and fewer in every week of the month; and fewer persons received outdoor relief in every week of December, 1860, than in the corresponding week of December, 1859. In the metropolis, where the cry of distress seemed so great, 95,237 persons were in the receipt of relief at the close of the fourth week of December, 1860, 91,665 at the corresponding period of 1859, an increase of 3,572; but in every week of December, 1860, the numbers relieved were fewer than in 1858; and the number relieved at the end of the fourth week of last December was only 3,920 more than at the end of the first week, when the cold weather had not begun.

* * * * *

At the end of the fourth week in December, though the cold had already become so severe, the number of persons receiving relief (835,129) was not at all extraordinary for the time of year; but the continuance of the

* Quoted from *The Times*.

inclement weather then began to tell, and at the end of the third week in January the number had risen to 948,379, more than 14 per cent above the corresponding period of 1860, and even at the end of the month, with changed weather, it was still 10 per cent above the previous year. But we find that the highest numbers here reported as relieved only show an increase, for all England and Wales, of 118,382 above the numbers in January, 1860, which was a month of mild weather. The distribution of this increase is not less remarkable. In the metropolis it was no less than 42 per cent above the previous year, the numbers relieved were more by 38,851, and the large demands upon private charity seem to prove that this did not meet the necessities of the case; but in the country the increase was not to be compared with this. In the South-Western district it was not 2 per cent. That district has at all times a greater proportion of its population pauperized, and there may be a smaller body for sudden pressure to affect. The difference, again, in the way in which the additional relief was dealt out in different districts is remarkable. In London it was nearly all outdoor relief; at the end of the third week of December the indoor poor were 28,740, and a month later they were only 29,959, though above 37,000 persons more were then receiving relief. On the other hand, in the eastern counties, with not near half that additional number of persons receiving relief at the end of the third week in January, the increase of indoor poor was more than double what it was in the metropolis.'

Now comes a diary of the charitable work at some of the London police-courts, extracted from the newspapers. It shows how the applications for relief, and the funds for relieving, ceased with the approach of fine weather.

To what extent the knowledge that no more money was to be given away acted upon the different crowds who flocked round the magistrates, will always, perhaps, remain a mystery. One thing may, however, be safely assumed: the degrading public exhibition of so much mixed poverty and imposition, and the knowledge that they had only to ask to have, must have had a very demoralizing effect upon the poor.

THAMES POLICE-COURT

December 31st, 1860.—An immense number of poor and destitute creatures, principally widows with families, and old women whose misery was apparent, applied at the Thames Police-court, in the course of Saturday, for a little relief from the poor-box fund. The want of employment, and the unusual severity of the weather, combined with the dearness of fuel and the high price of provisions, have caused an enormous amount of distress in the densely populated district assigned to the court. Mr Selfe said he was compelled to limit his assistance to those whose honesty and good character were verified by the clergy of the district, and he could only relieve the most deserving of those. A poor ship-wrecked sailor boy, thinly clad, and very ill, was presented to the magistrate in the most deplorable condition. He was half starved, and in danger of perishing. Mr Selfe directed Howland, 83 H, an officer of the court, to provide the boy with food, a suit of warm clothing, and pay his railway fare to Newport, in Wales, where his friends are residing.

January 1st, 1861.—A poor woman named Sarah Smith, dwelling in Poplar, came before Mr Yardley, and stated that, owing to the inclemency of the weather, and to her husband being out of employ, she was in great distress, and upon applying to one of the relieving officers of the Poplar Union, he refused to relieve her and her family.

Mr Yardley: Upon what grounds did he refuse?

Applicant: He said there were too many of us.

Mr Yardley: How many children have you?

Applicant: Seven, sir. The eldest is fifteen years, and the youngest eleven months old.

Mr Yardley could hardly believe that any relieving officer would assign as a reason for refusing relief the number of a family. It was a most unlikely story, indeed. If the relieving officer had given as a reason for not relieving a man and his family that they were nine in number, he was a most inconsistent and unreasonable person. It was the first time he had ever heard of relief being denied to a man and woman in distress because they had a large family. That was an additional reason, in addition to the ordinary ones, for administering relief. He would write a letter to Mr Jeffreys, the principal relieving officer of the Poplar Union, calling attention to the case, and he was quite sure if the family were deserving, and the parents were persons of good repute, that they would be promptly and effectually relieved.

Mr Yardley said he wished it to be distinctly understood that it was no part of his duty to relieve the poor of the district, or to perform the functions of a relieving officer. The poor-box fund was applied to peculiar cases of destitution and distress in the court, to cases of a peculiar nature springing out of the investigations in the court. He could not attempt to relieve the destitution in the district, which he had no doubt was very great.

Mr Selfe has opened about 3,000 letters of recommendation, and afforded temporary relief to about 600 persons in the course of the last five weeks. Yesterday numerous destitute widows and others came to the court with recommendatory certificates, certifying their poverty and good character, and were informed it was useless for them to wait, and that they had better apply on Thursday next, when Mr Selfe will preside.

January 4th, 1861.—Mr Selfe said he could only return thanks through the medium of the public journals for the liberal donations forwarded to him on behalf of the poor. He quite agreed with the observations of his learned colleague, Mr Yardley, that it was only a subsidiary portion of the duty of the magistrate in the police-courts to relieve cases of distress, and that they were not relieving officers; but the system had grown with the police-courts, and had been productive of incalculable good. He also agreed with his colleague that the administration of the poor-box fund ought not to be allowed to interfere with the ordinary business of the court. It was true, as was observed by his colleague, that there was not a proper organization, and no relieving officers appointed to inquire into cases of distress presented in that court; but they did their best; and every one who had watched the administration of relief must be aware that very little imposition was practised. Everything possible was done to guard against imposition. If the magistrates erred at all, it was on the side of over-caution. He had turned away more urgent cases of distress than he had relieved, or than it was possible to inquire into. The relief at police courts was administered, and the money disposed of, without one farthing of expense. There were no treasurers, secretaries, collectors, inquiring officers, or rent of offices to pay. The principal contributions forwarded to the poor-boxes of the police-courts were subscribed by the nobility and gentry of the West End, a few of the influential Livery companies of the City of London, and some of the large firms both in the City and West End.

January 12th, 1861.—A great number of unemployed coal-whippers, dock labourers, lumpers, hammermen, and others, have been loitering about the court for the last two days, in expectation of obtaining some relief from the poor fund. They were all evidently in a state of great distress, and many stalwart men, anxious to obtain a living by honest industry, were suffering from cold and hunger, and very thinly clad. On Thursday evening Mr Yardley directed Mr Livingston, the chief usher, to relieve twenty poor fellows with 2*s*. 6*d*. each. After the business of the court had terminated yesterday evening, Mr Yardley directed Mr Livingston to distribute 20*l*. in small sums among poor men in want of employment who were assembled in the waiting-room and the avenues of the court. After the magistrate left the bench, the chief usher presented 150 of the poor men with 2*s*. 6*d*. each, and a few with 1*s*. 6*d*.

each, until the 20*l.* was expended.

January 14*th*, 1861.—On Saturday, soon after the night charges were disposed of at the Thames Police-court, a great number of unemployed coal-whippers, dock labourers, lumpers, and others, began to assemble in the street opposite the court, in hopes of obtaining some relief from the poor-box fund. At four o'clock the applicants for relief had increased to 700, and the gates of the station-house yard were thrown open, and ample room found for the poor fellows there. Mr Yardley, the presiding magistrate, believing the numbers would not exceed 600, directed Mr Livingston, the chief usher, to obtain 50*l.* worth of silver, and distribute the same among the crowd at his discretion. Every person among them was in a state of great distress and in want of food. A majority of them were married, with wives and children at home actually starving. Of course, with such a number assembled to crave a little assistance, inquiries were out of the question; but, in addition to the chief usher, there were other astute officers in attendance, who could tell, at a glance, whether the person soliciting aid was what he represented himself to be, and the only questions put were the following:—What are you? Are you married or single? How many children? And to some who were well known those questions were avoided. The number of destitute labourers increased every minute, and when the 50*l.* of silver was exhausted, there were at least 500 more clamouring for a bit of bread in the station-house yard. The chief usher took hasty counsel with his brother officers, and finding it impossible to send any of the destitute creatures away empty-handed, procured an additional 30*l.* worth of silver, and distributed that also to the best of his judgment. About 100 received 2*s.* 6*d.* each; a second hundred, 2*s.* each; a third hundred, 1*s.* 6*d.* each; 300, 1*s.* each; and 400, 6*d.* each. The total number relieved was exactly 1,500, including 50 women, and at least 1,000 of them were Irishmen, who always suffer naturally by the suspension of business in the docks, on the wharves, and on the river, and whose precarious earnings at all times are very small, though engaged in the most laborious and roughest work of the port of London. It was intended to confine the relief to unemployed labourers only, Mr Selfe having relieved about 800 destitute women in the course of the last three weeks; but fifty half-starved seamstresses got into the station-yard behind the men, and it was impossible to send them away without a shilling or a sixpence. It is believed that on Saturday there were 26,000 labourers out of employ in the district of this court.

January 16*th*, 1861.—Yesterday the applicants for relief from the poor-box were again very numerous, and Mr Yardley, on hearing that a vast number of unemployed labourers were assembled in front of the court gave instructions to Mr Livingston, the chief usher, to obtain 80*l.* worth of silver, and distribute it among them to the best of his judgment. A few words of inquiry only were addressed to each individual, but imposition was almost impossible. Mr Livingston gave 100 1*s.* each; 100, 6*d.* each; and about 200 more, 2*s.* and 2*s.* 6*d.* each. There were upwards of 100 poor women craving relief in attendance, and they were directed to attend with letters of recommendation from persons known to the magistrate, and their cases would be seen to.

January 17th, 1861.—The magistrates of this court have each adopted a different system of administering relief to the unemployed and destitute population of the district. Mr Selfe commenced by relieving poor women whose poverty and misery were verified by the clergy of all sects in the district, and others of repute known to him, and in this way gave temporary relief to about 700 women, principally widows, and a few men. Mr Yardley commenced by relieving a few unemployed labourers on Thursday evening last, and their numbers increased daily until Tuesday, when 1,100 out of 1,500 assembled were assisted; about 300 with 1*s.* each, 100 with 6*d.* each, and another 100 with 2*s.* or 2*s.* 6*d.* each. It was announced on Tuesday that women only would be relieved on the following day, and that letters of verification from the clergy or from ladies and gentlemen known to the magistrates only, would be attended to. At noon, a vast assemblage of poor women thinly clad, many suffering from cold and hunger, assembled in the street. They continued to increase until they amounted to at last 2,000, and as they completely blocked up Arbour-street East, directions were given to admit them into the station-house yard, the great gates of which were thrown open for that purpose. About 1,000 letters were handed to Mr Selfe in the course of the day by the half-famished creatures. A selection was absolutely necessary, and the letters from tradesmen and landlords not known to the magistrate, and not a few of whom were suspected of recommending applicants for the purpose of obtaining payments of debts and arrears of rent, were thrown aside. Soon after four o'clock not fewer than 3,000 women and about 200 men had assembled.

January 18th, 1861.—Mr Selfe said the conduct of the police and the officers of the court, during a very trying period, was beyond all praise, and he was much indebted to Mr Griffin and Mr Hayes for their attention, and the excellent manner in which they had carried out a most difficult duty. He asked how many there were assembled in the street now?

Mr Griffin: Upwards of 2,000 men and women.

Mr Selfe: I am sorry there are so many. I do not intend to relieve the men tonight. I cannot do it, but as many as possible will be provided by Mr Livingston with a loaf of bread.

Soon afterwards all the females, about 1,100 in number, were admitted into the yard, and, under the direction of the police, found an entry into the court in batches of twelve or fifteen at a time. The letters and recommendations of great numbers were from persons of whom the magistrate knew nothing. Others were satisfactory, and in the course of the evening 300 women were relieved at a cost of 45*l.*, in sums of from 1*s.* to 7*s.* each. 340 bread tickets were given away, one woman was relieved with 10*s.* 10*l.* was given to a Protestant minister for the relief of destitute persons belonging to his flock, and 20*l.* to a Roman Catholic priest for a similar purpose. The men, principally Irish labourers, and without employ, waited in the street opposite to the court until nearly eight o'clock, and finding there was nothing for them except the bread tickets, which only a small portion of them obtained, they departed sorrowfully enough.

January 19th, 1861.—The assemblage this day of destitute people seeking relief from the poor-box fund was greater than ever, and among them were several cases of appalling distress. Creed and country were not considered in the distribution of relief. The representatives of the High Church, Low Church, and Broad Church were on the bench at one time, soliciting aid for the humble members of their flocks who were in want. At three o'clock upwards of 4,000 men and women were assembled, and a large force of police of the K division were in attendance, under the direction of Mr Howie, superintendent, and Inspectors Griffin and Hayes, of the K division. The greatest eagerness was manifested by the people, many of whom had been waiting several hours to obtain relief; and if it had not been for the great care, forbearance, and firmness of the police, numerous accidents, if not loss of life, would have occurred. The rush occasionally was tremendous. About 200 at a time were admitted into the yard between the station-house and the court, and, under well-managed regulations, were admitted into the court thirty and forty at a time. Mr Selfe personally inquired into and ordered relief to those who produced the printed forms filled up. Nine-tenths of them were poor women, the rest were coal-whippers and labourers, recommended by that well-known philanthropist, Mr Gowland.

January 22nd, 1861.—Notwithstanding the favourable change of the weather, and the partial resumption of business on the river and in the docks, great numbers of poor and hungry persons besieged the Thames Police-court in hopes of obtaining relief.

Mr Yardley said the cases he wished to relieve were those of poor men who had been thrown out of employment by the stoppage of business on the river and in the docks. He was in hopes the whole of them would have been employed with this favourable change in the weather, but it was not so, and the magistrates were overwhelmed with applications, and with letters containing money. It was impossible to go on day after day relieving, or attempting to relieve, unemployed workmen and labourers from all quarters, who flocked to the court. Relief had been given to many thousands last week, and there must now be some limit to it.

Mr Selfe was engaged in a private room for several hours in making inquiries, and relieving persons who presented the printed forms issued by the court, properly filled up by trustworthy and honourable persons who had been supplied with them by the magistrate. Mr Selfe attaches great value to this system of giving relief, as preventing the possibility of imposition, for he not only makes every person responsible for the accuracy of the statements made in those papers, but he inquires of each person calling upon him with them whether they are fit objects of relief or not. He relieved 150 deserving persons of both sexes yesterday in sums varying from 3s. to 7s. each.

January 23rd, 1861.—In the afternoon Mr Livingston, the chief usher, relieved 500 unemployed dock-labourers, coal-whippers, and workmen, by order of Mr Yardley. Some received 2s., others 2s. 6d., and the remainder 3s. each. In all 75l. worth of silver was distributed. There were at least 400 hungry and destitute men turned away empty-handed.

January 25th, 1861.—There was an immense gathering of poor and destitute persons in the vicinity of this court yesterday, to solicit relief from the poor-box, and incessant applications were made in the course of the day by clergymen of various creeds, deputations from relief committees, and others, for assistance. Mr Selfe shortly investigated their various claims, and awarded upwards of 400l. among those who waited upon him. Mr Selfe relieved about 500 persons with sums varying from 3s. to 20s. The average was about 5s. each applicant. The forms revealed an appalling amount of distress in every conceivable shape, and many of them contained such entries as their family starving, not an atom of furniture, children huddled together on the floor or on straw, and other similar details. Mr Selfe more than once remarked that many of the cases ought to be visited and relieved by parochial officers, and effectually dealt with by them, as they were beyond the range of the temporary relief that could be afforded by a police-court poor-box. The magistrate, whose patience, perseverance, and humanity, during a very trying season, has been above all praise, did not terminate his useful and humane labours until midnight, when he retired in a most exhausted state.

January 26th, 1861.—A considerable number of poor individuals collected in front of the court, in expectation of obtaining some relief from the poor-box fund, but there were of a very different class to those who have hitherto sought for and obtained assistance. There were few coal-whippers and labourers among them, and it was reported to Mr Selfe that the various dock companies were now employing a great many hands, and that the Victoria Dock Company, at Plaistow, sent 'over the border' to Middlesex for 500 labourers yesterday. The large engineering firms and proprietors of chemical works in Ratcliff, Limehouse, Stepney, and Poplar, are about to resume their operations on the same scale as before the frost commenced, and there is no doubt that should the present mild weather continue, 10,000 workmen and labourers, in addition to those who have been taken on in the course of the last three days, will resume their industrial occupations. Mr Selfe announced that, for obvious reasons, there would be a discontinuance of the general relief of the poor after tomorrow evening, and that he should attend to no applications for temporary relief (urgent and pressing cases of want excepted) unless the applicants produced one of the printed forms issued by the court, properly filled up by some honourable and trustworthy gentleman known; and he expected, before they recommended any one, they would make themselves personally responsible by visiting, and inquiries about the applicant's position, character, cause of distress, and number of family.

Mr Selfe relieved upwards of 100 destitute persons. In the course of the last five weeks his labours have been often protracted until nearly midnight. He has opened upwards of 4,000 letters recommending deserving persons as objects of temporary relief, examined 3,000 printed forms, received numerous clergymen of all creeds, committees, laymen, and others soliciting, and has been engaged day after day in corresponding with various persons on the necessities of the district.

The amount received and distributed at this court during the month of January, 1861, was about 3,000*l*.

WORSHIP-STREET POLICE-COURT

January 14th, 1861.—Mr Knox was again engaged the greater part of the day in listening to and relieving the numerous melancholy cases introduced to him by the warrant officer and other dependable persons. Sergeant Gee, of the H division, brought a wretched-looking man into court for assistance under these circumstances:—It appeared that, at an early hour that morning, some market people engaged in Spitalfields saw the old man standing with a basket on his head. Suddenly he fell to the ground, was picked up, and taken to the station-house. The immediate attendance of Dr Edmunds, the divisional surgeon, restored him, and that gentleman then announced that the patient was perishing for want of sustenance. This was, of course, at once afforded, and when able he was brought to this court.

The poor creature stated that he was eighty-two years of age, lived by carrying heavy loads in the market, but he had not had food for many hours.

The sergeant said he had visited the old man's lodging in Bowl-court, Shoreditch, where he found a young girl, a niece with a piece of bread she had procured from the workhouse for her relative.

Mr Knox ordered instant relief in this instance.

January 19th, 1861.—Again Mr Knox devoted hours to inquiries into applications for relief from the poor-box fund, and the minute questioning of this worthy gentleman elicited much that was satisfactory on one hand, and most distressing on the other. A large sum is now laid out in the purchase of coals and bread, which is supplied by tickets, and this is essentially the most prudent course to pursue. Despite the relief that has been bestowed, hundreds flock to the doors of this court, bearing with them indisputable evidence of sickness and destitution. Mr Knox took the opportunity of observing that above 300 letters were received daily on behalf of the bearers, and there were but four persons to open them. Under such circumstances, all he could do was to devote every minute possible to spare from the general business to their consideration. This evening great difficulty was experienced in clearing the court from those applicants who asserted that they had been in waiting day after day—some weeping, and others seeming resolved to remain.

January 23rd, 1861.—Mr Knox, at the conclusion of the day's business, made the following remarks relative to the disposal of the poor-box funds, and the district over which he presided:—'The course I and my colleague, Mr Leigh, have followed, has been this—the district has been divided into four portions for the purpose of facilitating the duty of serving warrants, summonses, notices, and such like, and one officer is appointed to the charge of each of these portions. Now each of these officers, Farrall, Bull, Haynes, and Edis, at the end of a long and heavy day's work in the court, has each night visited the homes of as many poor persons as he could at all accomplish in the time, reporting the result of each visit to the magistrate the next day, and in every case which he has so verified adequate relief in money and bread has been immediately granted. And here I should be very imperfectly discharging a moral duty if I did not most sincerely render my cordial thanks to those officers, for their exertions have been not only willingly made, but the extra duties so imposed upon them, trying and arduous as they were, have proved most effective and satisfactory. Indeed, I may truly say that, without their assistance, the vast amount of relief granted to the starving population of this district would have been entirely lost sight of. Every shilling disbursed has been so after a house to house visitation by them, and my most sincere thanks are due for the services they have rendered me. The chief destitution of this district appears to me to have fallen upon three great classes—dockyard labourers, shoemakers, and weavers. The thaw which has now set in may be the means of at once restoring the two former, but, with regard to the Spitalfields weavers, it is different, I greatly fear. I am informed that in this district alone there are 20,000 persons who follow this trade, their average earnings being only from 7s. to 10s. per week, and for seven or eight weeks past these have been almost entirely deprived of all occupation. Whether the system of relief by police-courts is to become one of the regular duties of such tribunals is not a point upon which I as one of the younger magistrates upon the bench can express any opinion. I only trust that we may receive some positive rule for our own guidance, which may enable us to carry the business through in a proper and efficient manner, or that we may be enabled to state to the public that it is considered injudicious that police magistrates should be any longer charged with such a responsibility. The relief given by this court has been partly in the form of bread, coals, and blankets, and part in sums of ready money, and I most sincerely hope that a real amount of good has been effected with as small as possible a percentage of that rascality and imposition which is and ever must be inseparable from such proceedings. The number of cases attended to since about the 19th of December, when the frost set in with such severity, I find to embrace no less than one thousand four hundred persons, and this, taking the usual average number that families are found to consist of, gives a total number so assisted over want and starvation of about 5,600 persons, who, but for the funds so left at our disposal, must have been left to themselves in misery and want.'

GUILDHALL POLICE-COURT

January 9th, 1861.—Alderman Allen, having disposed of the ordinary business of the day, devoted the whole of the afternoon to the investigation of the numerous applications for temporary assistance from the funds of the poor-box. Upwards of one hundred letters of recommendation were opened and examined, and although some were evidently attempted impositions, and others from interested persons, such as landlords, bakers, and other tradesmen with whom the poor people dealt, the number relieved with amounts, varying, according to circumstances, from 2*s*. 6*d*. to 1*l*., or 1*l*. 10*s*. each, was between eighty and ninety. The majority of these were old women, almost on the verge of the grave either from sickness or old age, and some apparently from starvation. One poor creature said she was seventy-nine years of age, and had upon her hands a son fifty-eight years of age, who was paralyzed, and unable to do anything for a living. The magistrate kindly advised her to go into the union; but, like all the respectable poor, she entertained an aversion to entering an institution which would have separated her from her helpless son. She said she had 3*s*. per week from the parish, and if she could obtain a trifle to help her over the bad weather, she would attend her son 'very carefully', and work for both. Another case was that of a very decent-looking woman, eighty-seven years of age, who said she got her living by hard work as a charwoman.

January 10*th*, 1861.—From an early hour this court was literally besieged by poor persons of all ages applying for some temporary assistance from the poor-box.

Alderman Allen very carefully investigated every case in which the applicant came with a letter of recommendation from some respectable person known to the court, and whose position placed such person above the influence of interested motives; but from the number of poor who were arriving in a continuous stream throughout the afternoon, it became obvious that it would be utterly impossible to relieve them all, and the magistrate, therefore, after he had assisted about seventy of those who appeared the most deserving with small sums, according to the circumstances of their cases, announced publicly that the remainder of the applications could not be attended to unless the parties came better recommended. He wished also to impress upon the poor people who came here for charity that he could not accept the recommendation of a landlord or petty tradesman, as he feared that such recommendations were more often given with the view of settling back scores and arrears of rent rather than that of satisfying the craving appetites of the starving tenants and their famished children, and it was evident that this rule could not be too widely known or too rigidly adhered to, as he had already noticed some half-dozen names of persons, landlords of small tenements, who had issued their recommendations wholesale.

January 11*th*, 1861.—Alderman Allen directed the officers to admit the poor, who thronged every avenue of the court, in order that their applications for assistance might be heard, and such as were deemed deserving relieved. The worthy alderman was engaged from one until nearly six o'clock in the evening, during which nearly three hundred letters were opened; but although the suggestions thrown out on the previous day with regard to the class of persons from whom letters of recommendation should be obtained had been complied with to a very considerable extent, there were yet a vast number whose recommendations were unavailable in consequence of the writers not occupying any of the positions which would bring them within the knowledge of the magistrate or the officials connected with this court. Notwithstanding the intimation from the bench that any one recommended by inspectors of police would be certainly relieved, not more than two or three have been received, and in the course of the afternoon Inspector Cole explained that the class of deserving persons that they generally came in contact with were not without friends, to whom their first application for a recommendation would naturally be made; but there was another class of persons, if anything, more deserving—equally respectable, but suffering from destitution far beyond what any one unacquainted with them could conceive. A class of persons neither seeking nor receiving relief either from the parish or private individuals, except their own friends, and who would rather exist upon a crust of dry bread or starve than venture to supplicate alms of a stranger. Many cases of that kind came under his observation, which would never be heard of unless visited in the wretched localities where they obtained a shelter.

January 12th, 1861.—Alderman Allen was engaged until past six o'clock in the evening in administering the funds placed at his disposal for the relief of the distressed poor of the district. At one time during the afternoon there could not have been less than 600 or 700 persons waiting for assistance, and among them were recognized many who were evidently prepared to exercise all their powers of dissimulation to impose upon the magistrate; but every recommendation was most carefully scrutinized, and the applicants closely interrogated, and any discrepancy in their statement, when compared with the letters of recommendation, proved fatal to their application, unless there were circumstances apparent to the magistrates which rendered them, if not so deserving as many others, fit objects for the sympathy of the benevolent.

January 15th, 1861.—Alderman Mechi, as soon as the ordinary business was disposed of, stated that as the applicants for relief were so numerous and daily increasing, and the funds at present in the poor box for the relief of the poor were very much diminished—in fact, all but exhausted—it behoved him to distribute pecuniary aid only to those who were in most urgent need of immediate relief. The alms given away during the past week amounted to nearly 300*l*.; but to continue assistance at the same rate for one day would be sufficient to swallow up the remaining balance in hand. A notice was posted up outside the court stating that no relief would be given that day, but that all letters of recommendation might be left, which would be examined, and those who were deserving, after due inquiry into their cases, would be relieved at their homes, which had the effect of dispersing a crowd of strong, able-bodied Irishmen who have assembled during the last few days, and kept back many of the deserving English poor by force, in order that their countrywomen might be relieved before the money ran short.

January 17th, 1861.—Alderman Mechi was engaged for several hours administering the relief placed at his disposal to about seventy poor and distressed families, and as every case had been previously visited and fully inquired into by the police, there was no possibility of imposition. It was found necessary to confine the distribution to the City poor belonging to this district, as, in many instances, the parties relieved at this court proceeded immediately after and endeavoured to get relief at the Mansion House, and those relieved at the Mansion House repeated their application at this court.

January 18th, 1861.—Alderman Phillips, who attended this day for the purpose of assisting Alderman Conder, while the latter disposed of the criminal charges, in the relief of the poor, was engaged the whole of the day administering temporary assistance to such as came provided with a recommendation from an inspector of police, certifying that their cases had been inquired into and found deserving. During the day no less than 250 distressed women were relieved with various sums, amounting in the aggregate to between 70*l*. and 80*l*., but although this number is greater than the numbers who have hitherto been relieved at this court in one day, it must not be taken as a fair criterion of the actual amount of distress now existing. Hundreds of families have within the last two or three weeks been relieved.

January 23rd, 1861.—Alderman Phillips and Alderman Conder, the latter having disposed of the ordinary night charges and summonses between the usual hours of twelve and two, were engaged the rest of the day in relieving about 250 poor families, whose circumstances had been previously inquired into by the police—the amount distributed being about 70*l*., exclusive of bread and soup, and coal tickets.

January 25th, 1861.—Alderman Mechi opened the court at an early hour this morning, and with the exception of a short interval, during which he disposed of the ordinary criminal business of the day, was engaged the whole time, up to half-past six in the evening, in relieving the distressed applicants whose circumstances had been previously investigated by the police, and whose cases were certified by the inspectors of the different police divisions in this district as deserving. The number of families relieved during the day was nearly 200, and the amount disbursed about 80*l*. The total sum received and distributed at this court during January, 1861, was about 900*l*.

MANSION HOUSE POLICE COURT

January 17*th*, 1861.—The number of applications at this court for relief continues very great, and the benevolence of the public still enables his lordship to afford relief to a great number. Yesterday no less than 300 applied for assistance, and after strict inquiries had been made, all who were found deserving received, to the number of 180, sufficient for the relief of their present wants.

January 26*th*, 1861.—His lordship, in the course of the day, stated that the necessity for subscriptions for special charity had passed, and that by a merciful Providence we had been allowed to get back into the ordinary condition of things, that all those people who were thrown out of work by the late severe weather, are now in most cases enabled to continue their labours; consequently there was no more necessity for him to solicit the public assistance, or to keep up that machinery by which he had been enabled to dispense public charity. During the last few weeks no less than 3,000 persons had been relieved from the funds so liberally supplied by the benevolent public, all cases having first been strictly inquired into. No case of distress had been brought to that court that had not received the fullest investigation, and the result went to show that while there were a great number of cases of extreme distress, there had been also a great many cases which were totally undeserving. He was sorry to state that even now there were still a vast number of applicants, and probably there might be some few who might require to be attended to, and he should for the next two days continue to relieve those who were really in distress, and whose cases would bear investigation, and that after that he should not consider it necessary to afford relief except in cases of the most urgent necessity.

The sum received and distributed at this court during the month of January, 1861, was nearly 2,000*l*. At the Southwark police-court, during the same period, nearly 1,400*l*. was received and distributed, and at the Westminster police-court about 850*l*., besides coals, soup, and bread were distributed to about 2,000 applicants. The accounts of the other police-courts are not published.

Notes

p.2   **1** The ten articles, each under the title 'London Horrors', were:
1 'The Back of Whitechapel', 21 January 1861, p.4.
2 'St George's-in-the-East', 22 January 1861, p.4.
3 'Behind Shoreditch', 23 January 1861, pp.4-5.
4 'Near Regent Street', 24 January 1861, p.5.
5 'Clerkenwell and the City Borders', 25 January 1861, p.5.
6 'Near King's Cross', 26 January 1861, p.5.
7 'Over the Water', 28 January 1861, p.5.
8 'Marylebone and the Outskirts', 29 January 1861, p.4.
9 'Near Westminster Abbey', 30 January 1861, p.5.
10 'Conclusion', 31 January 1861, p.5.

INTRODUCTION

p.5   **1** This chapter appeared on 21 January 1861 as a section of 'The Back of Whitechapel'.

2 *The Times*, 18 January 1861, also devoted considerable space to the bread riots; it quoted the law court reports of 'the terror induced by this lawless gang' which attacked bakers' and chandlers' shops in Stepney, St George's, and Ratcliff, and spoke of the 'formidable mob'.

p.6   **1** The Dorcas Societies, named after Dorcas ('full of good works and alms-deeds') in the Acts of the Apostles, were philanthropic groups offering relief to the poor.

2 Ragged schools were schools for the very poor; as Lord Shaftesbury, the President of the Ragged School Union (founded in 1844), put it, almost every pupil 'would have been a vagabond or thief' if not rescued and educated by the ragged schools. The Field Lane school (see p.10, n.1), in which Dickens showed great interest, was perhaps its best known endeavour. N. Pope, *Dickens and Charity*, (New York, 1978), pp. 152-3.

† 'with a favourable turn in the bitter weather'. On the 21st the temperature went above freezing for the first time since 1 January, although by only one degree. By 25 January it was 43°.

†† Hollingshead had originally written, rather more compassionately, 'at any period of exceptional want'.

††† 'are secrets that will never be fully exposed until the appearance of the census of 1861'. In the original article

Hollingshead then laid out his geographical schema for the articles to follow. The remainder of this introduction, with the exception of the last paragraph, first appeared in Hollingshead's article on overcrowding in London, 'Huddled together in London', in *Good Words*, Vol.II (1861), p.110. See also my notes to pp.36, 44 and 49 of the text.

p.7   **1** For Hollingshead's confused analysis of the immobility of the working classes, see my introduction, p. xxii.

  2 The Tothill Fields area, off Victoria Street, was demolished by the Metropolitan Board of Works (hereafter referred to as MBW) in its Metropolis (Old Pye-Street Westminster) Scheme of 1877, London County Council, (hereafter referred to as LCC), *The Housing Question in London* (1900), pp. 143ff.

CLERKENWELL AND THE CITY BORDERS

p.9   **1** This is certainly questionable, for the infant death rate among urban working-class children was certainly higher than that for middle-class children.

p.10   **1** The Saffron Hill area (including Field Lane), off Holborn Hill, attracted considerable attention, and its moral and physical state were exposed by Lord Shaftesbury in the parliamentary speech referred to by Hollingshead on pp. 19 and 118. Saffron Hill was held to be the district where Fagin lived. It was partly demolished in the Farringdon Road clearance scheme. The Field Lane Dormitory, built in 1851, was a temporary shelter or 'refuge' for the utterly destitute pupils of the Field Lane Ragged School, see Pope, *Dickens and Charity*, pp.180-1. During the harsh winter months of 1860-61 the newspapers gave considerable publicity to the generous donations which poured into the refuge. See for example, *The Times*, 1 January 1861, p.9. For an illustration of Field Lane, see A. King, ed., G. Godwin, *Town Swamps and Social Bridges* (1859, reprinted Leicester, 1972), p.10. The area was also publicized in *Our Homeless Poor. The Results of a Visit to the Field Lane Ragged School, and Night Refuge for the Homeless* (1859).

† 'the dwellings and'. The omission of this phrase is significant, for in the original newspaper article Hollingshead was perhaps conforming to the editorial argument that the condition of the dwellings influenced the morals and habits of the inhabitants. Hollingshead was himself unclear on the causal connection.

2 This area was cleared by the MBW in its Metropolis (Whitecross-Street, St Luke) Improvement Scheme of 1877, LCC, *The Housing Question in London*, pp.135ff. The cleared land was sold to the Peabody Trust for the erection of model dwellings.

p.11 † 'they must be rooted out'. The omission of this phrase would suggest that Hollingshead had second thoughts about the desirability of large clearance schemes, see my introduction, p.xxvi.

1 This was a rough paraphrase of Derby's speech. See *Hansard*, Third Series, Vol. 161 (28 February 1861), 1060-69. Derby was presenting a petition on behalf of property owners and leaseholders in the Paddington vicinity against the Metropolitan Railway Company's building in the area, and Derby used the occasion to attack the evictions that were an inevitable consequence of 'improvements' and railway construction.

p.13 1 Samuel Prout (1783-1852), an English water-colourist, painted landscapes and sea scenes, but was better known for his foreign townscapes.

† 'dear'.

p.14 1 The slums of this area were demolished by the MBW in its Metropolis (Pear-tree Court, Clerkenwell) Improvement Scheme of 1877. The half-wood, half-brick houses in the neighbourhood were said to be the last of their kind in London. The cleared land was sold to the Peabody Trust, see LCC, *The Housing Question in London*, pp.132ff.

2 Quinten Massys (also Metsys, Matsys) was a Flemish painter (1466-1530), who painted marvellous grotesques of old men, see L. Silver, *The Paintings of Quinten Massys* (Oxford, 1984).

p.17 1 In 1858 the City Corporation agreed to subscribe £200,000 towards the building of a terminus at Farringdon Street for the Great Western Railway. The terminus added to the evictions in the area. The Metropolitan Railway Company's line from Paddington to Farringdon Street (opened in January 1863) was the first underground railway in the world. F. Sheppard, *London, 1808-1870. The Infernal Wen* (1971), pp.139, 141.

p.18 1 H.J. Dyos estimated that over 50,000 people were displaced by railway schemes in London and that 37,000 of them were evicted during the period of greatest railway activity (1859-1867). H.J. Dyos, 'Railways and Housing in Victorian London: Part I', *Journal of Transport History*, Vol.I, No.II (May 1955), pp.13ff. See also J.R. Kellett, *The Impact of Railways on Victorian Cities* (1969), p.327.

p.19 1 For a slightly different version of the speech see *Hansard*, Third Series, Vol.161 (28 February 1861), 1069-1074. See also p.90 note 1.

THE BACK OF WHITECHAPEL

p.23 **1** This chapter appeared on 21 January 1861, with the exception of the first paragraph, which formed the opening paragraph of the second article, 22 January 1861.

p.25 † 'are struggling for want of funds, and'.

†† For 'privy' Hollingshead had originally written, far less accurately, 'water closet'. See Wohl, *Endangered Lives. Public Health in Victorian Britain* (1983), Ch.4, for the slow introduction of water closets.

1 The Common Lodging Houses Act (14 & 15 Vict. cap. XXVIII), 1851, one of two housing acts Lord Shaftesbury was able to steer through Parliament that year, introduced compulsory registration and police inspection to all dwellings where single rooms were let on a nightly basis to more than one family. By mid-century some 80,000 people were accommodated nightly in the common lodging houses (see Wohl, *The Eternal Slum*, p.74).

2 The Irish were held by the mid-Victorians to be responsible for the deterioration of inner city areas and for lowering domestic standards, see p.75, and Wohl, *The Eternal Slum*, pp.9, 10.

3 The adjoining area was cleared by the MBW in the Metropolis (Goulston-Street, and Flower and Dean-Street, Whitechapel) Improvement Scheme of 1877. LCC, *The Housing Question in London*, pp.118ff.

p.27 **1** Most Jewish charity in London came under the direction of the Board of Guardians for the Relief of the Jewish Poor (generally known as the Jewish Board of Guardians), founded in 1859. The Poor Law Board generally referred cases involving poor Jews to it.

ST GEORGE'S IN THE EAST

p.29 **1** This chapter appeared on 22 January 1861 and began with the first paragraph on p.23 above. St George's in the East later became part of the Borough of Stepney created in 1899.

p.35 † Originally 50,000.

BEHIND SHOREDITCH

p.36 **1** This paragraph is based on a similar description in Hollingshead's article, 'Huddled together in London', *Good Words*, Vol.II (1861), p.111.

p.37 **1** The Philoperisteron Society was a bird society: in 1868 it merged with the National Columbrian Society to become the National Peristeronic Society, *The Times*, 6 January 1904.

† 'A thorough clearance – a clean sweep for miles and miles – is wanted to improve Bethnal-green; and competent authorities – even the proprietors of the commonest, filthiest dust-holes of dwellings – state that new buildings, let to the same class of tenants, would pay a net dividend of 5 per cent upon the outlay.' See my introduction, p.xxvi.

p.38 † Originally 'water closet'.

p.39 **1** Henry Peter, Lord Brougham (1778-1868) seems to have been a great favourite of the working classes, perhaps because as a 'Radical' Whig he had attacked the often repressive Whig ministries and had been a leading supporter of the abolition of slavery. He became Lord Chancellor and, at the time Hollingshead wrote, he was President of the Social Science Association.

2 The French Treaty was the Cobden free-trade treaty with France, 1860, which was the final nail in the coffin of the East London silk-weaving industry. In 1824 some 50,000 workers had been employed in that industry; by the 1830s 30,000 were said to be unemployed, by 1860 under 10,000 were employed, and by 1880 only 3,300. Stedman Jones, *Outcast London*, p.101.

p.42 **1** The Old Nichol area of Bethnal Green was the locale for Arthur Morrison's celebrated novel, *A Child of the Jago* (1896). The area, one of the last and certainly the most widely known of the old criminal 'rookeries' was cleared in the LCC's Boundary Street Scheme, begun in 1890.

2 'Box-clump-making' possibly refers to the domestic production of wooden soles or clogs which were worn to protect pedestrians from the filth in the (often unpaved streets in a horse-driven age.

p.44 **1** The remainder of this chapter is additional material. The section beginning, 'peep on one side of the hay-bundle (p.44) and ending, 'is full of these holes and corners' (p.46) is, with minor changes, taken from his article, 'Huddled together in London', *Good Words*, Vol.II (1861), pp.111-12.

p.45 **1** The metropolitan slaughter houses constituted one of the worst sanitary nuisances, see Wohl, *Endangered Lives*, p.84.

p.49 **1** The following paragraph first appeared in Hollingshead's article, 'Huddled together in London', *Good Words*, Vol.II (1861), pp.112-113.

NEAR WESTMINSTER ABBEY

p.53 1 The word 'slum' was first popularized by Cardinal Wiseman (1802-65), Archbishop of Westminster, in his *An Appeal to the Reason and Good Feeling of the English People on the Subject of the Catholic Hierarchy*, written in 1850, the year he became a cardinal; in this tract Wiseman condemned the 'congealed labyrinths of lanes and courts, and alleys and slums', close by Westminster Abbey, (p.30). 'Slum' first appeared in Vaux's *Flash Dictionary* (1812) and was probably derived from slumber, or a sleepy back alley. See E. Partridge, *Origins; a Short Etymological Dictionary of Modern English* (1958), p.633, and Dyos, *Victorian Studies*, Vol.XI, No.I (September 1967), pp.7-10.

2 Victoria Street was developed by the Westminster Improvement Commission under an act of 1845. For its slow development see P. Metcalf, *Victorian London* (1972), p.22.

p.54 1 For the subsequent demolition of much of this area see p.7, n.2 above. The Pye Street scheme embraced Pye Street and Orchard Street mentioned by Hollingshead, see pp.56, 57.

2 For the full speech see *Hansard*, Third Series, Vol.161 (28 February 1861), 1070-79.

p.55 1 This description certainly recalls the illustrations of Doré for *London Pilgrimage*.

p.58 † The original article ended with the paragraph (with minor changes) which opened his 'Conclusion', pp.117-25.

NEAR REGENT STREET

p.62 1 There was a practical reason behind the fear of moving; to move meant giving up known credit facilities at pub or pawnshop.

p.64 1 The quality of milk in London did not improve greatly until the end of the century. Wohl, *Endangered Lives*, pp.21-2, 53.

NEAR KING'S CROSS

p.67 1 Agar Town was a notorious slum before the building of St Pancras Station, and its lines in the 1860s cut through it, displacing and dispersing its population (without compensation or re-housing), see Kellett, *The Impact of Railways*, p.64, and J. Simmons, *St Pancras Station* (1968), pp.9, 25.

p.68 † Hollingshead's original article was less condemnatory of the Ecclesiastical Commissioners. Perhaps the *Morning Post* toned down his indictment and he is here speaking his mind. The original read: 'Now, thanks to the efforts of the Rev. R.P. Clemenger, the active and long-resident minister; the Rev. Thomas Dale, late of St Pancras; and others, the Ecclesiastical Commissioners have been brought to some sense of their duty, and while they have repurchased the property, they have given it lamps and pavements.'

1 Chadwick's 1842 *Report on the Sanitary Condition of the Labouring Population of Great Britain* (M. Flinn, ed., Edinburgh, 1965), pp.82-4, had drawn attention to the county's insanitary condition, but Hollingshead was probably thinking of the series of articles by 'Our Own Correspondent' which appeared in *The Times* in the summer of 1846 and which drew a barrage of fiery letters from the great crusader, the Rev. Lord Sidney Godolphin Osborne.

p.71 † 'Starting with a Sunday School held in a shed near a gas-factory'.

p.72 † '(the Rev. Mr Clemenger and his curate)'.

1 Part of the Somers Town slums were demolished by the LCC in its London (Churchway, St Pancras) Improvement Scheme of 1895, LCC, *The Housing Question in London*, pp.213ff.

MARYLEBONE AND THE OUTSKIRTS

p.74 † Hollingshead had originally written, with some exaggeration, 'Eight or ten families'.

††4 'and each house will thus contain about 50 or 60 people'.

p.76 1 See p.78, note 1.

p.78 1 Rev. J. Llewelyn Davies, 'Metropolitan Distress', *Macmillan's Magazine*, Vol.III (February 1861), pp.334-5.

p.79 † 'The rector is now calling in fresh help in his work, and is building a new church in the very worst part of the Bell-street district.'

1 The Potteries were notoriously insanitary, partly as a consequence of the pigsties in the district. In 1849 pigs outnumbered people by three to one, and according to one local estimate between 25 and 30 per cent of the heads of families were professional pig-keepers. Not until the early 1870s was pig-keeping ruled a sanitary nuisance and the pig-keepers finally closed down or driven out. See P.E. Malcolmson, 'Getting a Living in the Slums of Victorian Kensington', *The London Journal*, Vol.I, No.I (May 1975) pp.34, 53, 55.

2 'Health by Act of Parliament', *Household Words*, Vol.I (10 August 1850), p.463. The author, W.H. Wills, called the Potteries 'a plague spot scarcely equalled for its insalubrity by any other in London', where 'discontent, dirt, filth and misery, are unsurpassed by anything known even in Ireland', *ibid*.

p.80 1 John Hampden was the hero of the Ship Money Case of 1637 which challenged the prerogative taxation of Charles I.

'OVER THE WATER'

p.86 1 Pariatelia may have been derived from parietinae, fallen or ruined walls (see *Oxford English Dictionary*). I am grateful to my colleague, Professor Ben Kohl, for assistance with this reference.

2 Hollingshead has the date incorrectly. This passage appeared in the *Morning Post* on 31 January 1861 and not on 30 January 1860. It was in response to Hollingshead's articles, and the passage quoted began 'the misnamed courts and alleys he [Hollingshead[mentions are many of them in the immediate vicinity of the soup kitchen and hundreds' etc.

p.87 1 After the publication of *Oliver Twist*, Jacob's Island, the setting for Bill Sykes's capture, became something of a tourist spot.

p.88 1 Hollingshead was here using the word (interchangeable with amuck or amok) literally: it referred to frenzied Malays (or, variously, Indians or Javanese) who went out into the streets to fight or kill indiscriminately.

p.89 1 Smollet called Kent Street, which ran into the junction of Great Dover Street and the Old Kent Road, 'a most disgraceful entrance to such an opulent city. A foreigner, in passing through this beggarly and ruinous suburb, conceives such an idea of misery and meanness, as all the wealth and magnificence of London and Westminster are afterwards unable to destroy.' See Tobias Smollet, *Travels through France and Italy* (1766, reprinted 1907), Letter I, p.3.

p.90 1 Hollingshead's veiled references to sexual promiscuity were much more delicate than those of Lord Shaftesbury in the speech in the House of Lords which Hollingshead quoted on pp.19 and 118.

A NEW CHAMBER OF HORRORS

p.97 **1** This material did not appear in the original 'London Horrors' series, but is based on an article under the same title which he wrote for *All the Year Round*, Vol.4, No.97 (2 March 1861), pp.500-1. Additions to the original are marked by square parentheses. From its opening in Baker Street in 1835 Madame Tussaud's had a room designated 'The Dead Room', which *Punch* called the 'Chamber of Horrors', J.T. Tussaud, *The Romance of Madame Tussaud's* (New York, 1920), p.174.

OUR LONDON MODEL LODGING-HOUSES

p.102 **1** This chapter did not appear in the original 'London Horror' series, but was an article in *Good Words*, Vol. II (1861), pp.170-4. The article, originally entitled 'London Model Lodging-Houses' began with the sentence, 'The task of digging out, etc.' (quoted in my introduction, p.xvii): apart from the omission of this sentence and the additions on pp.112 and 113, marked by square parentheses, this chapter is identical to the *Good Words* article.

2 The General Board of Health was established under the Public Health Act of 1848, but it always laboured under the stigma of intolerable state interference and opposition to Edwin Chadwick, its most prominent member, and in 1858 it was abolished and replaced by the Privy Council's Medical Department (led by John Simon), constituted under the 1858 Local Government Act. Hollingshead's criticism of this change was hardly justified, see Wohl, *Endangered Lives*, pp.149-59. In 1871 the Local Government Act finally created a unified public health administration, combining as it did under the Local Government Board the staffs of the Poor Law Board, the Local Government Act Office, the Registrar-General, and the Privy Council, *ibid*., pp.159ff.

3 See page 25, note I, above.

4 For cellar dwellings (or kitchens as they were sometimes called), see Wohl, *Endangered Lives*, pp.296ff. Effective legislation controlling cellar dwellings was not passed until the Sanitary Act of 1866 condemned all such dwellings as 'unfit for human habitation'.

p.103 1 The Metropolitan Association was the oldest of the model dwelling companies, and was founded in 1841, not in 1842, as Hollingshead stated. By 1881 it had accommodated approximately 6,000 people and was at that time the third largest of the model dwelling companies. Wohl, *The Eternal Slum*, pp.146-9.

2 Hollingshead is here reflecting the contemporary London prejudice against block dwellings.

p.104 1 For the Association's tenants, see *ibid.*, p.148. In 1875 of the total rent roll of £12,257, only £156 was lost in unpaid rent, *ibid.*

p.105 1 In the 1870's the average wage of the Association's poorest tenants was given as between 15s. and 20s. a week at a time when the average wage for labourers in London was probably under 15s. a week, *ibid.*

2 Hollingshead is here quoting the evidence supplied by Earl Granville, see p.106. The Association's charter prevented it from paying more than five per cent, but the company had financial difficulties in its early years, and this figure was not reached until 1873, *ibid.*, p.147.

p.106 1 For a slightly different version of the speech, see *Hansard*, Third Series, Vol.161 (28 February 1861), 1075-79.

p.107 1 The Columbia Square Buildings of Angela, Baroness Burdett-Coutts (1814-1906), were completed in 1862. The heiress to a vast fortune from the Duchess of St Albans, Burdett-Coutts was inspired by Charles Dickens, who worked closely with her on the scheme. One hundred and eighty-three tenants were housed in an enormous structure, complete with gothic market hall, see Wohl, *The Eternal Slum*, p.145 and Pope, *Dickens and Charity.*, pp.235ff.

p.108 1 The murder of the 'Italian Boy' – he was never referred to by name – took place in 1831 and occupied the pages of *The Times* in late November of that year. Bishop and Williams were accused (along with May and Shields) of having drugged the boy with laudanum and then suspending him, head first, in a well. 'The next day his body was hawked round the London hospitals', see D. Orton, *Made of Gold. A Biography of Angela Burdett Coutts* (1980), p.155. Thereafter Nova Scotia Gardens became known as 'Burker's Hole', after William Burke, who, together with William Hare, was the most notorious of the body-snatchers. Murdering to sell bodies to medical students became known as 'burking'. See also K.J. Fielding, 'Dickens's work with Miss Coutts – I', *The Dickensian*, Vol.LXI, No.346 (May 1965) p.115.

p.109   **1** They did, in fact, accept costermongers, unlike most of the other model dwelling companies, see Wohl, *The Eternal Slum*, p.145.

p.110   **1** The Society for Improving the Condition of the Labouring Classes, an offshoot of the Labourers' Friend Society, was founded in 1844 and received its charter in 1850. Prince Albert served as its President, Lord Shaftesbury as its Chairman, and Henry Roberts, one of the leading housing reformers of the day, as its architect. The Society was the most prominent evangelical housing agency at this time and its rules were strict – those for its George Street Lodging House (opened in 1847), for example, prohibited alcohol, smoking, gambling, card-playing, and profane language, and the Bible was read every night in the common room. See Pope, *Dickens and Charity*, p.286, note 38. The Society, under the direction of Prince Albert, erected the model dwellings in the 1851 Crystal Palace Exhibition. For a history of the Society, see *ibid.*, pp.208-12.

2 Dickens was extremely interested in the work of the Society and the Wild Court renovations were the subject of two articles in his *Household Words*, 'Conversion of a Heathen Court', Vol.X (16 December 1854) and 'Wild Court Tamed', Vol.XII (25 August 1855), both written by Henry Morley. Inevitably, 'improvement' meant eviction and dislocation: Wild Court once housed a thousand people, and the new building of the Society provided accommodation for only one hundred families. See Pope, *Dickens and Charity*, p.242.

3 Hollingshead seems here to be using the summary from the Society's own magazine, *The Labourers' Friend*, January 1860, p.2, but with minor errors, *ibid.*, table 5.1, p.209.

p.112   **1** Hollingshead would have had little cause to change this criticism had he revised the book at the end of his life. The Peabody Trust certainly did not reach the 'lowest of the low', nor did the later model dwelling companies, such as the Four Per Cent Industrial Dwellings Company and the East End Dwellings Company. For this, and Hollingshead's other criticism of the appearance of the model dwellings and the dislocations which their construction caused, see Wohl, *The Eternal Slum*, ch.6.

2 'Muscular Christianity', or the Christian Socialism of Charles Kingsley, J.M. Ludlow, and Frederick Denison Maurice, did in fact spread the gospel of sanitary reform and health visiting. Kingsley directly inspired the formation of the Ladies' Sanitary Association which published pamphlets such as *The Power of*

Soap and Water and which brought women directly into the field of public health, see Wohl, *Endangered Lives*, pp.67-9.

p.113 1 By the time of Hollingshead's death in 1904 the principal model dwelling companies and trusts in London had housed roughly 123,000 or so people, see Wohl, *The Eternal Slum*, p.172.

MISTAKEN CHARITY

p.114 1 Although none of this material appeared in the original *Morning Post* articles, it develops themes presented there.

CONCLUSION

p.117 1 This chapter appeared on 31 January 1861, with the exception of the opening paragraph (pp.117-18) which concluded the penultimate article, 30 January 1861.

p.118 1 See p.117 note 1, above.
2 'One-third' originally read 'one-half'. For London as a whole one-third is probably more accurate, although there were large areas of inner London where one-half and more of the inhabitants were living in overcrowded conditions. For census purposes overcrowding was defined as more than two people to a room.
3 See p.19 note 1 and p.90 note 1, above.

p.120 1 'pugilistic exhibitions' originally read '*posé-plastique* exhibitions'.

p.124 1 Hollingshead was correct to question if sanitary reform was always in the best interests of the poor. Building and sanitary codes involved the landlords in expenses which they passed on to the tenants in the form of higher rents, and legislation which was directed at overcrowding often simply forced the poor when they were evicted to huddle elsewhere. Medical officers of health, who were responsible for the enforcement of much of this legislation, were often reluctant to act, since they realized that to do so would only add to the hardships of the poorer class of tenants. See Wohl, *The Eternal Slum*, pp.117-18.

p.125 1 The Sanitary Act of 1866 (29 & 30 Vict.cap.XC) authorized local authorities to make by-laws for houses let in lodgings. Those few London vestries which chose to adopt the Act generally set a minimum requirement of 400 cubic feet for each adult in a room occupied both day and night and 300 cubic feet for each adult in a bedroom; for children under ten years of age these measurements were halved.

2 In 1860 the Ragged School Union had 15,437 day scholars, 9,413 evening students, and 3,741 pupils enrolled as industrial students, see Pope, *Dickens and Charity*, table 4.2, p.177.

APPENDIX

p.132   **1** In 1855 the Metropolis Local Management Act compelled local authorities throughout London to appoint medical officers of health. It will be apparent from this extract that medical officers could use their annual reports to their vestries to advance social reforms and public health measures, although by so doing they ran the risk of incurring the wrath of rate-conscious men on whom their re-appointment depended. For the insecure tenure and powers of the medical officers of health, see Wohl, *The Eternal Slum*, ch.5.

p.157   **1** For an analysis of this budget and the one on p.160 below, see *ibid.*, pp.40ff., and *ibid.*, pp.308ff., for late nineteenth-century budgets.

p.162   **1** Co-operative building societies were tried, without marked success, in the north of England, but not in London.